Georgian Cuisine

T. P. SULAKVELIDZE

ISBN-10: 1481993453
ISBN-13: 978-1481993456

CONTENTS

INTRODUCTION

Food of the republics of the Caucasus region of the former Soviet Union is virtually unknown in the United States. Food of Georgian, Armenian, and Azerbaijani kitchens is simply amazing. Our goal is to introduce you to these cuisines.

The first book we are going to translate is called "Georgian Dishes" which was published in 1959. Unfortunately we could not find any information about its author, doctor Sulakvelidze. The book itself has only a short foreword by the author. He wrote "The book contains technology of preparing more than 400 Georgian dishes. Some of the listed dishes are also present in the kitchens of Armenian and Azerbaijani cuisines (for example bozbashi, buglama, tolma, pilaf, shashlik, and so on); however, the ingredients and method of preparation differs in every republic. This book lists recipes of the most famous Georgian dishes. Using these recipes a housewife can, if desired, increase or decrease suggested quantity of herbs and spices listed. If dried suneli (mix of dried herbs) is not available, dishes can be cooked without it."

When discussing Georgian food, it is worth mentioning the fundamental differences between Western and Eastern Georgian cuisine. These differences are caused not only by nature and climate, but also by Turkish influence on Western Georgia and Iranian influence on Eastern Georgia. As the result, several key ingredients are used differently until this day.

In Western Georgia, bread and corn flour flat bread

(mchadi) are very popular, while in Eastern Georgia wheat bread is preferred. As far as meat, in Eastern Georgia lamb is very popular (in addition to beef) and animal fats comprise a large part of the diet. In Western Georgia, meat is mostly replaced by poultry – chicken and turkey.

Western Georgia is characterized by dishes that are spicier, sauces are somewhat different. Long existence of the Georgian nation at the crossroads of different cultures led to none of the meat sources being dominant – Georgian meat dishes can be made with pork, lamb, beef or poultry. Such tolerance is not typical of the other Eastern nations. Overall, beef and poultry are more popular choices.

Different types of nuts are widely used in Georgian cuisine – hazelnuts, almonds, etc. – although walnuts are used most often. They are a required ingredient for many dressings and sauces equally suitable for poultry, vegetable and even fish dishes. Nuts are added to meat soups, pastry, cold salads and hot entrées. It is impossible to fathom Georgian food without nuts.

Herbs are very important in Georgian cuisine also. They are used throughout the year and some examples are tarragon, basil, cilantro, savory, leeks, scallions, mint.

Frequent and generous use of cheese also sets Georgian cuisine apart. Cheese is not only an appetizer, but also an ingredient in a wide variety of soups and entrées.

As typical for all cuisines of the Caucasus region, skewer is widely used not only for meat dishes, but also for vegetable, fish and cheese dishes.

Special techniques are employed for preparing various dishes, such as creation of sour, sour-fat and sour-egg environments for soups and sauces.

Similar to French cuisine, Georgia is famous for sauces. Georgian sauces have different ingredients and methods of preparation, however. Most often it is sour berry and fruit juices or purees with blackthorn, pomegranate, blackberry, barberry and tomatoes. Nut-based sauces are also very popular. Chicken may be served with several different sauces – sacebeli, sacivi, garo, tkemali, garlic-wine, nut, barberry, etc. Variety of Georgian cuisine is largely accomplished by switching between different sauces for entrées. Sauces are consumed with lentils, eggplants and poultry, etc., but sometimes Georgian sauces act as separate dishes and are eaten with bread.

SOUPS

SOUPS WITH MEAT AND POULTRY

Soup-Artala (A)

Ingredients:
Beef shin and udder - 1 kg
Celery (with root) - 4 stalks
Celery leaves - to taste
Garlic and salt - to taste

Thoroughly wash beef shin and udder (or just shin) in warm water, cut it into pieces, and put into a pot with boiling water (8-10 cups), cover the pot and cook, skimming the foam with a skimmer from time to time. When water returns to boil lower the heat to prevent rapid boiling, otherwise the soup will turn murky. Add celery stalks and root to the pot and continue cooking until tendons start separating from the bones.

Remove celery from the cooked soup, season it with salt and crushed garlic. If desired - add finely chopped celery leaves. Crushed garlic and chopped celery leaves can also be served on a side.

Soup-Artala (B)

Ingredients:
Beef shin - 1 kg
Celery root - 2
Parsnips - 2
Onion - 1
Garlic and salt - to taste

Thoroughly wash beef shin in warm water, cut it into pieces, put into a pot, cover with cold water (8-10 cups), cover the pot, and bring to boil skimming the foam as it rises to the top.

Add celery roots, parsnips, and onion to the pot and continue cooking until tendons easily separate from the bone. Remove roots from the finished soup, season the soup with salt and add finely chopped celery leaves.

Serve the soup with crushed garlic on a side.

Soup-Hashi with Beef or Lamb Tripe and Feet (A)

Ingredients:
Beef or lamb feet and tripe - 1 - 1.5 kg
Garlic and salt - to taste

Put thoroughly cleaned, washed in warm water, and cut into pieces beef or lamb feet and trip into a pot with boiling water and return to boil. When water in the pot comes to boil - pour it out and add fresh boiling water (10-12 cups). Skim the foam rising to the top with a skimmer. Stop cooking when soup is thickened and tendons easily separate from bones.

Soup-hashi can also be cooked as follows - put prepared beef or lamb feet and tripe into a pot, add enough milk to cover, cover the pot and leave for 5-6 hours. Pour the milk out, transfer tripe and feet into a clean pot, put the pot on heat and roast for about 15 minutes. Pour the juice from cooking out into some bowl, return the pot back top the heat and continue roasting another 30-40 minutes, pouring the juice out from time to time. After 30-40 minutes add boiling water to the pot, pour back all the accumulated cooking juice, return the pot to boil, and cook for 5-6 hours.

Serve soup-hashi with salt and garlic pounded with a small quantity of salt. If desired - serve wine vinegar. This soup can be cooked with only tripe or only beef or lamb feet.

Soup-Hashi with Beef or Lamb Tripe and Feet (B)

Ingredients:
Beef or lamb feet and tripe - 1 -1.5 kg
Garlic and salt - to taste

Put thoroughly cleaned and cut into pieces beef and lamb feet and tripe into a cold flowing water (ed. note - Georgia is a mountainous country. The idea here is to soak feet and trip in the water of a mountain stream or river) for 15 hours. Separate feet from tripe, put into boiling water and cook without salt on a low heat in separate pots. When tripe is cooked transfer them into the pot with feet and continue cooking over low heat until done (approximately 5-6 hours longer). Serve the soup with salt and pounded garlic on a side.

Soup-Hashi with Beef Tripe and Feet

Ingredients:
Beef tripe and feet - 1 - 1.5 kg
White bread (Georgian) - 200 g
Garlic and salt - to taste

Put thoroughly cleaned, cut into pieces, and washed in warm water beef tripe and feet into a pot, add enough water to reach half-way up, and set to cook on high heat. When half of the liquid evaporates, add soaked in milk white bread (Georgian), mix everything well and cook another 30 minutes. Then add enough boiling water to cover the contents of the pot and cook (without salt) in a covered pot another 1-2 hours. Serve the soup with salt and crushed garlic on the side.

Soup-Kharcho with Beef (A)

This soup is perhaps the best known and most popular Georgian soup in the territories of the former Soviet Union.

Ingredients:
Beef - 500 g
Onions - 3-4
Rice - 1/2 cup
Tomatoes - 500 g
or Tomato paste - 1/2 cup
Cilantro - 8 sprigs
Parsley - 8 sprigs
Tkemali or sour fruit leather, dried suneli (mix of dried herbs) - to taste
Garlic and salt - to taste

Wash fatty beef (brisket, ribs), cut into small pieces, put into a pot, add 8-10 cups of cold water and set it to cook. Remove rising to the top foam using a skimmer. After about 1.5-2 hours of cooking add washed rice, finely chopped onions, 2 sprigs each of cilantro and parsley (tied together into a bouquet), and continue cooking until meat is done.

About 10-15 minutes before the end of cooking add finely chopped cilantro and parsley, crushed garlic, chili peppers, salt, prepared tkemali (sour sauce made from plums) or sour fruit leather (made from tkemali) and dried suneli.

This soup can be cooked with tomatoes or tomato paste, or seasoned with wine vinegar; however, in this case tkemali or sour fruit leather (tklapi) are not used.

If desired - sprinkle with finely chopped cilantro or parsley just before serving.

Soup-Kharcho with Beef (B)

Ingredients:
Beef - 500g
Onions - 3-4
Rice - 4 tbsp
Tomatoes - 500-700 g
or Tomato paste - 1/2 cup
Bay leaves - 1-2
Whole black pepper - 4-5
Cilantro - 4 sprigs
Parsley - 4 sprigs
Red chili pepper - to taste
Dried suneli - to taste
Salt - to taste

Cut fatty beef (ribs, brisket) into small pieces, wash, put into a pot, cover with 8-10 cups of cold water, bring to boil, and cook until the meat is half-done. Skim the foam before the water comes to boil.

In a separate pot sauté finely chopped onions with some fat skimmed from the broth for 10 minutes. Take the meat out of the broth and add it to the pot with onions, cover this pot and continue cooking 15-20 minutes. Add tomato paste (paste can be replaced with tomatoes cooked and passed through a sieve, or peeled and diced tomatoes) and braise 10-15 minutes longer. Add strained broth to the pot, and, when the broth returns to boil, add rice.

Approximately 10 minutes before the end of cooking add pounded garlic, chili pepper, finely chopped parsley, cilantro, dill, whole black pepper, dried suneli, bay leaf, and salt. Remove bay leaf from the finished soup.

Soup-Kharcho with Beef and Walnuts

Ingredients:
Beef - 500 g
Shelled walnuts - 1 - 1.5 cups
Corn flour - 1 tbsp
Whole coriander seeds - 1 tsp
Dried suneli - 1 tsp
Tkemali or sour fruit leather - to taste
Cilantro - to taste
Chili pepper - to taste
Garlic and salt - to taste

Wash fatty beef and cut it into small pieces, put into a pot, cover with 8-10 cups of water and bring to boil. Skim the foam as it rises to the top before water comes to boil. After 2 hours of cooking add crushed walnuts, pounded together chili pepper, garlic, and salt, corn flour mixed with a small quantity of broth, sour fruit leather (tklapi) or tkemali sauce or wine vinegar. Approximately 10 minutes before the end of cooking add crushed coriander and dried suneli.

Soup-Kharcho with Lamb or Beef (A)

Ingredients:
Beef or lamb - 500 g

Onions - 4-5
Rice - 1/2 cup
or Vermicelli - 3/4 cup
Whole black pepper - 3-4
Whole coriander - 1/2 tsp
Tkemali or grape vinegar - to taste
Cilantro - to taste
Chili pepper - to taste
Garlic and salt - to taste

Wash fatty lamb or beef (brisket), cut it into small pieces, put into a pot and sauté 10-15 minutes. Add finely chopped onions and continue braising a while longer. Add boiling water (7-8 cups), return water to boil, and cook for 1 hour. Add rice and continue cooking until meat is done.

Approximately 10-15 minutes before the soup is done add pounded garlic, finely chopped cilantro, chili pepper or crashed black pepper, tkemali or wine vinegar (if desired), and salt.

Soup-Kharcho with Lamb or Beef (B)

Ingredients:
Beef or lamb - 500 g
Onions - 4
Rice - 4 tbsp
Tomato paste - 1/2 cup
Allspice - 5-6
Garlic - 2-3 cloves
Cilantro - 4-5 sprigs
Parsley - 3 sprigs
Dill - 4 sprigs
Bay leaf - 1
Dried suneli - to taste
Chili pepper - to taste
Salt - to taste

Cut fatty lamb or beef (brisket) into small pieces, wash it, put into a pot, cover with water (7-8 cups) and cook 2 hours from the moment it comes to boil. Skim foam before the water comes to boil.

Into a separate pot put onions passed through a meat grinder, add fat skimmed from the broth, and saute 10-15 minutes. Add tomato paste and continue cooking 15 minutes longer.

Strain broth, and, together with meat, add it to the pot with onions. Return to boil, and previously soaked rice and cook 20 minutes, then add pounded garlic and chili pepper, finely chopped herbs (cilantro, parsley, and dill), dried suneli, allspice, bay leaf, salt, and let it simmer for 10-15 minutes longer. Remove bay leaf from finished soup.

Soup-Kharcho with Pork

Ingredients:
Pork - 500 g
Onions - 5
Millet - 4 tbsp
or Vermicelli - 50-60 g
Crashed coriander seeds - 1/2 tsp
Dried suneli - 1 tsp
Garlic - 2 cloves
Cilantro - 4 sprigs
Parsley - 4 sprigs
Tkemali or sour fruit leather or wine vinegar - to taste
Dried savory and basil - to taste
Chili pepper - to taste
Black pepper - to taste
Salt - to taste

Wash fatty pork, cut it into small pieces, put into a pot together with finely chopped onions and brown everything nicely. Add boiling water (7-8 cups), return to boil, add millet or vermicelli and cook until done.

About 10-15 minutes before the end of cooking add boiled and passed through a sieve tkemali or soaked and passed through a sieve sour fruit leather (tklapi) (or just use wine vinegar to season the soup), crushed coriander seeds, ground cinnamon and cloves, dried suneli, dried and crushed savory and basil, ground black pepper, chili pepper pounded with salt, pounded garlic, and chopped herbs (cilantro and parsley).

Soup-Kharcho with Chicken and Walnuts (A)

Ingredients:
Chicken - 1
Onions - 4
Wheat or corn flour - 1-2 tbsp
Tkemali - 1/2 cup
or Tomatoes - 500 g
Walnuts - 1 1/2 cups
Garlic - 3 cloves
Dried suneli - 1 tsp
Crushed coriander seeds - 1 1/2 tsp
Cilantro - 4-5 sprigs
Chili pepper, allspice, black pepper, cinnamon, cloves, saffron, bay leaf, salt - to taste

Singe and gut a fatty chicken, thoroughly wash the carcass and cut it into small pieces, put into a pot, add cold water (2- 2.5 liters), cover the pot, and cook until chicken is half-done.

In a separate pan sauté finely chopped onions in the fat skimmed from broth until browned. Take chicken out of the broth and add it to onions. Cover the pot and continue cooking for 10-15 minutes longer, mixing the contents of the pot from time to time. Add wheat or corn flour to the pot and fry 5 minutes longer, then pour chicken broth in and simmer 10-15 minutes. Then add boiled and passed through a sieve tkemali or tomatoes, and let simmer 5 minutes longer. Add following ingredients dissolved in a small quantity of slightly cooled broth - crushed walnuts, pounded garlic, chili pepper, black pepper, allspice, cinnamon and cloves, saffron, dried suneli, crushed coriander seeds, finely chopped cilantro, bay leaf, salt. Simmer the soup for 10 minutes longer.

Tkemali or tomatoes can be replaced with wine vinegar.

Soup-Kharcho with Chicken and Walnuts (B)

Ingredients:
Chicken - 1
Onions - 4
Shelled walnuts - 2 cups
Parsley - 5 sprigs
Cilantro - 5 sprigs
Crushed coriander seeds - 1/2 tsp
Garlic - 2 cloves
Tkemali or sour fruit leather, saffron, dried suneli, chili pepper, salt - to taste

Prepare chicken as indicated in the previous recipe, cut it into small pieces, put into a pot, add enough cold water to barely cover the chicken, cover the pot, and bring it to boil. Skim the foam as it rises to the top. After 1 - 1.5 hours after water came to boil add finely chopped onions and continue cooking until chicken is almost done.

Add cooked and passed through a sieve tomatoes or tkemali, or soaked and passed through a sieve sour fruit leather. When the soup returns to boil add finely chopped cilantro, parsley, and following ingredients mixed with a small quantity of slightly cooled broth -- crushed walnuts, saffron, coriander seeds, dried suneli, pounded garlic, chili pepper, and salt. Return the soup to boil and simmer for 10 minutes longer.

Sprinkle with chopped parsley just before serving.

Soup-Kharcho with Chicken, Turkey, or Goose (A)

Ingredients:
Chicken - 1
Rice - 1/2 cup
Onions - 300 g
Sour fruit leather - 50 g
Cilantro - 4 sprigs
Chili pepper, salt - to taste

Cut into small pieces prepared carcass of a chicken, turkey, or a goose, put into a pot, add enough water to just cover the meat, cover the pot and bring to boil. Skim the foam as it rises to the top.

Add cracked rice, finely chopped onions, pieces of sour fruit leather (tklapi), chili pepper, and continue cooking until the meat is cooked through.

About 3-5 minutes before the end of cooking season the soup with salt. Sprinkle with chopped cilantro just before serving.

Soup-Kharcho with Chicken, Turkey, or Goose (B)

Ingredients:
Chicken, turkey, or goose - 1
Onions - 400 g + 1 whole
Celery - 1 stalk
Parsley - 1 sprig
Eggs - 3-4
Chili pepper, chopped cilantro or parsley, salt - to taste

Put prepared carcass of a chicken, turkey, or goose into a pot, add cold water, cover the pot and bring to boil, skimming the foam as it rises to the top. Add parsley sprig, celery, and whole onion and cook until meat is done.

Remove cooked carcass from the pot, strain the broth, and return it to boil together with chopped onions, chili pepper, and salt. Cut cooked bird into small pieces and return to the simmering broth. Return soup to boil, then gradually add beaten eggs to the soup while constantly stirring.

Sprinkle the soup with chopped cilantro or parsley just before serving.

Soup-Kharcho with Sturgeon and Walnuts

Ingredients:
Sturgeon - 500 g
Onions - 4
Carrot - 1
Parsley - 2 sprigs
Celery - 2 stalks
Bay leaf - 1
Allspice - 3
Wheat flour - 1 tbsp
Garlic - 2-3 cloves
Whole coriander - 1/2 tsp
Dried suneli - 1 tsp
Shelled walnuts - 1 cup
Tkemali, tomatoes, or sour fruit leather - to taste
Herbs (parsley, cilantro, and dill) - to taste
Chili pepper and salt - to taste

Cook sturgeon in one piece until half-done together with onion, carrot, parsley, celery, bay leaf, allspice, and salt. Take the fish out of the broth and cut into small pieces. Skim fat from the top of the broth and put into a different pot, strain the broth.

Return pot with skimmed fat to the heat, add finely chopped remaining onions and brown them nicely. Add flour to the onions and saute for 5 minutes longer, then add strained broth. Return broth to boil, add pieces of fish and simmer 10 minutes, then add pounded garlic and coriander seeds, finely chopped parsley and dill, dried suneli, chili pepper, boiled and passed through a sieve tkemali or tomatoes, or sauce Tkemali, or tomato sauce, or soaked in hot water and passed through a sieve sour fruit leather (tklapi), and, mixed with a small quantity of lightly cooled broth, crushed walnuts. Continue simmering for 10 more minutes.

Just before serving sprinkle the soup with finely chopped cilantro, parsley, or dill.

Soup-Tatariahni with Beef (A)

Ingredients:
Beef - 500 g
Carrots - 2
Onion - 1
Celery - 2 stalks
Parsley - 2 sprigs
Bay leaf - 1
Pounded garlic, chili and black pepper, chopped parsley, salt- to taste

Cut fatty beef (brisket, rump, shank) into small pieces, wash, put into a pot together with 6-8 cups of cold water and bring to boil. Skim the foam as it rises to the top.

Approximately 20-30 minutes before the end of cooking add sliced carrot and "bouquet" of parsley with celery. Season the soup with salt and add bay leaf and chili pepper about 1o minutes before the soup is done.

Just before serving sprinkle the soup with chopped parsley, dill, and pounded garlic.

Soup-Tatariahni with Beef (B)

Ingredients:
Beef - 500 g
Parsley - 5 sprigs
Celery - 5 stalks
Onion - 1
Pounded garlic, chili and black pepper, chopped parsley, salt - to taste

Cut beef brisket into small pieces, wash it, put into a pot with 6 cups of cold water, cover the pot and bring it to boil. Skim the foam as it rises to the top.

After 2 1/2 hours, when the meat is almost done, take it out of the broth and rinse with a warm water, the add to the strained broth and return to boil. Add cleaned and washed celery, parsley, onion and simmer for 30 minutes. Season the soup with salt, add chili pepper and simmer for 5 minutes longer.

Just before serving sprinkle the soup with chopped parsley. Served pounded garlic on a side.

Beef and Tomatoes Soup

Ingredients:
Beef - 500 g
Onion - 1
Celery - 1 stalk
Parsley - 1 sprig
Dill - 1 sprig
Bay leaf - 1
Allspice - 2
Tomatoes - 500 g

Eggs - 2
Finely chopped herbs (parsley, cilantro) and salt - to taste

Cut beef into small pieces, put into a pot with 6 cups of water, bring to boil skimming foam as it rises to the top. Add onion, celery, bay leaf, and allspice to the pot. Cook the broth until meat is done. Take beef out of the pot and rinse with warm water, put into a clean pot, add strained broth and return to boil.

Meanwhile wash tomatoes, cut into pieces, put into a clean pot, bring to boil and simmer for until cooked. Pass cooked tomatoes through a sieve. Add prepared tomatoes to the soup and continue cooking 15-20 minutes longer.

Just before serving gradually add beaten eggs to the soup stirring all the time. Sprinkle the soup with chopped cilantro and parsley.

Soup-Bozartma with Lamb

Ingredients:
Lamb - 500 g
Onions - 200 g
Cilantro - 4-5 springs
Salt and pepper - to taste

Cut fatty lamb into small pieces, wash, put into a pot, add enough cold water to cover the meat, and bring to boil over a low heat. Skim the foam as it rises to the top. Approximately 1 1/2 -2 hours later remove meat from broth.

Finely chop onion and brown it in the fat skimmed from broth, then add lamb to the onion and continue to cook for a while longer. Add strained broth to the pot with meat and onion, season with salt and pepper, sprinkle with finely chopped cilantro, return to boil and remove from heat.

Soup-Bozartma with Young Chicken

Ingredients:
Young chicken - 1
Onions - 4-5
Clarified butter - 1 tbsp
Cilantro - 4-5
Salt - to taste

Cut young chicken into servings, wash, put into a pot, add finely chopped onions, clarified butter, and saute everything together until nicely browned. Add enough water to cover the chicken and bring to boil. About 5 minutes before the end of cooking season the soup with salt and add finely chopped cilantro.

Soup-Bozartma with Chicken or Turkey

Ingredients:
Chicken or turkey - 1
Onions - 500 g
Cilatnro - 5-6 sprigs
Parsley - 3 sprigs
Dill, mint, saffron, salt - to taste

Cut one fatty chicken or medium turkey into pieces, wash, put into a pot, cover the pot and braise the bird. From time to time pour the juice released during cooking into another container. Add finely chopped onions to the braised meat, return the meat juice back, and braise everything together for 10-15 minutes. Add boiling water (2 - 2.5 liters), bring to boil, and let it simmer for 10 minutes. Add finely chopped herbs (cilantro, parsley, dill, mint), crushed saffron, ground black pepper, salt, return to boil and simmer for 10 minutes longer.

Soup-Bozartma with Goose

Ingredients:
Goose - 1
Onions - 500 g
Cilantro - 6 sprigs
Wine vinegar - 1-2 tbsp
Chili pepper and salt - to taste

Cut prepared carcass of a medium-sized fatty goose into pieces, wash them, put into a pot, cover with water and bring to boil. Skim the foam as it rises to the top. Cook until meat is cooked through.

In a separate pot brown sliced onions in fat skimmed from the goose broth. To the pot with onions add pieces of goose and strained broth and return it to boil. When broth returns to boil, add finely chopped cilantro, chili pepper, season with salt and wine vinegar, let it simmer 5 minutes longer, then remove from heat.

Soup-Bozartma with Spring Chicken

Ingredients:
Spring chicken - 1
Onions - 300 g
Butter - 50-70 g
Cilantro - 4 sprigs
Basil - 3 sprigs
Mint - 2 sprigs
Tarragon - 2 sprigs
Garlic - 2 cloves
Wine vinegar - 1-2 tbsp
Chili pepper and salt - to taste

Cut prepared carcass of a spring chicken into pieces, wash them, put into a pot together with thinly sliced onions and butter, cover the pot and brown chicken and onions nicely. Add boiling water (6-7 cups), return to boil, simmer for 5 minutes, then add finely chopped herbs (cilantro, basil, mint, tarragon, parsley, and dill), finely pounded garlic, chili pepper, and saffron with salt, wine vinegar. Continue simmering for 10 minutes longer, then remove from the heat.

Soup-Buglama with Lamb

Ingredients:
Lamb - 500 g
Onions - 500 g
Tomatoes - 1 kg
or Tomato puree - 1 cup
Potatoes - 500 g
Cilantro - 4-5 sprigs
Salt and ground black pepper - to taste

Peel and thinly slice onions. Cut lamb into pieces and wash them. Peel and dice tomatoes. Peel potatoes and cut them into large pieces. Put ingredients in layers in a pot in the following order -- onions, meat, potatoes, then add 1 cup of water, next, put tomatoes, season with salt and pepper, sprinkle with chopped cilantro. Tightly cover the pot and cook over low heat until meat is done.

If using tomato puree instead of tomatoes -- use just 1/2 cup of water.

Soup-Buglama with Lamb and Eggplant

Ingredients:
Lamb - 500 g
Tomatoes - 1200 g

Onions - 400 g
Potatoes - 4-5
Eggplants - 2-3
Cilantro - 2-3 sprigs
Chili pepper and salt - to taste

Cut lamb into medium-sized pieces and wash them. Peel and cut tomatoes. Slice onions, peel potatoes and cut into large pieces. Slice eggplants across.

Put ingredients in layers in a pot: sliced onions, meat, potatoes, tomatoes, eggplants, add chili pepper, finely chopped cilantro, season with salt, add 1/2 cup of water.

Cover the pot tightly and cook over low heat. Meat will be done in about 2 hours. During cooking leave the pot completely undisturbed.

Soup-Buglama with Chicken

Ingredients:
Chicken - 1
Butter - 50 g
Onions - 3
Tomatoes - 600 g
Green beans - 300 g
Cilantro - 4 sprigs
Parsley, basil, dill - 1 sprig each
Chili pepper and salt - to taste

Cut prepared fatty chicken into pieces, put into a pot with 1 cup of water and braise until half-done.

Cook string beans in salted water until half-done. Peel and wash onions, dice them, and brown in butter.

Scald washed tomatoes, peel them, and cut into wedges. Put all ingredients into one pot -- chicken, green beans, browned onions, tomatoes. Season everything with salt and add finely chopped parsley, basil, dill, cilantro, chili pepper, and cook until done.

Lamb Soup

Ingredients:
Lamb - 500 g
Onions - 500 g
Water - 5-6 cups
Cilantro, salt - to taste

Cut fatty lamb into pieces, put into a pot, add finely diced onion, and brown everything gently. Add boiling water and continue cooking until meat is done. About 5 minutes before the end of cooking season the soup with salt and add finely chopped cilantro.

Lamb's Head and Feet Soup

Ingredients:
Lamb's feet, head, and stomach - 2 kg
Garlic - 10-15 cloves
Salt - to taste

Put prepared, thoroughly washed and cut into pieces lamb's feet, stomach, and head (whole) into a pot with cold water, cover the pot and cook for 5-6 hours. Strain the broth and transfer it into a clean pot. Remove bones from feet and head, cut stomach into small pieces, return the meat into the simmering broth and simmer for another 10-15 minutes. Season broth with salt and pounded garlic.

Lamb Soup with Rice

Ingredients:
Lamb - 500 g
Onions - 200 g
Rice - 100 g
Prunes - 200 g
Cilantro - 2-3 sprigs
Parsley, salt - to taste

Cut fatty lamb into pieces, wash, put into a pot, add 8 cups of cold water and bring to boil. Skim the foam as it rises to the top. Approximately 30 minutes after the water comes to boil skim the fat and use it to brown finely chopped onions. Put browned onions into broth, add finely chopped cilantro, washed rice, salt, and continue cooking until meat is done. Just before the end of cooking add prunes. Sprinkle soup with chopped parsley just before serving.

Lamb Soup with Meatballs

Ingredients:
Lamb - 500 g
Potatoes - 300 g
Egg - 1
Rice - 1/4 cup
Onions - 3
Cherry plums or Tkemali - 1/2 cup
Cilantro - 4 sprigs
Parsley, salt, pepper - to taste

Separate lamb meat from bones. Make a stock from the bones and strain it. Pass lamb through a meat grinder twice, add rice, raw egg, salt, and ground black pepper. Thorough mix ground lamb with other ingredients and roll into walnut-sized meatballs.

Put diced potatoes into strained boiling stock and cook for 10 minutes. Add meatballs to the soup and continue cooking 10-15 minutes longer, then add pitted cherry plums or tkemali and browned onions. Just before serving sprinkle soup with chopped parsley and cilantro.

Lamb Soup with Vegetables

Ingredients:
Lamb - 500 g
Onions - 200 g
Rice - 3/4-1 cup
Potatoes - 3-4
Carrots - 2-3
Tomatoes - 300 g
or Tomato puree - 80-100 g
Garlic - 1-2 cloves
Whole black pepper - 5-6
Parsley, cilantro, salt - to taste
Sour milk - to taste

Cut fatty lamb into pieces, add to the pot with water (6-8 cups) and cook until half-done, skimming foam as it rises to the top.

Remove lamb from the pot and brown in a fat skimmed from the broth. Add diced onions and salt and continue frying 5-10 minutes longer. Add fresh tomatoes passed through a sieve of tomato puree, continue cooking 10-15 minutes more.

Meanwhile, strain the broth, return it to boil in a clean pot, add washed rice, diced carrots and potatoes, and simmer until rice and vegetables are cooked through. Add garlic pounded with salt and ground black pepper to taste.

Return fried meat to the broth and simmer for 1-2 minutes longer.

Just before serving season soup with sour milk and sprinkle with finely chopped parsley or cilantro.

Lamb Soup with Peas

Ingredients:
Lamb - 500 g
Peas - 200 g
Lamb tail fat - 50 g
Onions - 100 g
Potatoes - 300-400 g
Herbs, salt - to taste

Pick over and thoroughly wash peas. If peas are not hulled - soak them in cold water for 4-5 hours, then drain.

Bring 8-10 cups of water to boil. When water comes to boil add washed and cut into small pieces lamb tail fat and lamb meat. About 15-20 minutes after the water returns to boil add prepared peas, a bouquet of cilantro and parsley, continuing cooking until meat and peas are falling apart.

When lamb tail fat is half done -- take it out of the soup, finely chop it, then return back into the pot.

15-20 minutes later add browned onions, salt, peeled and cut into pieces potatoes, finely chopped cilantro (4 sprigs). To spice up the soup (if desired) add pepper and tkemali 15 minutes after adding potatoes.

Remove and discard herb bouquet from the soup. Just before serving sprinkle the soup with finely chopped cilantro and parsley.

Soup-Bozbashi (A)

Ingredients:
Lamb - 500 g

Lamb tail fat - 30-50 g
Onions - 150-200 g
Cracked rice - 1 tbsp
Cilantro - 7-8 sprigs
Parsley - 2 springs
Fine salt and ground black pepper - to taste

Thoroughly wash fatty lamb with cold water and cut it into pieces, put into a pot together with finely chopped lamb tail fat and cilantro, add 8-10 cups of water, and bring to boil. Skim the foam as it rises to the top. When the water starts boiling and foam is no longer rising -- add finely chopped onions, cracked rice, and cook until meat is done.

Before the end of the cooking season the soup with salt and ground black pepper, sprinkle with finely chopped cilantro (2-3 sprigs) and parsley.

Soup-Bozbashi (B)

Ingredients:
Lamb - 500 g
Lamb tail fat - 50 g
Onions - 30-40 g
Cilantro - 8-10 sprigs
Tkemali, cherry plums, or plums - to taste
Parsley leaves, salt, pepper - to taste

Bring to boil 8-10 cups of water. Put cut into pieces and thoroughly washed fatty lamb into the pot with boiling water together with a piece of lamb tail fat, cover the pot, and return to boil. Skim the foam as it rises to the top. Peel onions, pass it through a meat grinder and add it to the simmering soup. Take out of the pot still somewhat uncooked lamb tail fat, pass it through a meat grinder together with cilantro and return it back to the pot. Approximately 20-25 minutes later season the soup with salt and ground black pepper, return the soup to boil and remove from heat. If desired - add to the soup boiled and passed through a sieve tkemali plums, cherry plums, or some other sour plums, let the soup simmer for 3-5 minutes longer. Sprinkle with chopped parsley before serving.

Soup-Bozbashi (C)

Ingredients:
Lamb - 500 g
Lamb tail fat - 50 g
Rice - 1/4 cup
Onions - 3-4
Egg yolks - 2
Cilantro - 4-5 sprigs
Tarragon - 2 sprigs
Salt and ground black pepper - to taste

Cook washed lamb and lamb tail fat just like in the previous recipe.

Strain cooked broth into a clean pot, transfer meat and fat into this pot, add rice, diced onions, and cook until rice is done. Gradually add egg yolks mixed with a small quantity of broth, return soup to boil, then remove from heat. Add finely chopped cilantro and tarragon, season soup with salt and ground black pepper.

Soup-Bozbashi with Meatballs (A)

Ingredients:
Lamb - 300 g
Lamb bones - 200 g
Peas - 100 g
Rice - 1/2 cup
Onions - 2

Tomatoes - 200-300 g
or Tomato puree - 70-100 g
Carrot - 1
Egg - 1
Cinnamon, cloves, salt - to taste

Make broth with lamb bones, strain.

Pass lamb through a meat grinder twice, add half-cooked rice, salt, ground black pepper, ground cinnamon and cloves, raw egg, and mix everything well. Roll walnut-sized meatballs from this meat mixture.

Brown diced onions in the fat skimmed from the broth, then add it to the broth. Return soup to boil, add diced carrot, peeled and cut into wedges tomatoes (or tomato puree).

Add meatballs gradually, one after another, then season the soup with salt and cook until done.

Soup-Bozbashi with Meatballs (B)

Ingredients:
Lamb - 500 g
Lamb tail fat - 30 g
Onions - 150 g
Cracked rice - 1 tbsp
Cilantro - 3 sprigs
Salt - to taste
For meatballs -
Onions - 100 g
Egg - 1/2
Cilantro - 4 sprigs
Cracked rice - as needed
Cinnamon, ground black pepper, salt - to taste

Separate meat from bones. Wash bones and lamb tail fat, put into a pot, add 8-10 cups of cold water and bring to boil.

Skim foam as it rises to the top. Take tail fat out of the broth and finely chop it together with cilantro, strain the broth into a clean pot. Return chopped tail fat and cilantro to the strained broth together with diced onions, cracked rice, salt, and continue cooking.

Pass lamb meat through a meat grinder twice together with cilantro and onions. Thoroughly mix ground meat with black pepper, ground cinnamon, salt, and egg, then shape walnut-sized meatballs from the mixture. Coat meatballs with cracked rice, lower them into the simmering soup one at a time, and cook until done.

Soup-Bozbashi with Meatballs (C)

Ingredients:
Lamb - 500 g
Onions - 3
Rice - 1/2 - 3/4 cup
Egg - 1
Egg yolks - 2
Carrot - 1
Parsley - 1 sprig
Cilantro, pepper, salt - to taste

Separate meat from bones. Make broth from bones, adding carrot, onion, and a sprig of parsley after water came to simmer and all the foam has been skimmed. Strain finished broth.

Brown diced onions in the fat skimmed from the broth, then add it to the simmering strained broth.

Make meatballs - pass meat through a meat grinder, mix in half-cooked rice, season with salt, ground pepper, and add an egg. Roll walnut-sized balls from the mixture, and gradually add them to the simmering broth.

Just before serving dress soup with egg yolks mixed with a small quantity of broth, season with salt, and sprinkle with chopped cilantro.

Soup-Bozbashi with Eggplant and Green Beans

Ingredients:
Lamb - 500 g
Onions - 2
Eggplants - 200 g
Sweet bell peppers - 2
Green beans - 150-200 g
Tomatoes - 3-4
Cilantro, garlic, salt - to taste

Cut fatty lamb into pieces, add 6-8 cups of water, and cook until done.

Remove cooked meat from the broth and brown it in the fat skimmed from the broth. Pour strained broth over browned lamb.

Brown diced onions in the fat from the broth, then add it to the pot with broth. When the broth returns to boil, add washed and cut eggplants, green beans, sweet bell peppers, and cook until done.

Just before the end of cooking add finely chopped cilantro and garlic mashed with salt to the soup.

Soup-Chihirtma with Chicken or Lamb

Ingredients:
Chicken - 1
or Lamb - 500-700 g
Onions - 5
Eggs - 2-3
Wine vinegar - 1-2 tbsp
Cilantro - 4 sprigs

Ground cinnamon - 1/4 tsp
Salt and ground black pepper - to taste

Finely dice or pass through a meat grinder peeled onions, and lightly brown them in a pot in lamb or chicken fat. Add washed and cut into small pieces lamb or chicken to the pot and continue sautéing for 10-15 minutes. Add cold water (8-10 cups) to the pot and cook 2-2 1/2 hours. About 10 minutes before the end of cooking add finely chopped cilantro, salt, and ground cinnamon to the soup. If desired -- season soup with ground black pepper.

Just before serving beat 2-3 eggs with a little vinegar, then gradually add them to the soup while constantly stirring. Return soup to simmer and remove from heat.

Soup-Chihirtma with Chicken (A)

Ingredients:
Chicken - 1
Onions - 300-400 g
Wheat flour - 1 tbsp
Eggs - 3-4
Cilantro and parsley - 3-4 sprigs each
Wine vinegar, lemon acid, black pepper, cinnamon, coriander, salt - to taste

Pure prepared fatty chicken into a pot, add 8-10 cups of cold water, bring to boil, and simmer for 1-2 hours until chicken is completely cooked. Remove foam as it rises to the top. Transfer cooked chicken to a plate and season it with salt.

Skim fat from the top of the broth, put it into a clean pot, and brown diced onions in it. To prevent onions from burning stir it with a spoon from time to time. Mix wheat flour with 1 tbsp of broth, the ad it to the pot with onions.

Pour in strained broth, return it to boil, then add

"bouquet" of cilantro. 30 minutes later season the soup with cinnamon, black pepper, crushed coriander seeds, wine vinegar, salt, and cook 15 minutes longer. Remove soup from heat and discard "bouquet" of cilantro. Gradually add eggs beaten with a small quantity of broth stirring all the time. Return soup to boil and instantly remove from heat. If desired - add lemon acid or saffron infusion (to taste) to the soup.

To serve - put pieces of chicken meat back into the soup and sprinkle it with finely chopped parsley. Prepared soup can also be served without chicken, in which case used cooked chicken to make some other dish.

Soup-Chihirtma with Chicken (B)

Ingredients:
Chicken - 1
Onions - 5
Egg yolks - 2-3
Mint - 3 sprigs
Basil - 2 sprigs
Salt - to taste

Put prepared fat chicken into a pot together with its giblets, add 8-10 cups of cold water, bring to boil skimming the foam as it rises to the top. Cook until chicken is down. Transfer cooked chicken with giblets into a clean container and cover it. Skim fat from the top of the broth and use it to soften onions in another pot. Add strained broth to sautéed onions and return it to boil.

Cut chicken into serving pieces and return to the simmering broth together with its giblets.

Beat egg yolks and mix them with small quantity of cooled broth, then pour it into the soup, season the soup with salt and sprinkle with finely chopped mint and basil.

Soup-Chihirtma with Chicken (C)

Ingredients:
Chicken - 1
Onions - 5
Wheat flour - 1 tbsp
Eggs - 2-3
Cilantro, black pepper, coriander seeds, wine vinegar, salt - to taste

Cut prepared fatty chicken into pieces, wash them, put into a pot, cover with cold water, and cook until chicken is half-done.

In another pot render chicken fat, add some fat skimmed from the top of the broth, and soften finely chopped onions in it. Add more fat skimmed from the broth with wheat flour, and continue cooking for about 10 minutes. Transfer pieces of chicken from the broth to the onions and continue cooking 15 minutes longer. Add strained chicken broth, return to boil, and cook 10 minutes longer. Season the soup with wine vinegar, ground black pepper, salt, crushed coriander seeds, and let it simmer 10 minutes longer, then gradually add eaten eggs. Just before serving sprinkle with finely chopped cilantro.

Soup-Chihirtma with Young Chicken

Ingredients:
Young chicken - 1
Onions - 4-5
Clarified butter - 1 tbsp
Egg yolks - 3-4
Vinegar, herbs, salt - to taste

Cut young medium sized chicken into serving pieces, wash, put into a pot, season with salt, add chopped onions, and braise with clarified butter until almost cooked. Add enough water to the pot to cover the chicken, bring to boil, add chopped cilantro and let it simmer 15 minutes.

Just before serving remove soup from the heat and slightly cool it, at the same time beat egg yolks with a little vinegar and a small quantity of broth. Gradually add beaten eggs to the soup, stirring all the time. Return the pot to the stove and warm it up without returning the soup to boil to prevent yolks from curdling. Pour soup into bowls and sprinkle it with chopped cilantro.

Soup-Chihirtma with Chicken Giblets

Ingredients:
Giblets - From 1 chicken
Onions - 4
Wine vinegar - 2 tbsp
Egg yolks - 2
Ground cinnamon - 1/2 tsp
Wheat flour - 1 tbsp
Cilantro - to taste
Salt and ground black pepper - to taste

Sauté chicken giblets with finely chopped onions until nicely browned, sprinkle with wheat flour and mix well, then add 1/4 cup of boiling water and braise for 5-10 minutes, then add more boiling water (5-6 cups), add cilantro sprigs and let it simmer. About 10-15 minutes later remove cilantro from the pot and season the soup with salt. Mix ground cinnamon and pepper with vinegar and add it to the soup.

Just before serving dress the soup with egg yolks beaten with a small quantity of soup. To prevent egg yolks from curdling - gently heat up the soup but do not boil it.

Summer Soup

Ingredients:
Lamb - 500 g
Onions - 3
Tomatoes - 300 g
Green beans - 200 g
Apples - 2, medium
Chili pepper, parsley, salt - to taste

Wash fatty lamb and cut it into medium-sized pieces, add to the pot with 6-8 cups of water and bring to boil. Skim fat from the broth, transfer it into another pot and sauté chopped onions in it until softened. Transfer cooked lamb to the onions and lightly brown it. When meat is browned -- add chopped tomatoes to the pot and braise for 5-10 minutes longer. Add strained broth to the pot, return it to boil and let it simmer 3-5 minutes before adding cut green beens, chili pepper, salt, cut into wedges sour apples, and cook until done. Just before serving sprinkle the soup with finely chopped parsley.

Soup-Hashlama

Ingredients:
Veal - 1 kg
Parsnips - 2
Celery - 2 stalks
Garlic, parsley, salt - to taste

Cut veal (brisket) into pieces, put into a pot, cover with water, and bring to boil. Skim the foam as it rises to the top before boiling. Once water comes to boil add parsnips and celery which should be removed once the soup is done. Just

5 minutes before the end of cooking season the soup with salt.

Before serving put meat, mashed garlic, and finely chopped parsley into each bowl, and fill the bowl with broth. Taste of garlic should be clearly pronounced in this dish.

Soup with Pork

Ingredients:
Pork - 500 g
Eggs - 2
Cilantro and parsley - 2 sprigs each
Sour fruit leather, salt - to taste

Cut pork into small pieces, wash, put into a pot, cover with 5-6 cups of water and bring to boil. Remove the foam as it rises to the top, then add herbs.

Remove the meat from the pot when it is cooked. Strain broth and transfer it into a clean pot, add sliced sour fruit leather (tklapi) and cook 15 minutes longer. Season the soup with salt, remove the pot from the heat and let it cool slightly.

Meanwhile, beat eggs, and gradually add them to the soup, stirring all the time. Return the pot to the stove and heat it up without letting it boil.

Just before serving return cooked pork to the soup, or serve it on a side.

Soup with Goose and Dried Dogwood Berries

Ingredients:
Goose - 1 kg
Onions - 500 g
Dried dogwood berries - 1 cup

Cilantro and parsley - 3 sprigs each
Salt - to taste

Cut prepared goose into pieces, wash, then put them into a pot, add 8-10 cups of cold water, and bring to boil. Skim foam as it rises to the top. Add sliced onions and sprigs of parsley and cilantro to the soup. About 5-10 minutes later add throughly washed pitted dry dogwood berries and continue cooking until meat is done. Season the soup with salt.

Chicken Soup

Ingredients:
Chicken with giblets - 1
Parsnips - 3
Carrots - 3
Celery - 3 stalks
Rice - 1/2 cup
Garlic - 8-10 cloves
Parsley, salt - to taste

Put prepared washed chicken together with giblets into a pot, add peeled carrots, parsnips, celery, parsley, cover with 8-10 cups of cold water, and bring to boil, skimming foam as it rises to the top.
Test if chicken is ready with a help of a fork (if it goes in easily -- the bird is cooked), transfer chicken and giblets into another container, season it with salt, and keep covered. Strain the broth, put into a clean pot together with rice and 3-4 cloves of garlic, and return to boil. About 30 minutes later add chicken cut into pieces together with giblets back to the simmering soup, add chopped parsley and sliced coked

carrot from the first step. Remove pot from the heat 5 minutes later.

Just before serving add mashed garlic (remaining cloves) to the soup, and, if desired, sprinkle with more chopped parsley.

VEGETARIAN SOUPS

Soup-Chihirtma

Ingredients:
Onions - 300 g
Butter - 500 g
Flour - 1 tbsp
Eggs - 2-3
Wine vinegar, black pepper, cinnamon, lemon acid, herbs, salt - to taste

Finely dice or pass onions through a meat grinder, put into a pot and lightly brown in 30 g of butter. Add 6-7 cups of boiling water to the pot together with cilantro sprigs and let it simmer for 5-10 minutes. Add flour mixed with a little of broth and wine vinegar, season the soup with ground cinnamon, ground black pepper, salt, and continue cooking for 15 minutes longer. Take the pot off the heat, remove cilantro, and gradually add eggs beaten with a small quantity of broth. Just before serving sprinkle soup with finely chopped parsley or cilantro, add remaining butter, and, if desired, add lemon acid.

Soup-Chihirtma with Tomatoes

Ingredients:
Onions - 4

Tomatoes - 800 g
Flour - 1 tbsp
Butter - 70 g
Eggs - 2-3
Cilantro, parsley, salt - to taste

Finely dice onions, put them into a pot, add 30 g of butter and sauté onions until lightly browned. Add flour and 20 g of butter and continue sautéing 5-10 minutes, then add cooked and passed through a sieve tomatoes together with remaining butter, and simmer 10-15 minutes longer. Add 5-6 cups of boiling water, return the pot to boil, and simmer 20 minutes. Add finely chopped parsley and cilantro and simmer 5 minutes. Gradually add beaten eggs and once eggs are cooked remove pot from the heat.

Soup-Kharcho

Ingredients:
Onions - 300 g
Butter - 30-35 g
Rice or vermicelli - 3/4-1 cup
Herbs, sour fruit leather, garlic, chili pepper, dried suneli, salt - to taste

Finely dice onions, put into a pot and sauté in butter, then add boiling water (6-7 cups) and bring to boil. Add washed rice or vermicelli, simmer for 20 minutes, then add finely chopped herbs, pieces of sour fruit leather (tklapi), mashed garlic, thinly sliced chili pepper, dried suneli and salt. Soup will be done in 5-10 minutes.

Soup-Kharcho with Walnuts

Ingredients:
Onions - 200 g
Butter - 30-50 g
Shelled walnuts - 100 g
Tomatoes - 300-500 g
Cilantro - 4 sprigs
Rice - 1/2 cup
or Vermicelli - 3/4 cup
Chili pepper, garlic, herbs, salt - to taste

Put finely diced onions into a pot, add butter, cover the pot and sauté onions stirring from time to time to prevent onions from burning.

Mix crushed walnuts with cilantro, garlic, and chili pepper pounded in mortar, add 7 cups of water, then pour this mixture into the pot with onions, add rice or vermicelli, season with salt and let it simmer.

Meanwhile, cut tomatoes, braise them, pass them through a sieve. Put tomato puree into a clean pot and simmer until thickened, then add tomato puree to the soup. Return soup to boil, then add finely chopped parsley and cilantro and remove from the heat.

Soup-Kharcho with Eggs

Ingredients:
Onions - 300 g
Butter - 60 g
Eggs - 4-5
Rice - 1/2 cup
Shelled walnuts - 3/4 cup
Sour fruit leather or tkemali, herbs, pepper, salt, garlic - to taste

GEORGIAN CUISINE

Finely chop onions, put into a pot and brown in 30 g of butter, then add 6 cups of boiling water, rice, return to boil and cook 15-20 minutes. Pound shelled walnuts together with cilantro, garlic, chili pepper, and salt, and crush everything together in a mortar, mix with 2 cups of boiling water, and add to the soup. Approximately 5-10 minutes later add pieces of sour fruit leather (tklapi) or tkemali puree and return to boil. Break eggs, one after another, over the soup pot. Remove pot from the heat when eggs are completely cooked. Just before serving sprinkle the soup with finely chopped herbs and dress with a little butter.

Soup-Kharcho with Bread

Ingredients:
Georgian bread - 1 kg
Onions - 200 g
Butter - 100 g
Eggs - 2-3
Salt - to taste

Finely dice onions, pout into a pot with some butter and salt and lightly brown them.
Cut Georgian bread into small pieces, add to the pot with onions, add enough boiling water to cover bread and bring everything to boil. When bread is falling apart, add 2-3 beaten eggs to the pot, and continue cooking until done.

Soup with Walnuts

Ingredients:
Shelled walnuts - 1 cup
Onions - 200 g

Flour - 1 tbsp
Butter - 30-50 g
Egg yolks - 2-3
Herbs, wine vinegar, salt - to taste

Thoroughly crush shelled walnuts. Finely dice onions and put into a pot together with walnuts, add 1/2 cup of water and simmer until the onions are soft. Add 6 cups of boiling water and flour mix with a small quantity of wine vinegar. About 15-20 minutes after the sour returns to boil add finely chopped cilantro, parsley, and dill, return to boil and remove the pot from the heat. Beat egg yolks in a tureen, and gradually pour the soup in stirring it all the time. Sprinkle soup with finely chopped parsley and add a little butter before serving.

Asparagus Soup

Ingredients:
Asparagus - 500 g
Onions - 200 g
Butter - 1 tbsp
Eggs - 3
Herbs, salt - to taste

Peel asparagus, cut the spears carefully making sure not to break the tips of the spears - the best part of asparagus, wash in cold water, put into a pot with boiling water (6-7 cups) and cook.

Finely chop onions and soften them in butter, then add to the simmering soup. Season the soup with salt and chopped herbs. Remove the pot from the heat when asparagus is cooked through. Beat eggs in a separate container with a small quantity of soup, gradually pour beaten eggs into the soup, mix, then heat the soup up without letting it boil.

Sprinkle with finely chopped parsley leaves before serving.

Sweet Pea Soup

The soup is made with Sweet Pea (Lathyrus roseus) - plant growing in the Caucasus Mountains

Ingredients:
Sweet Pea - 500 g
Onions - 200 g
Clarified butter - 1-2 tbsp
Shelled walnuts - 1/2 cup
Eggs - 2
Cilantro, parsley, salt - to taste

Clean Sweet Pea from leaves, trim dried ends of stems, wash, and put into a pot with boiling water.

Brown finely chopped onions in butter, then add to the soup and continue cooking.

Crush shelled walnuts with salt and cilantro in a mortar and also add to the simmering soup.

About 20 minutes later, when the soup is done, remove the pot from heat, and gradually pour in 2 beaten eggs. Just before serving sprinkle soup with finely chopped parsley.

Pea Soup with Rice

Ingredients:
Peas - 800 g
Onions - 3-4
Vegetable oil - 1/3 cup
Rice - 1 tbsp
Potatoes - 3

Parsley, dill, salt - to taste

Wash peas in a few changes of cold water and soak it in 5-6 cups of water. One hour later put peas to cook in the water it was soaking in and cook until it is cooked. Remove husks from cooked peas.

Finely chop onions, cook them until softened in vegetable oil, add peas to onions and continue cooking for a while. Pour strained pea cooking broth together with rice, peeled, diced potatoes, finely chopped cilantro, season with salt, and continue cooking for 15-20 minutes longer. Just before serving sprinkle the soup chopped parsley and dill.

Red Kidney Bean Soup

Ingredients:
Red kidney beans - 300 g
Shelled walnuts - 100 g
Onions - 1-2
Herbs, pepper, salt - to taste

Pick red kidney beans over, wash them a couple of times with cold water, put into a pot, cover with boiling water (8-10 cups) and bring to boil. When beans are cooked through mash them thoroughly so there are no whole beans left. Add crushed walnuts, finely chopped onions, ground pepper, salt, mix everything, and cook 5-7 minutes. Then add finely chopped herbs (parsley, cilantro, celery leaves, dill, and mint) and cook 3-5 minutes longer, then take the soup off the heat.

Beans in Vegetable Oil Soup

Ingredients:

Beans - 500 g
Crushed shelled walnuts - 50 g
Vegetable oil - 50 g
Onions - 2-3
Herbs, chili pepper, salt - to taste

Put prepared beans into a pot, cover with boiling water and return to boil. Add cilantro stalks while beans are cooking. When beans are soft take it out with a skimmer, pass it through a sieve, and return back to cooking liquid.

Finely chop onions, soften them in vegetable oil and add to the simmering soup. Five minutes later add chili pepper, crushed walnuts, and salt, mix everything well and cook for five minutes longer. Just before serving season the soup with wine vinegar or boiled tkemali, finely chopped parsley, mint, cilantro, and dill.

Bean Soup with Butter and Eggs

Ingredients:
Beans - 500 g
Onions - 2-3
Butter - 50 g
Eggs - 3-4
Herbs, salt - to taste

Put beans into a pot, add boiling water (6-8 cups) and bring to boil. Strain beans preserving the cooking liquid, mash beans well, then return cooking liquid back into the pot, and return pot to boil. Add finely chopped and browned in butter onions, season the soup with salt, add finely chopped cilantro and celery leaves, and cook 2-3 minutes longer. Beat eggs and gradually add them to the simmering soup, stirring all the time. The moment eggs are cooked, remove pot from the heat and sprinkle soup with herbs (dill, mint).

Soup-Shechmandy with Yogurt (Matsoni) (A)

Ingredients:
Matsoni - 2 cups
Wheat flour - 1 tbsp
Onions - 1-2
Butter - 50 g
Eggs - 2-3
Herbs, salt - to taste

Sauté diced onions in butter. Beat matsoni well to break any clumps, add 1 cup of cold water, wheat flour, and salt, and pour it into the pot with onions. Bring the pot to boil, then lower the heat and simmer 15 minutes, then gradually add beaten eggs, stirring all the time. Remove pot from the heat when eggs are cooked. Just before serving put chopped cilantro, mint, or dill into bowls.

Soup-Shechmandy with Yogurt (Matsoni) (B)

Ingredients:
Matsoni - 3 cups
Milk - 3 cups
Onions - 2-3
Flour - 1 tbsp
Butter - 50 g
Rice - 1/2 cup
Egg yolks - 2
Herbs, salt - to taste

Sauté dice onions in butter for about 10 minutes. Add flour to the onions and continue sautéing for another 5 minutes.

Meanwhile mix matsoni with milk thoroughly, add to the pot with browned onions, and bring to boil. When contents of the pot come to boil add cooked in water rice, season with salt, and simmer 5 minutes longer. Remove soup from the heat and gradually add egg yolks mixed with a small quantity of cooled soup.

Just before serving sprinkle the soup with finely chopped tarragon and dill.

Soup-Shechmandy with Yogurt and Rice (A)

Ingredients:
Matsoni - 2 cups
Water - 2 cups
Onions - 2
Butter or clarified butter - 50 g
Rice - 1/2 cup
Eggs - 2
Herbs, salt - to taste

Finely dice onions, put into a pot, and brown in butter. Meanwhile mix matsoni with water, mix well to break any lumps, pour this mixture into the pot with browned onions, add washed rice and bring to boil. Season the soup with salt and add chopped herbs while it is cooking. Cook until the rice is done. Remove pot from the heat, and, constantly stirring, add beaten eggs to the soup.

Soup-Shechmandy with Yogurt and Rice (B)

Ingredients:
Matsoni - 2-3 cups
Cold water - 2 cups
Boiling water - 1 cup
Onions - 3
Butter or clarified butter - 50-70 g

Rice - 1/4-1/2 cup
Egg yolks - 2
Herbs, salt - to taste

Finely dice onions, add to a pot, and brown in butter. Add 1 cup of boiling water and washed rice to the browned onions, and cook 15 minutes.

Mix matsoni with water, add to the pot with onions and rice, return to boil, and simmer for 10 minutes. Add tarragon and cilantro (fresh or dried), season with salt, simmer for 5 minutes longer, then remove pot from the heat. Beat egg yolks with a small quantity of cooled soup and add to the pot.

Soup-Shechmandy with Buttermilk

Ingredients:
Buttermilk - 1 cup
Onions - 2
Butter - 50 g
Eggs - 3
Mint, salt - to taste

Finely dice onions, put into a pot, add butter, and brown onions. Add 1 cup of buttermilk mixed with 4 cups of water, season with salt, bring to boil, and simmer 15-20 minutes, then gradually add 3 beaten eggs, and, stirring all the time, return soup to boil and immediately remove from heat. Sprinkle finely chopped mint into the finished soup.

Milk Soup with Eggs and Herbs

Ingredients:
Milk - 1 1/2 l
Savory - 3-4 sprigs

Garlic - 2-3 cloves
Eggs - 3-4
Salt - to taste

Season boiling milk with salt, add finely chopped savory, mashed garlic, and beaten eggs. Soup is done when eggs are curdled.

Cheese Soup (Gadazelili)

Translating this recipe was somewhat of a challenge - Imeretinsky cheese is available in some Russian stores in New York area, but otherwise, can't be found in a local grocery. Neufchatel cheese is perhaps the closest substitution, but try mozzarella or queso fresco as well when cooking this soup.

Ingredients:
Cheese Imeretinsky - 500 g
Milk - 2 l
Mint - to taste

Divide young, unsalted, or lightly salted, fresh Imeretinsky cheese in half, put into a pot, add hot milk and bring the pot to boil. When cheese becomes soft take it out of the pot and put it in a bowl. Take some of the milk from the pot with a ladle and pour it over cheese. Mash cheese with a spoon, then pour the liquid from the bowl back into the pot. Add another ladle of milk from the pot to the cheese and continue mashing the cheese. Repeat the process a number of times, until the cheese is mashed well and liquid in the pot thickens. Before serving cut cheese into serving pieces and put into bowls.

Add finely chopped mint leaves into the milk-cheese and continue simmering for 2 minutes, then remove pot from the heat and pour the soup into bowls with cheese.

Soup-Chrianteli with Sour Cherries or Blackberries

Ingredients:
Sour cherries or blackberries - 1 kg
Garlic, scallions, cucumbers, cilantro, salt - to taste

Pick sour cherries or blackberries over, wash, mash berries, and squeeze juice from them. If the juice is too sweet - add a little water to it. Season the juice with mashed garlic, chopped cilantro, dill, salt, and leave in a cool place. Just before serving add finely chopped scallions, and peeled, diced cucumbers to the soup.

Soup-Shechmandy with Dogwood Berries (A)

Ingredients:
Fresh dogwood berries - 500 g
or Dried dogwood berries - 200 g
Wheat flour - 2 tbsp
Garlic - 2-3 cloves
Salt - to taste

Wash fresh or dried dogwood berries, put into a pot, add 4-5 cups of water and bring to boil. When dogwood berries are cooked and soft, strain berries, preserving the cooking liquid, and pass them through a sieve. Save a little of cooking liquid and cool it, then mix it with flour to make a slurry. Meanwhile return remaining cooking liquid to boil and then add flour slurry to the boiling liquid and let it cook for a while, then add dogwood berry puree. Season the soup with salt and mashed garlic. This soup can also be made with sour cherry or blackthorn berries. It can be served warm or cold.

Soup-Shechmandy with Dogwood Berries (B)

Ingredients:
Dogwood berries - 1 kg
Water - 1.5-2 l
Wheat flour - 2 tbsp
Onions - 2
Mint, salt - to taste

Wash fresh, ripe dogwood berries and pass them through a sieve. Transfer dogwood berries puree into a clean container and cover it. Cover remains of berries with water, bring to boil, and cook for 5 minutes, then pass everything again through a sieve, pour it into a clean pot, add finely chopped onions and wheat flour mixed with a small quantity of cooking liquid, and cook for 15 minutes. Add finely chopped mint, dogwood berry puree, season soup with salt, and serve.

Soup with Dogwood Berries and Walnuts

Soup with dogwood berries and walnuts is cooked following instructions of the previous recipe. Add 1/2 cup of crushed walnuts to the soup during the last stage of cooking.

Soup-Shechmandy with Sour Fruit Leather (Tklapi)

Soup-shechmandy with sour fruit leather (tklapi - fruit leather made with juice of sour cherry plums tkemali) is cooked following instructions of the soup made from dogwood berries, just instead of dogwood berries use 150 g of sour fruit leather (if it is made from tkemali). If it is made from sweet fruit (blackthorn berries or plums) - take 200 g. of fruit leather.

Soup-Shechmandy with Herbs

Ingredients:
Leeks - 2
Dill - 3 sprigs
Parsley - 2 sprigs
Celery - 2 stalks
Cilantro - 3 sprigs
Mint - 3 sprigs
Wheat flour - 2 tbsp
Onions - 1
Shelled walnuts - 2 tbsp
Salt - to taste

Finely chop leeks and all the herbs, put into a pot with boiling salted water, add finely chopped onion and cook. During cooking add flour mixed with cold water, crushed walnuts, and season with more salt if necessary.

Soup with Tomatoes (A)

Ingredients:
Tomatoes - 1 kg
Onions - 3
Crushed shelled walnuts - 1/2 cup
Cilantro, salt - no taste

Cut slightly unripe tomatoes into thin wedges, put into a pot with crushed walnuts, finely chopped onions, cilantro, season with salt, and cook until done. Serve cooled.

Soup with Tomatoes (B)

Pour boiling water over medium sized tomatoes, peel them, cut each in half, seed them, put into a pot and bring to boil. Add finely diced onions.

Just before the end of cooking season the soup with salt and pepper. Sprinkle with finely chopped parsley just before serving.

Soup with Unripe Grapes

Cook unripe grapes in four cups of water, mash them and pass through a sieve. Separate a small quantity of broth and mix it with flour. Bring remaining broth to boil. Add flour slurry to the boiling broth, and continue cooking, stirring from time to time to prevent burning. Add crushed walnuts, finely chopped onions, season with salt, and cook until the flour can't be tasted or smelled. This soup can be served warm or cold.

FISH

FISH

Tsotshali

Gut live fish (brook trout), wash it, cut large fish into serving pieces, leave small ones whole. Cook fish in salted boiling water with a small quantity of alum (2-3 g of alum for 500 g fish). Remove cooked from the pot with a help of skimmer, put on a board, drizzle with cold water to cook. Transfer cooked fish to a serving plate, decorate with sprigs of parsley and celery leaves.

Sturgeon or Stellate Sturgeon with Walnut Sauce

Ingredients:
Fish - 500 g
Shelled walnuts - 1 cup
Cilantro - 2-3 sprigs
Garlic - 1 clove
Onion - 1
Chili pepper, vinegar, salt - to taste

Wash cleaned sturgeon or stellate sturgeon, cook in boiling water in one piece, then let it cool. Cut cooked fish into serving pieces and transfer to a serving plate.

Pound walnuts, cilantro, garlic, chili pepper, and salt in a mortar. Mix walnut mixture with 1 1/2 cups of cold boiled water, add to taste wine vinegar and finely chopped onion, mix well. Pour the sauce over fish and serve. If desired - squeeze oil from walnuts and drizzle it over the dish.

To make this dish with fried fish - cut prepared fish into serving pieces and fry until done in vegetable oil or clarified butter. Fish can be coated with wheat or corn flour prior to frying. Put fried fish on a serving dish and pour the sauce over it.

Boiled Fish (Sturgeon, Stellate Sturgeon or Beluga) with Vinegar Sauce

Ingredients:
Fish - 500 g
Wine vinegar - 1/2 cup
Cilantro - 5-6 sprigs
Onions - 2
Bay leaves - 1-2
Carrot - 1
Salt - to taste

Put prepared, washed sturgeon, stellate sturgeon or beluga in one piece into a medium pot with enough boiling salted water to cover the fish. Add bay leaves, peeled carrot, one onion, and cook 30-40 minutes.

Cool cooked fish, cut it into serving pieces, put on a serving plate, pour sauce over it and sprinkle with thinly sliced onion.

To make sauce mix vinegar with fish broth (1/2 cup) and finely chopped cilantro. The sauce can also be made without cilantro.

Sturegon or Stellate Sturgeon in Broth (A)

Ingredients:
Fish - 1 kg

Onions - 3-4
Garlic - 2 cloves
Bay leaves - 2
Cilantro, parsley, sweet bell pepper, salt - to taste

Cut cleaned, prepared sturgeon or stellate sturgeon into serving pieces, wash, put into a pot, season with salt, add water mixed with wine vinegar (water should barely cover the fish), finely chopped onion (1), crushed garlic, bay leaves, cover the pot and bring to boil. When the fish is cooked - remove bay leaves from the pot and add thinly sliced onions, finely chopped cilantro and diced sweet bell pepper. Remove the pot from the heat and let it cool.

Transfer fish together with broth into a serving bowl and sprinkle with finely chopped parsley.

Sturegon or Stellate Sturgeon in Broth (B)

Ingredients:
Fish - 1 kg
Wine vinegar - 3/4 cup
Onion - 1
Bay leaves - 2
Parsley - 2 sprigs
Celery - 2 stalks
Garlic - 2 cloves
Parsley, dill, cilantro - to taste
Cinnamon, cloves, black pepper, allspice salt - to taste

Cut cleaned, prepared sturgeon or stellate sturgeon into servings, sash, put into a pot, season with salt, add enough mixed with water wine vinegar to cover the fish, bay leaves, allspice (whole), black pepper (whole), cinnamon, cloves, parsley, celery, cover the pot and bring to boil. When the fish is cooked remove the pot from the heat, sprinkle with finely chopped parsley, cilantro, and dill, and let it cool.

Sturegon or Stellate Sturgeon in Broth (C)

Ingredients:
Fish - 1 kg
Onions - 300 g
Garlic - 2 cloves
Cilantro - 5 sprigs
Dill - 4 sprigs
Tarragon - 2 sprigs
Lemon juice - From 1/2 of lemon
Sliced lemon - 1/2
Saffron, ground black pepper, salt - to taste

Cut cleaned, prepared sturgeon or stellate sturgeon into servings, wash, put into a pot, season with salt and ground black pepper and add enough water to cover the fish. Add finely chopped onions, crushed garlic, finely chopped herbs (cilantro, dill, tarragon), crushed saffron, cover the pit and bring to boil. Remove the pot from the heat when the fish is cooked. Transfer contents of the pot into a serving bowl, drizzle it with lemon juice, sprinkle with finely chopped dill (2 sprigs) and decorate with lemon slices.

Fried Sturgeon or Stellate Sturgeon with Tomato Sauce

Ingredients:
Fish - 500 g
Onions - 2-3
Tomatoes - 500 g
Vegetable oil - 2-3 tbsp
Garlic - 1 clove
Parsley - 2 sprigs

Chili pepper and salt - to taste

Coat prepared pieces of fish in flour (whet or corn) and fry on both sides in vegetable oil. If desired - fish can be fried without flour coating.

Peel and finely chop onions, put them into a pot, add 1/2 tbsp of vegetable oil, and lightly brown. Add tomatoes passed through a sieve or through a meat grinder, and simmer until tomatoes are thickened. Closer to the end of the cooking season the sauce with chili pepper, garlic, and salt.

Transfer fried fish to a serving plate, pour the oil used to fry the fish and sauce over the fish, sprinkle with finely chopped parsley.

Sturgeon or Stellate Sturgeon Head in Broth

Ingredients:
Fish head - 1 kg
Onions - 400-500 g
Cilantro - 3-4 sprigs
Lemon - 2 slices
Salt and ground black pepper - to taste

Remove gills and eyes from fish head, wash it in cold water and cut into pieces.

In alternating layers set slices of onions and pieces of fish head in a pot - starting and finishing with a layer of onions (two-three layers). Sprinkle contents of the pan with chopped cilantro, season with salt, add 1 1/2-2 cups of water, bring to boil, and cook until cartilage becomes soft - approximately 1 1/2-2 hours.

About 30 minutes before the end of cooking add lemon slices and ground black pepper to the pot.

Fish (Sturgeon, Stellate Sturgeon, Salmon, Beluga) with Garlic Sauce

Ingredients:
Fish - 500 g
Bay leaf - 1
Carrot - 1
Parsley - 1 sprig
Celery - 1 stalk
Allspice - 4
Onion - 1
Garlic - 8-10 cloves

Cook cut into pieces fish (sturgeon, stellate sturgeon, salmon, beluga) in water with bay leaf, allspice, carrot, celery, onion, parsley, then transfer into a serving bowl.

Add boiling water to broth (to adjust for saltiness) and simmer for 5 minutes, then strain.

Mix one cup of broth with crushed garlic and pour it over fish, or serve it on a side in a sauce boat.

Fried Fish with Walnut-Tomato Sauce

Ingredients:
Fish - 500 g
Flour - as needed
Tomato puree - 1/2 cup
Vegetable oil or clarified butter - 2-3 tbsp
Shelled walnuts - 3/4 cup
Wine vinegar, chili pepper, garlic, cilantro, saffron, salt - to taste

Coat cleaned and cut into pieces fish (sturgeon, stellate sturgeon, beluga, trout, flounder, carp, sterlet,
horse mackerel) in flour (wheat or corn) and fry on all sides in vegetable oil or clarified butter. Pour tomato puree over

fish, bring to boil, add walnut sauce, simmer 2-3 minutes, remove from heat, transfer to a serving plate, and sprinkle with finely chopped parsley.

Make walnut sauce. Pound walnuts, chili pepper, cilantro or coriander seeds, saffron, and salt in a mortar. Mix walnut mixture with cooled boiled water (2 cups) and a little of wine vinegar.

Satsivi with Fish

Satsivi is another famous Georgian dish.

Ingredients:
Fish - 500 g
Shelled walnuts - 1-1 1/2 cups
Wine vinegar - 1/2-3/4 cup
Onions - 3-4
Garlic - 2 cloves
Ground cloves and cinnamon - 1 tsp
Whole coriander seeds - 1 tsp
Bay leaves - 2
Allspice - 8
Saffron, ground black pepper, chili pepper, dried suneli, salt - to taste

Cover cleaned and cut into serving pieces fish (sturgeon, stellate sturgeon, beluga) with salted water so the fish is completely submerged. Add bay leaves, allspice, and cook approximately 45-50 minutes. Transfer cooked fish to a serving plate.

Pound shelled walnuts with garlic, chili pepper, and salt in a mortar. Add crushed coriander seeds and crushed saffron to the walnut mixture, and mix well, then add fish broth and fat skimmed from the broth. If broth is too salty - dilute it with a bit of boiling water. Put everything into a pot, add finely chopped onions, bring everything to boil, and cook for 10 minutes. Add mixed in vinegar ground cinnamon, ground cloves, ground black pepper, dried suneli (if desired) and continue cooking 10 minutes longer.

Finished satsivi can be dressed with egg yolks (mix 2-3 egg yolk with a small quantity of cooled satsivi before adding it to the pot).

Pour hot satsivi over fish, let it cool, then serve.

Pomegranate or unripe grape juice can be used instead of vinegar.

This dish can also be cooked as follows: lightly coat fish in flour and fry in vegetable oil or clarified butter. Use water instead of fish broth to make satsivi.

Baked Sturgeon, Stellate Sturgeon, or Salmon

Put cleaned, washed fish in one piece onto a baking sheet, season with salt , and bake in a preheated oven. Cut baked fish into serving pieces, sprinkle with finely chopped onions or scallions and decorate with lemon slices. If desired - serve sauces tkemali, masharabi, kvatsarahi in a sauce boat on a side.

Salmon in Broth

Ingredients:
Fish - 500 g
Onions - 400 g
Cilantro, ground black pepper, salt - to taste

Cut cleaned fish into medium-sized pieces and wash with cold water.

Cover the bottom of a pan with two-three layers of sliced onions, put a layer of fish on top of onions. Season everything with salt and pepper. Add enough water just to cover the contents of the pot, cover the pot, and cook over low heat.

Transfer finished dish into a serving bowl and sprinkle with finely chopped cilantro.

Bozartma with Salmon

Wash cleaned and cut into serving pieces salmon. Slice onions and mix it with finely chopped cilantro, parsley, dill, and tarragon. Cover the bottom of a pan with half of the onion and herb mixture, put pieces of fish on top of onions, season fish with salt and top with remaining onion mixture.

Add enough water to just cover the contents of the pot, bring to boil, lower the heat and cook until done. Transfer finished dish into a serving bowl, drizzle it with lemon juice, decorate with slices of lemon and serve hot or cold.

Trout with Walnut-Vinegar Sauce

Ingredients:
Fish - 500 g
Shelled walnuts - 1/2 cup
Garlic - 1 clove
Wine vinegar - 1/2 cup
Water - 1/2 cup
Salt - to taste

Wash cleaned and cut into serving pieces trout and cook until done in salted boiling water. Take cooked fish out of the pot and let it cool.

Thoroughly pound walnuts, garlic, and salt in a mortar, then mix it with vinegar diluted with water. Pour the sauce over cooled fish.

Poached Trout with Walnut Sauce

Ingredients:
Trout - 500 g

Shelled walnuts - 100 g
Garlic - 2-3 cloves
Salt - to taste

Clean, wash, and cut trout into serving pieces. Cook it in boiling salted water until done, then transfer to a serving plate.

Crush shelled walnuts, garlic, and salt in a mortar. Mix with cooled boiled water until the sauce has consistency of a thin sour cream. Pour the sauce into a sauce boat and serve on a side with fish.

Carp can be substituted for trout in this recipe

Trout with Sauce

Ingredients:
Fish - 500 g
Dried dogwood berries - 1/2 cup
Onions - 2
Crushed shelled walnuts - 2 tbsp
Salt - to taste

Poach cut into serving pieces of trout and transfer it to a serving plate.

Pour 1 1/2-2 cups of water into a clean pot, add dried dogwood berries (without pits), diced onions, crushed walnuts, season with salt and cook 15-20 minutes.

Pour finished sauce over the fish and serve.

Fried Trout with Pomegranate Sauce

Ingredients:
Fish - 500 g
Vegetable oil or clarified butter - 50 g
Shelled walnuts - 1/2 cup
Pomegranate juice - 1 1/2 cups

Onion - 1
Cilnatro - 2-3 sprigs
Chili pepper, salt - to taste

Cut large washed and cleaned trout into serving pieces (do not cut small fish), season with salt, coat with flour or crushed breadcrumbs, and fry in a hot skillet in vegetable oil or clarified butter. Transfer cooked fish to a serving dish.

Thoroughly mix pomegranate juice with garlic mashed with salt, finely chopped cilantro, chili pepper, walnuts, diced onion. Pour the sauce over fish.

Cold Fish with Walnut-Vinegar Sauce

Ingredients:
Fish - 500 g
Garlic - 2 cloves
Bay leaf - 1
Parsley - 1 sprig
Wine vinegar - 3/4 cup
Shelled walnuts - 1/4 cup
Salt - to taste

Cut cleaned fish (trout or catfish) into serving pieces and was in cold water.

Put crushed garlic, bay leaf, parsley into a pot with boiling salted water. Add prepared fish and cook until done. Transfer cooked fish to a serving plate and let it cool.

Finely crush garlic with salt, then mix with wine vinegar. Pour sauce over cooled fish and serve.

Trout Fried in Breadcrumbs

Ingredients:
Fish (trout) - 500 g
Eggs - 2

Butter - 50-70 g
Wheat flour and crushed breadcrumbs - as needed
Onion, lemon, salt - to taste

Gut and scale small trout, season with salt and instantly coat in flour, then dip in beaten eggs and coat fish in crushed bread crumbs. Put prepared trout into a heated skillet and fry in butter on all sides.

Transfer cooked fish to a heated serving plate, drizzle with juices from the pan, decorate with parsley leaves, lemon slices, and thinly sliced onion. Serve with sauces tkemali or masharabi.

Fried Trout with Garlic Sauce

Ingredients:
Fish (trout) - 500 g
Butter - 50 g
Garlic - 10-12 cloves
Water - 1/4-1/2 cup
Salt - to taste

Gut the fish, leave small fish whole, cut large fish into serving pieces, season fish with salt, put into a heated frying pan with butter and fry on all sides. Transfer cooked fish to a serving plate and pour garlic sauce over it.

To make sauce thoroughly mash garlic together with salt then mix it with cooled boiled water.

Catfish in Sauce

Ingredients:
Fish - 500 g
Bay leaves - 2
Cilantro - 4-5 sprigs
Whole black pepper - 2

Sour fruit leather - 30 g
Salt - to taste

Put cleaned, cut into pieces, and washed cat fish into a pot, add enough water to cover the fish and cook until the fish is done, skimming the foam as it rises to the top. Add salt, bay leaves, sour fruit leather, whole black pepper, chopped cilantro after when the liquid comes to boil. If desired - use 2 tbsp of tomato puree instead of sour fruit leather.

Fried Catfish

Wash cleaned, and cut into medium-sized pieces catfish, coat in flour (wheat or corn) and fry on both sides in vegetable oil or clarified butter. Transfer fried fish to a serving plate and sprinkle with finely chopped cilantro. Serve with sauce tkemali or masharabi on a side.

Mullet, Flounder, Trout with White Wine

Ingredients:
Fish - 1 kg
Onions - 400 g
White wine - 3/4 cup
Cilantro, salt - to taste

Pour wine into salted boiling water, add finely chopped onions and prepared in advance washed and cut into serving pieces fish and coked until done. Sprinkle cooked dish with finely chopped cilantro and serve.

Fried Flounder with Barberry Fruit

Ingredients

Fish - 1 kg
Vegetable oil or clarified butter - 2-3 tbsp
Onions - 2-3
Ground barberry fruit, salt - to taste

Season prepared serving pieces of fish with salt, coat with flour, dip in beaten eggs, coat in crushed breadcrumbs, and fry on all sides in a preheated skillet in vegetable oil or clarified butter until nicely browned.

Transfer cooked fish to a serving plate, sprinkle with finely chopped onions and dried barberry fruit. Serve hot.

Flounder in Wine Sauce

Ingredients:
Fish - 500 g
Red table wine - 1 cup
Parsley - 1 sprig
Onion - 1
Bay leaf - 1
Cloves - 4
Shelled walnuts - 1/2 cup
Cilantro - 1 sprig
Garlic and salt - to taste

Cut prepared fish into medium-sized pieces, put into a pot together with parsley, onion, cloves, bay leaf, salt, and red wine mixed with water (1 cup each). Cover the pot and cook until fish is once, approximately 20-25 minutes.

Take cooked fish out of the pot, strain broth, transfer into a clean pot, return to boil and simmer 10-15 minutes, then add walnuts crushed together with garlic, let it simmer another minute, then remove from heat.

Pour finished sauce over fish and sprinkle with finely chopped cilantro.

Barbel with Pomegranate and Walnut Stuffing

Ingredients:
Fish - 500 g
Salt - 1/2 tbsp
Flour - as needed
Vegetable oil or clarified butter - 2 tbsp
Crushed walnuts - 1/4 cup
Onion - 1
Pomegranate - 1
Ground cloves and cinnamon - 1/4 tsp
Chili pepper - to taste

Clean and gut barbel, season with salt and set aside for 30 minutes.

Meanwhile, crush shelled walnuts, then add mashed chili pepper, ground cloves and cinnamon, salt, finely chopped onion, and thoroughly mix everything, then add pomegranate seeds and mix carefully to avoid breaking seeds.

Stuff prepared barbel with the walnut-pomegranate mixture, then coat the fish in flour and fry on both sides in vegetable oil or clarified butter on a hot skillet.

Poached Catfish with Cilantro and Vinegar

Ingredients:
Fish - 500 g
Cilantro - 8-10 sprigs
Wine vinegar - 1/2-3/4 cup
Salt - to taste

Poach cleaned, washed, and cut into medium-sized pieces catfish in salted simmering water. Transfer cooked fish to a cutting board, drizzle it with cold water and let it cool. Move cooled fish to a serving plate and decorate with parsley sprigs.

Mix finely chopped cilantro with wine vinegar and pour the sauce over the fish just before serving. Sauce can also be served on a side in a sauce boat. Carp can be used instead of catfish in this recipe.

Fish in Broth

Ingredients:
Fish - 1 kg
Onions - 600 g
Cilantro - 5-6 sprigs
Bay leaves - 2
Salt and ground black pepper - to taste

Any fish can be used for this recipe. Wash selected fish, cut large fish into serving-sized pieces, leave smaller fish whole, put into a pot, season with salt, add sliced onions, bay leaves, 1/2 cup of water, cover the pot and cook over low heat. Just before the end of the cooking season the contents of the pot with ground black pepper and sprinkle with finely chopped cilantro.

Fish with Spicy Sauce

Ingredients:
Sour fruit leather - 50 g
Cilantro, garlic, chili pepper, salt - to taste

Cook any fish cut into serving size pieces by poaching in salted water or frying in butter in a heated skillet until nicely browned. Transfer poached or fried fish to a serving plate, decorate with parsley leaves and serve spicy sauce made from sour fruit leather (tklapi) or tkemali. Sauce can also be made from cherry plums or other varieties of sour plums.

To make sauce - cut sour fruit leather into pieces, cover with boiling water (3/4-1 cup) and let it stand 4-5 hours. Mash fruit leather right in the water in which it was softening, pass everything through a sieve, add to taste chopped cilantro (or crushed coriander), garlic, chili pepper, salt, mix everything well and transfer the sauce into a sauce boat.

Other sauces that can be served with this fish are tkemali, masharabi, or spicy tomato sauce.

Fish in Pomegranate Sauce

Ingredients:
Fish - 500 g
Butter - 1-2 tbsp
Flour (wheat or corn) - 1-2 tbsp
Pomegranate juice - 1 1/2 cup
Chili pepper, pomegranate seeds, salt - to taste

Poach any fish, cut into serving pieces, in salted water until half-done. Then coat in flour and fry in butter in a heated skillet until nicely browned.

Squeeze juice from a pomegranate and mix it with mashed chili pepper. Pour the sauce over fried fish set on a serving plate and sprinkle with pomegranate seeds.

Poached Fish with Tomatoes

Ingredients:
Fish - 500 g
Onions - 3
Cilantro - 3 sprigs
Tomatoes - 500 g
Chili pepper and salt - to taste

Serving size pieces of fish - steaks or fillets - put in one layer in a shallow pan, season with salt, add finely chopped onions and cilantro, and add water to go just halfway up the fish. Cover the pot and cook over low heat.

Put fresh tomatoes into boiling water for 2-3 minutes, then peel them and fry in a frying pan.

Transfer cooked fish to a serving plate, add fried tomatoes, season with salt and sprinkle with chopped green chili pepper.

Fish in Tomato Sauce

Ingredients:
Fish - 500 g
Onions - 4-5
Vegetable oil - 50-70 g
Flour - as needed
Cilantro, garlic, chili pepper, salt - to taste

Season serving size pieces of fish (fillets) with salt, coat them with flour in fry in vegetable oil.

Dice onions and brown them in vegetable oil. Dip fresh tomatoes in boiling water for 2-3 minutes, peel them. Cut tomatoes in half and remove all seed. Add tomatoes to the browned onions and braise 10-15 minutes. Season tomatoes with garlic mashed with salt, crushed chili pepper, and finely chopped cilantro while they are cooking.

Add fish to the simmering sauce, let it simmer one minute longer, then remove from heat.

Fried Fish in Walnut-Pomegranate Sauce

Ingredients:
Fish - 1 kg
Vegetable oil - 3 tbsp
Onions - 3

Shelled walnuts - 1/2 cup
Water - 1 cup
Pomegranate juice - 1/2 cup
Tomato puree - 2 tbsp
Bay leaf - 1
Garlic, chili pepper, salt - to taste

Cut cleaned, washed fish fillets into pieces, dry them with paper towels, season with salt, coat in flour, and fry on all sides in vegetable oil. Transfer cooked fish to a pot and cover with finely chopped onions browned in vegetable oil.

Thoroughly crush shelled walnuts, salt, garlic, red chili pepper in a mortar, mix this mixture with water (1 cup), add bay leaf, tomato puree and simmer 5-8 minutes. Add pomegranate juice to the pot with the sauce. Pour the sauce into the pot with fish, return to boil, and let is simmer 1-2 minutes, remove from heat and take the bay leaf out.

Transfer finished dish to a serving bowl or plate, and sprinkle with pomegranate seeds just before serving. Serve cooled, with hot gomi or mchadi.

Fresh Fish with Garlic and Wine Vinegar

Ingredients:
Fish - 500 g
Shelled walnuts - 1/4 cup
Garlic - 1 clove
Onion - 1
Water - 1/4 cup
Wine vinegar - 3/4 cup
Salt - to taste

Poach cleaned and cut into pieces fish in salted water, then transfer it to a serving plate.

Crush shelled walnuts with garlic and salt in a mortar, transfer to a pot, add finely chopped onion and wine vinegar mixed with water, and let is simmer 8-10 minutes. Pour the sauce over fish and serve.

Fried Cod

Ingredients:
Fish - 1 kg
Flour - as needed
Vegetable oil or clarified butter - 3-4 tbsp
Tomatoes - 700 g
Onions - 4
Cilantro, ground black pepper, salt - to taste

Cut fish with skin and bones or fillet with skin but without bones into serving pieces, season with salt, coat in flour (wheat or corn) ad fry on both sides in clarified butter or vegetable oil until nicely browned. Transfer cooked fish to a serving plate.

Slice tomatoes across, then put it into the pan used for frying fish, and lightly fry them. Set fried tomatoes on top of the pieces of fish, sprinkle everything with finely chopped onions, ground black pepper, chopped cilantro, and serve hot.

Fish with Eggplants

Ingredients:
Fish - 500 g
Eggplants - 3-4
Flour - 1 tbsp
Vegetable oil or clarified butter - 100 g
Pomegranate juice - 1/2 cup
Parsley - 3 sprigs
Basil - 2 sprigs
Savory - 1 sprig
Pomegranate seeds, scallions, salt - to taste

Cut eggplants across into rounds, put into salted boiling water for two minutes, then take them out and put onto a cutting board. Cover eggplants with another cutting board with some weight. Hold under the weight for 30 minutes to let all the water and bitter juice to drain, then fry in vegetable oil or clarified butter over a medium heat.

Clean the fish, cut into medium-sized pieces, wash, dry with paper towels, season with salt, coat in flour and fry in a hot skillet in vegetable oil or clarified butter. On a serving plate surround cooked fish with fried eggplant slices, pour pomegranate juice over everything, sprinkle with finely chopped scallions, parsley, savory, basil, pomegranate seeds, and serve.

Baked Fish with Dogwood Berry Sauce

Ingredients:
Fish - 1 kg
Butter - 50 g
Fresh dogwood berries - 1 cup
or Dried dogwood berries - 1/3 cup
Garlic, dill, salt - to taste

Set fish in one piece or cut into serving pieces on a bottom of a skillet brushed with clarified butter, season it with salt. Put skillet into a preheated oven and bake fish until it is nicely browned.

Put dogwood berries (fresh or dry) into a pot and add enough water to cover, bring to boil and cook until berries are soft. Strain the contents of the pot preserving cooking liquid, mix berries with mashed garlic, chopped chili pepper (if desired), and season with salt. Pass this mixture through a sieve and add back to the cooking liquid. Mix well.

Transfer baked fish to a serving plate, cover with dogwood berry sauce and sprinkle with finely chopped dill. Serve hot. If desired - serve the sauce on a side.

Fried Fish (Small) with Pomegranate Sauce

Ingredients:
Small fish - 500 g
Vegetable oil or clarified butter - 2-3 tbsp
Pomegranate juice - 1 cup
Garlic - 1-2 cloves
Salt - to taste

Wash and thoroughly dry small scaled and gutted fish, season with salt, coat in flour (wheat or corn) and fry whole on both sides in vegetable oil or clarified butter in a hot skillet until nicely browned. Use cast-iron skillet if possible.

Fish can also be fried in breadcrumbs. In this case fish should be coated in flour, then dipped in beaten eggs, and then coated in breadcrumbs.

Transfer cooked fish to a serving plate and pour prepared pomegranate sauce over it.

To make the sauce - squeeze juice from pomegranate, add garlic mashed with salt, and mix well. If desired - add crushed chili pepper and chopped cilantro to the sauce. Sprinkle finely chopped onions over the finished dish.

Dried Salted Fish with Tkemali

Ingredients:
Fish - 300 g
Sour cherry plums or tkemali - 1 1/2-2 cups
Cilantro - 2 sprigs
Garlic - 2 cloves
Chili pepper, pennyroyal, dill, salt - to taste

Soak cleaned and washed dried salted fish in water for 3-4 hours, then fry or poach until done.

Meanwhile put sour cherry plums or tkemali into a separate pot, add enough cold water just to cover, bring to boil and cook until plums are done. Pass cooked plums through a sieve, add mashed together cilantro, garlic, finely chopped dill and pennyroyal and mix well.

Cut cooked fish into serving pieces, transfer to a plate and pour the sauce over it.

Boiled Fish Eggs

Ingredients:
Fish eggs - 200 g
Crustless white bread - 1 cup
Onion - 1

Put fish eggs into a pot together with crumbled white bread, diced onion, add enough water just to cover the ingredients, mash everything well, bring to boil, and cook 10-15 minutes, stirring from time to time.

Fried Fish Eggs

Ingredients:
Fish eggs - 200 g
Crustless white bread - 1 cup
Onion - 1
Vegetable oil - 30 g

Mix fish eggs with crumbled white bread, diced onion, 1 1/2 cups of water and mash everything together.

Put prepared fish egg mixture into a preheated skillet with vegetable oil and fry on all sides.

MEAT

BEEF

Boiled Beef Shoulder

Wash whole beef shoulder and put into a pot with boiling salted water (water should just barely cover the meat), return to boil and let it boil vigorously for a couple of minutes, then lower the heat and cook meat at a simmer until it is done. Do not overcook the meat — it should be soft but not falling apart. Skim the foam as it rises to the top. When meat is cooked (test if meat is done with a larding needle - if needle goes in easily and running juices are clear - cooking is over) take it out of the pot, put on a serving plate, drizzle with broth to prevent it from drying, and serve. Slice across grain in long thin strips as needed. Serve sauces tkemali, mustard, horseradish, and others on a side.

Fried ground meat (A)

Ingredients:
Boneless beef - 500 g
Onion - 2
Clarified butter - 3 tbsp

Ground black pepper, parsley, pomegranate seeds, salt - to taste

Pass boneless beef through a meat grinder together with parsley.

Dice onion and soften it in a skillet in 2 tbsp of clarified butter, then add ground meat, season with salt, add remaining clarified butter, and cook until meat is done.

Season meat with ground black pepper, add 3 tbsp of broth or water, mix well and continue cooking 5-8 minutes longer, then remove from heat. Add pomegranate seeds to the skillet and mix everything carefully to avoid crushing the seeds.

Fried Ground Meat (B)

Ingredients:
Boneless beef - 500 g
Onion - 2
Parsley - 3 sprigs
Cilantro - 4 sprigs
Butter - 50-70 g
Garlic - 3 cloves
Chili pepper, ground black pepper, salt - to taste

Pass beef through a meat grinder together with onion, parsley, and cilantro. Fry ground beef in a preheated skillet until cooked. Add butter, ground black pepper, crushed coriander, chopped chili pepper, mashed garlic to the meat mixture, season with salt, add hot water (3-4 tbsp), mix and cook for 10 minutes longer.

Beef Meatballs Fried in a Skillet

Ingredients:

Boiled meat - 300 g
Potato - 1
Shelled walnuts - 50 g
Raisins - 150 g
Egg - 1
Butter - 4 tbsp
Breadcrumbs - as needed
Parsley, ground black pepper, salt - to taste

Pass boiled beef, potato, walnuts, raisins (50 g), and parsley twice through a meat grinder. Season ground meat mixture with salt, ground black pepper, add beaten egg and thoroughly mix everything. Shape medium-sized meatballs from the mixture, coat them in crushed breadcrumbs, slightly flatten, and fry on both sides in butter in a hot skillet.

Heat a clean pot, melt some butter, then add cleaned and washed seedless raisins (100 g). Keep the pot over heat until raisins swell.

Transfer meatballs to a serving plate, pour butter with raisins over meatballs, and serve.

Tenderized Beef with Tomato Sauce

Ingredients:
Beef - 500 g
Onions - 300 g
Fat - 80-100 g
Tomatoes - 1 kg
Cilantro, parsley - to taste
Garlic, black pepper, salt - to taste

Wash rib steaks in cold water. Tenderize them with meat mallet (this action softens the connective tissue and evens out the thickness if meat). If using tenderloin - do not tenderize it.

Season prepared meat with salt, put into a sizzling hot skillet with fat and fry until nicely browned on all sides. Transfer cooked meat into a pot.

Slice onions across and fry them in the same skillet that was used to cook meat. Put fried onions on top of cooked meat.

Wash tomatoes in cold water, cut them into pieces, bring to simmer, and cook for 10 minutes, then pass cooked tomatoes through a sieve. Transfer tomato puree to a clean pot, return to simmer and cook for 5 minutes longer. Pour tomato sauce over meat and onions and braise everything together 10-15 minutes.

Pound cilantro, salt, chili pepper, and garlic in a mortar, add the mixture to the pot with beef, let it simmer for 1 minute longer, then remove from heat.

Transfer everything to a serving plate, sprinkle with finely chopped parsley and serve.

Beef Tenderloin with Eggplants

Ingredients:
Beef tenderloin - 600-700 g
Eggplants - 6-7
Onions - 500-600 g
Tomatoes - 1000-1200 g
Sweet bell peppers - 4-5
Garlic - 3-4 cloves
Herbs (parsley, cilantro, savory, basil, dill) - to taste
Salt - to taste

Wash and trim beef tenderloin removing all silver skin, then cut into medium-sized pieces.

Wash and finely chop herbs (parsley, cilantro, savory, basil, dill).

Peel eggplants, cut them in half lengthwise, sprinkle with salt, set aside for 20 minutes, then carefully squeeze to remove bitter juices.

Cut sweet bell peppers into large pieces. Scald tomatoes with boiling water, peel and cut them in half.

Put meat in a layer in a pot, top with a layer of eggplants, followed by a layer of onions, herbs, garlic mashed with salt, then again a layer of meat, and so on. Top everything with a layer of chopped sweet bell peppers and tomatoes. Season with salt, add 1 cup of water, tightly cover the pot and cook over low heat until completely done.

Chahohbili with Beef

Ingredients:
Beef - 500 g
Onions - 3
Wheat flour - 1 tbsp
Tomatoes - 500 g
Herbs (cilantro, parsley, basil, savory) - to taste
Garlic, chili pepper, salt - to taste

Cut fatty beef into pieces, dust with flour, and brown in pot. Add sliced onions and continue cooking 10 minutes longer. Add peeled and chopped tomatoes (or tomato puree), mashed garlic and chili pepper, and braise 10-15 minutes longer. Add finely chopped cilantro, parsley, basil, savory, return to boil and remove from heat. Sprinkle with more chopped parsley just before serving.

Chahohbili with Beef Tenderloin

Ingredients:
Beef tenderloin - 500 g
Onions - 4

Butter - 70 g
Potatoes - 4-5
Salt and ground black pepper - to taste

Wash beef tenderloin and trim it from silver skin and fat, cut into small piece, put into a pot, and put the pot on a stove. After 5 minutes of cooking add 50 g of butter and continue cooking until nicely browned. Add finely chopped onions and remaining 20 g of butter and continue cooking until onions are browned.

Meanwhile peel potatoes, cut them into small pieces, put into a pot, season with salt, add enough boiling water to cover, bring to boil, and cook until potatoes are done. Add boiled potatoes together with cooking liquid to the pot with meat, season everything with ground black pepper, mix and cook 5-8 minutes longer.

Beef with Prunes

Ingredients:
Beef - 500 g
Onions - 3
Wheat flour - 1 tbsp
Pitted prunes - 300 g
Cilantro, parsley, salt - to taste

Cut beef (rib, loin, or sirloin) into pieces, put into a Dutch oven, season with salt, sprinkle with flour and brown in beef fat. Add water (1 cup), chopped onions, chopped cilantro and parsley, braise for 10-15 minutes, then add washed pitted prunes and continue cooking until meat is done.

Beef with Tkemali

Ingredients:
Beef - 500 g
Onions - 4
Tkemali - 1-1 1/4 cup
Dill - 4 sprigs
Cilantro - 3 sprigs
Garlic - 2 cloves
Chili pepper, salt - to taste

Cut beef together with bones into small pieces, wash, season with salt, put into a skillet and brown on all sides in very hot fat. Transfer contents of the skillet into a pot, together with fat, add a couple of tablespoons of water and braise over low heat until meat is soft. Shortly before the end of cooking add onions sliced across, and lightly braised in water pitted tkemali. Before taking the pot from the heat add finely chopped dill, cilantro, crushed chili pepper and mix well.

Beef with Pickles

Ingredients:
Beef tenderloin - 500 g
Butter - 1 tbsp
Onions - 2
Pickles - 3-4
Scallions, garlic, black pepper, salt - to taste

Cut beef tenderloin into small pieces, season with salt, and brown in butter together with diced onions. Season beef with ground black pepper and mashed garlic, add 1/4 cup of boiling water and braise for 10 minutes, then egg diced pickles and continue braising 5 minutes longer, mixing from time to time. Serve with raw diced scallions or onions.

Beef Fried with Green Beans

Ingredients:
Beef tenderloin - 500 g
Beef fat - 100-150 g
Onions - 2
Green beans - 500 g
Herbs (cilantro, parsley, basil, savory) - to taste
Bay leaves, salt - to taste

Trim washed beef tenderloin removing silver skin, cut across the grain into pieces. Season beef with salt and brown on both sides in hot fat. Add finely chopped onions and continue frying for two minutes. Transfer beef with onions and fat into a pot, add blanched green beans with their cooking liquid, and braise everything together for 10-15 minutes, then add finely chopped herbs (parsley, dill, savory, basil), add bay leaf, season with salt and braise 5-8 minutes longer. Just before serving - remove bay leaf, transfer everything into a serving bowl and sprinkle with chopped parsley.

Beef Tenderloin in Walnut-Tomato Sauce

Ingredients:
Beef tenderloin - 500 g
Shelled walnuts - 100 g
Onions - 4
Chili peppers - 2-3
Tomatoes - 500 g

Garlic, cilantro, dill (with seeds), parsley, basil, saffron, salt - to taste

Trim middle part of beef tenderloin from fat and cut it into pieces. Pass fat through a meat grinder, render it, then brown meat and finely chopped onions in rendered fat. Pour the juice released during cooking into a separate pot.

Cook tomatoes, passed through the meat grinder, until they are thickened.

Pound shelled walnuts with salt and garlic in a mortar, draining released oil from time to time.

Mix together soaked in hot water chili peppers, salt, saffron, garlic, dill, parsley, basil and grind it well. Add this mixture to crushed walnuts, chopped cilantro and juice from cooked meat, and return it to the pot with meat. Bring the pot to simmer, then add tomatoes and cook for 5 minutes. Remove pot from the heat, transfer everything to a serving plate and drizzle with walnut oil.

Beef Tenderloin Pot Roast

Ingredients:
Beef tenderloin - 1-1.5 kg
Onions - 4
Bay leaf - 1
Parsley, salt - to taste

Wash whole beef tenderloin, trim it from silver skin, rub with salt, and tie with a kitchen twine into a desired shape. Put tenderloin into a pot, cover the pot and put the pot on fire. About 10 minutes later add 3-4 tablespoons of hot water to the pot and continue braising. About 15-20 minutes later add sliced onions, bay leaf, and continue braising until done.

Baste meat with cooking juices from time to time. Add more hot water or broth whenever the juices evaporate. Remove the string from the pot roast and cut it across into thin slices. Set slices of meat on a serving plate, pour sauce with onions from the pot over the beef and sprinkle with chopped parsley. Serve sauce tkemali on a side.

Roasted Beef Tenderloin with Wine

Ingredients:
Beef tenderloin - 1 kg
Table wine - 1-1 1/2 cup
Tomatoes, garlic, onions, scallions, parsley, salt - to taste

Wash whole beef tenderloin and trim it from silver skin. Thinly slice garlic, make small slits all over the tenderloin and slide garlic slivers into the slits. Season tenderloin with salt, set it on a baking sheet and put into a preheated oven.

About 10-15 minutes later pour 1/2 cup of hot water into the baking pan. From time to time baste beef, first - with wine, and then - with juices released during roasting.

Cut roasted tenderloin into serving pieces and set on a serving plate to resemble the whole piece. Pour cooking juices over meat, then sprinkle it with chopped parsley and decorate with sliced onions. Garnish meat with fresh tomatoes, scallions, and more parsley sprigs. Serve sauce tkemali on a side.

PORK

Boiled Pork with Sour Fruit Leather

Ingredients:
Pork - 500 g
Sour fruit leather - 30 g
Cilantro - 7 sprigs
Garlic - 2 cloves
Salt - to taste

Put washed and cut into pieces pork into a pot, add enough water just to cover the meat, and bring to boil, then lower the heat. Skim the foam as it rises to the top. Continue cooking until pork is done. Take cooked meat out of the broth, season with salt, and keep in a warm place. Add sour fruit leather to the broth, return it to boil, and simmer for 5 minutes. Pass broth and sour fruit leather through a sieve, then add cilantro, salt, and garlic mashed together. Pour the sauce over meat and serve.

Pork Loin Braised with Qunices

Ingredients:
Pork loin - 1 kg
Onions - 4
Quinces - 800-1000 g
Salt - to taste

Wash pork loin, dry it with paper towels, season with salt, and brown on all sides in sizzling-hot fat. Transfer meat into a pot, add a couple of tablespoons of hot water, and braise in covered pot until half-done. Add sliced onions, lightly browned in fat used to brown pork. Add hot water whenever braising liquid evaporates. Closer to the end of the cooking add cleaned, cored, and sliced quinces.

Take cooked meat out of the pot and thinly slice it across the grain. Set sliced pork on a serving plate together with onions and quinces from the pot and pour cooking juice over meat.

Fried Pork Loin with Dogwood Berry Sauce

Ingredients:
Pork loin - 500 g
Dried dogwood berries - 150 g

Cilantro, parsley, salt - to taste

Trim pork loin from any visible fat, wash, and cut into individual rib steaks. Make several slashes in the meat and lightly pound it. Season prepared meat with salt and coat it in flour. Fry in sizzling hot fat on all sides until cooked through and nicely browned.

Meanwhile put pitted dogwood berries into boiling water (3/4 cup) and simmer until they are soft. Transfer berries together with their cooking liquid into fat used to fry pork and continue braising another 5-8 minutes.

Transfer cooked meat to a serving plate, pour dogwood berry sauce over it and sprinkle with chopped parsley and dill.

Roasted Pork Ham or Shoulder

Ingredients:
Pork ham or shoulder (on a bone) - 1 kg
Onions - 3-4
Potatoes - 800-1000 g
Dried pitted dogwood berries, salt - to taste

Season washed whole piece of pork (ham or shoulder) with salt, put into a roasting pan fat side up, add peeled and sliced onions, 3-4 tbsp of water, put into a preheated oven and roast on medium heat until cooked (2 1/2-3 hours), basting pork with juices from time to time. Add hot water to the pan if juices evaporate.

When meat will be half-done add peeled, sliced, and seasoned with salt potatoes, and soaked dried pitted dogwood berries.

Cut cooked pork into thin slices and set on an elongated serving plate. Surround meat with roasted potatoes, sprinkle with dogwood berries and onions, and drizzle with pan juices.

Muzhuzhi with Pork

Ingredients:
Pork - 1 kg
Bay leaves - 2
Allspice - 10
Vinegar - 3/4 cup
Salt - to taste

Put washed and cut into pieces pork into a pot, add enough water to cover, bay leaves, allspice, bring to boil, lower the heat, and cook until done.

When meat is completely cooked (broth should just barely cover it), add vinegar to the pot, season everything with salt, return to boil, and instantly remove from heat. Transfer together with broth into a serving bowl and cool before serving.

Muzhuzhi with Pigs Feet

Ingredients:
Pigs feet - 10
Wine vinegar - 3 cups
Whole black pepper - 8
Allspice - 10
Bay leaves - 2-3
Salt - to taste

Scaled pigs feet with boiling water, remove all visible bristles, rub them with flour and singe, then wash with cold water, and cook in a pot until they are falling apart. Mix 3 cups of broth with wine vinegar, add whole black pepper, allspice, bay leaves, season with salt, bring to boil, and let it simmer for a while. Cut boiled pigs feet across, put into jars, cover with prepared hot marinade, tightly close jars and leave in a cool place. Cooked this way pigs feet can be store from up to 15 days.

Boiled Suckling Pig

Ingredients:
Suckling pig meat - 1-1.5 kg
Shelled walnuts - 1 cup
Wine vinegar - 1/4 cup
Water - 1 cup
Garlic - 2 cloves
Coriander, saffron, salt - to taste

Wash suckling pig meat (whole piece), put it into a pot with boiling water, and cook 1 1/2-2 hours over a low heat until done. Season with salt almost before the end of cooking. Cut cooked mead into serving pieces, set on a serving plate and serve with a sauce.

To make the sauce - mix walnuts, crushed together with garlic, coriander, and saffron, with water soured with wine vinegar, and season everything with salt (to taste).

Roasted Suckling Pig

Ingredients:
Suckling pig - 1
Chili peppers - 2-3
Parsley, coriander, savory, dill, garlic, salt - to taste

Lightly season whole gutted and washed suckling pig (with head and feet) with salt inside and outside, set into a clean roasting pan and put into a preheated oven.

While pig is roasting every 10-15 minutes baste it with fat and juices released during cooking, or brush it with melted butter.

Do not turn or move pig inside the roasting pan. If necessary - turn the whole pan. To prevent years from burning over them with caps made from paper.

The oven should not be too hot; otherwise, bubbles that will form under its skin will ruin the appearance of the dish. Any bubbles that do form should be instantly pricked with a fork.

To test if pig is cooked through - prick it with a larding needle in the thickest section (around its head). If the needle goes in easily, and juices running from the hole are clear - cooking is done.

Take suckling pig out of the roasting pan, cut into serving pieces, transfer to a serving plate, decorate with parsley sprigs and serve.

Suckling pig can also be served whole, also decorated with parsley sprigs. It can be cut at the table as needed.

To spice up this dish pig can be basted from time to time with a special sauce. To prepare the sauce soak 2-3 chili peppers in boiling water for a couple of hours. Transfer soaked peppers to a mortar and thoroughly crush them together with some rock salt. Add to the mortar coriander seeds, dill, savory, garlic, and pound everything together.

Take the mixture out of the mortar, add walnut oil, and mix everything well.

Roasted Suckling Pig Stuffed with Offal

Ingredients:
Suckling pig - 1

Wash pig intestines under a running water, outside and inside - turning them out with a help with a stick. Twice rub washed and turned inside out intestines with salt, wash again with water, clean with flour, and wash once more.

Put intestines into a pot, cover with cold water, bring to boil, and drain the water. Add heart, lungs liver, kidneys, and spleen to the intestines, cover everything with boiling water and cook until half-done. Drain and finely chop contents of the pot, season to taste with ground coriander, crushed chili peppers, salt, finely chopped tarragon, dried suneli, and mix everything well.

Stuff suckling pig with prepared stuffing, close the opening with a kitchen twine, and roast as described in the previous recipe or on a spit. Remove the twine when the pig is cooked.

Roasted Suckling Pig Stuffed with Imeretinsky Cheese

To make stuffing boil heart, lungs, liver, kidneys, and spleen of a medium-sized suckling pig until half-done, then finely chop everything. Add to the chopped offal cut into pieces Imeretinsky cheese (1/2-3/4 kg) or feta cheese (unsalted), finely chopped tarragon and mint, season everything with salt and mix well.

Stuff suckling pig with prepared stuffing, close the opening with a help of kitchen twine and roast in an oven or on a spit. Remove kitchen twine before serving.

Roasted Suckling Pig with Rice Stuffing

Prepare stuffing as follows: thoroughly pick over rice (1 1/2-2 cups), wash it with cold water, put into a pot with a boiling water, and cook until half-done, then drain in a colander.

Meanwhile boil until half done offal of the pig - heart, kidneys, liver, lungs, cut them into small pieces and mix with drained rice. Season to taste with ground black pepper, ground cinnamon and cloves, chili peppers crushed with salt, garlic, cilantro, finely chopped tarragon, dried suneli (if available), crushed saffron, coriander, and mix everything well.

Use prepared stuffing to stuff gutted, cleaned, and seasoned with salt suckling pig. Close the opening with kitchen twine and roast pig in an oven or on a spit. Remove kitchen twine before serving.

Muzhuzhi with Suckling Pigs Feet

Ingredients:
Suckling pigs feet - 1 kg
Carrots - 2
Onions - 3
Allspice - 8
Bay leaves - 3
Wine vinegar - 3/4 cup
Salt - to taste

Cut cleaned, washed suckling pigs feet along in half, put into a pot, cover with cold water so it completely covers the meat and cook until half-done. Transfer pigs feet into a clean pot. Strain broth and add wine vinegar to it (3/4 cup of vinegar to 2 1/2 cups of broth), add broth to the pot and continue cooking until pigs feet are completely cooked.

Approximately 30-40 minutes before the end of cooking add sliced onions and carrots, bay leaves, allspice, and salt to the pot.

Finished dish should be served warm, in bowls.

VEAL

Boiled Veal Brisket

Cut veal brisket into pieces, wash, put into a pot with boiling water and return the pot to boil. After 1-1 1/2 hours from the moment the water returns to boil add cut into large pieces parsnips and celery, onions, bay leaf, whole black pepper, season with salt, and continue cooking until meat is done.

Just before serving transfer meat to a serving plate, sprinkle with finely chopped parsley, and serve sauce from blackthorn plums or tkemali on a side.

Fried Minced Veal with Eggs

Ingredients:
Veal - 200 g
Water or broth - 2 tbsp
Onion - 1
Cooking fat - 1 tbsp
Parsley - 1-2 sprigs
Egg - 1
Tarragon, black and chili pepper, garlic, salt - to taste

Cut trimmed from sinews veal into pieces and pass it together with onion through a meat grinder or finely chop with a knife. Add water or broth to the minced meat, put into a preheated skillet and braise over low heat 10-12 minutes. Add cooking fat, and then, 2-3 minutes later - season with salt and add ground pepper, mashed garlic and crushed chili pepper, finely chopped parsley and tarragon, and finally, add beaten egg, and continue cooking until egg is done. Serve the dish in the skillet.

Fried Minced Veal with Tomato Sauce

Ingredients:
Veal - 500 g
White bread - 50 g
Onion - 1
Potato - 1
Egg - 1

Flour - as needed
Vegetable oil - 2-3 tbsp
Parsley - 1 sprig
Garlic, cinnamon, cloves, allspice, salt - to taste
For the sauce: -
Tomatoes - 700 g
Vegetable oil - 1/2 tbsp
Onions - 2
Cilantro - 1 sprig
Garlic, parsley, chili pepper, salt - to taste

Cut veal, separated from bones and trimmed from sinew, into pieces and pass it through a meat grinder. Add bread soaked in water and squeezed, potato, parsley, onion, and garlic to the minced meat, and pass everything again through a meat grinder. Moisten the mixture with 1/4 cup of water from soaked bread and egg, season with salt and ground allspice, cinnamon, cloves, mix everything well, then roll into cigars (6-8 cm long and 2 cm thick), coat in wheat or corn flour, and fry oil in a sizzling hot skillet. Turn cigars to insure even cooking on all sides. Cook for approximately 10-15 minutes.

To make sauce wash tomatoes, cut them into pieces and simmer until cooked, then pass them through a fine sieve. Finely dice onions and brown them in clarified butter. Add tomato puree to the browned onions and continue cooking until the sauce thickens. While it is cooking season the sauce with cilantro, chili pepper, garlic, and salt mashed together in a mortar, then add finely chopped parsley.

Transfer veal "cigars" to a serving plate, pour the sauce over and serve. Sauce can also be served on a side.
This dish can also be cooked with beef or lamb.

Roast Veal

Wash and rub veal loin or veal leg (approximately 1.5-2 kg) with garlic and salt. Set it in a roasting pan and put into a preheated oven. Starting with medium heat gradually increase the heat as meat cooks until it is done (about 1 1/2-2 hours).

From time to time baste veal with juices released from cooking, and brush it with garlic mashed with salt. Cut cooked meat into slices, set on a serving plate and decorate with parsley sprigs.

If desired, meat can be roasted with potatoes.

LAMB

Boiled Young Lamb (Hashlama)

Cut lamb into serving-size pieces, wash, put into a pot with boiling salted water and cook (no less than 1-1 1/2 hours). Meat should be completely submerged. Remove foam as it rises to the top.

Take cooked meat out of the pot with a skimmer. Put in on a serving plate and let cool slightly before serving.

Young lamb can also be cooked in unsalted water, and should be seasoned with salt when taken out of the broth, while still hot.

Boiled Young Lamb with Garlic Sauce

Ingredients:
Young lamb - 500 g
Garlic - 10-12 cloves
Broth - 3/4-1 cup
Salt - to taste

Wash a piece of lamb, put into a pot, add enough boiling salted water to cover the meat, and return to boil. Then lower the heat and simmer until meat is cooked.

Take cooked meat out of the pot, cut into serving piece and put into a bowl.

Strain broth, mix in garlic mashed with a small quantity of salt, and pour the sauce over meat. This dish can be served hot or cold.

Young Lamb with Quinces

Ingredients:
Young lamb - 500 g
Lamb fat - 50 g
Quinces - 2-3
Onions - 2-3
Granulated sugar - 1 tbsp
Ground cinnamon - 1/2 tsp
Cilantro - 3-4 sprigs
Salt - to taste

Cut young lamb into medium-sized pieces, wash in cold water, put into a pot, add enough water just to cover the meat, and bring to boil. Remove foam as it rises to the top.

Peel and core quinces, then thinly slice them. Finely dice onions and brown them in lamb fat. Add quinces to browned onions and sauté a bit longer. Add strained broth (1/2-3/4 cup) to the pot with onions and quinces and simmer for 10 minutes, then add sugar and simmer 3-5 minutes longer.

Transfer contents of the pot with quinces to the pot with lamb, season everything with salt and ground cinnamon, sprinkle with finely chopped cilantro, simmer everything together 5 minutes longer, then remove from heat.

Lamb with Green Beans (A)

Ingredients:
Lamb - 500 g
Green beans - 600 g
Parsley, cilantro, tarragon, basil, savory - 2 sprigs each
Scallions - 1
Cinnamon, pepper, salt - to taste

Wash fatty lamb and cut it into small pieces, put into a pot, add enough water just to cover the meat, and bring to boil. Skim foam as it rises to the top. About 1-1 1/2 hours after water comes to boil add washed and cut into small pieces green beans and continue cooking. Add chopped parsley, basil, savory, tarragon, cilantro, scallion, season with salt, and continue cooking until meat and beans are falling apart (approximately 20 minutes longer). About 5-10 minutes before the end of cooking season lamb with ground black pepper and cinnamon.

If desired - add tomatoes passed through a meat grinder or passed through a sieve to the pot while lamb is cooking.

This dish can also be cooked with beef.

Lamb with Green Beans (B)

Ingredients:
Lamb - 500 g
Green beans - 600 g
Onions - 200 g
Parsley - 2 sprigs
Savory and basil - 3 sprigs each
Salt - to taste

Wash and cut fatty lamb into small pieces, put into a pot and fry for about 20 minutes, then add finely chopped onions and continue frying 10-15 minutes longer.

Remove strings from green beans and chop the pods, put into the pot with lamb and onion, season with salt, add enough hot water to cover everything and continue braising.

If desired - ad chopped savory and basil. When beans are cooked - remove pot from the heat. Transfer everything into a serving bowl and sprinkle with finely chopped parsley.

Lamb with Green Beans and Matsoni (Yogurt)

Ingredients:
Lamb - 500 g
Green beans - 600-700 g
Matsoni (yogurt) - 500 g
Dill, salt - to taste

Wash fatty lamb and cut it into medium-sized pieces, put into a pot and brown on all sides, then add cleaned from strings and cut into pieces green beans, add water to cover everything and cook in a covered pot until done. Just before the end of cooking season with salt and add chopped dill.

Transfer lamb and beans to a serving bowl, pour beaten matron and sprinkle with finely chopped dill.

Lamb with Beans

Ingredients:
Lamb - 500 g
Beans - 500 g
Onions - 3
Cilantro - 3-4 sprigs
Chili pepper and salt - to taste

Put dry beans and finely chopped onions (2) into a pot, cover with water (5-6 cups), bring to boil, and cook until beans are done (2 1/2-3 hours). About 10-15 minutes before the end of cooking add chili pepper, salt, and finely chopped cilantro.

Meanwhile wash fatty lamb, cut into small pieces, put into a pot together with chopped onion (1) and nicely brown everything.

Add contents of pot with beans to the pot with lamb, simmer 10 minutes longer, then remove from heat.

Braised Lamb with Eggplants and Tomatoes

Ingredients:
Lamb - 500 g
Onions - 300 g
Eggplants - 500 g
Tomatoes - 800 g
Chili pepper, parsley, salt - to taste

Cut fatty lamb into medium-sized pieces, wash with cold water, put into a pot, and brown on all sides. Add diced onions and continue frying until onions are softened.

Wash eggplants, cut them lengthwise into large pieces and set atop of the meat.

Wash tomatoes, cut them into pieces, pass through a meat grinder and add to the pot. Bring to boil, then lower the heat and simmer everything 50-60 minutes, seasoning with salt and chili peppers to taste.

Just before serving sprinkle with finely chopped parsley.

Braised Lamb with Pomegranate Sauce

Ingredients:
Lamb - 500 g
Lamb tail fat - 50 g
Pomegranate juice - 1/4-1/3 cup
Onions - 2
Cilantro - 1 sprig

Salt and ground black pepper - to taste

Wash fatty lamb with cold water, cut into medium-sized pieces, put into a hot skillet together with chopped lamb fat, brown on all sides, then transfer to a clean pot and season with salt and pepper.

Add a cup of water to the skillet used to fry meat, bring it to simmer, scraping all browned bit, then pour it into the pot with meat, return to boil, and simmer over low heat for 15-20 minutes. Drain all the cooking liquid from the pot, mix it with pomegranate juice, finely chopped onions and cilantro, and mix well.

Transfer meat to a serving bowl and pour prepared sauce over it.

Braised Lamb with Rice

Ingredients:
Lamb - 500 g
Onions - 3-4
Rice - 3/4-1 cup
Salt - to taste

Wash fatty lamb (breast), cut into pieces, and fry in a skillet over low heat, just to lightly brown. The meat should still remain soft. Transfer lamb to a pot, add peeled, chopped onions softened in the fat remaining from lamb, pour in 1 1/2 cups of hot water and bring to boil. When water comes to boil add rice to the pot, season with salt, cover the pot and braise over a low heat until rice absorbs all the water. Do not stir.

Lamb with Cherry Plums (A)

Ingredients:
Lamb - 500 g

Cooking fat - 50-100 g
Onions - 3-4
Wheat flour - 1/2 tbsp
Cherry plums - 300 g
Parsley, pepper, salt - to taste

Season lamb cut into pieces with salt and ground black pepper, put into a pot with cooking fat and nicely browned on all sides.

Meanwhile slice onions, coat in wheat flour and fry in large quantity of fat.

Scald cherry plums, pit them, and add to the fried meat. Bring meat with plums to boil and remove from heat. Transfer everything to a serving plate and sprinkle with fried onions and finely chopped parsley.

Lamb with Cherry Plums (B)

Ingredients:
Lamb - 500 g
Onions - 300 g
Cherry plums - 500 g
Cilantro, parsley, ground black pepper, salt - to taste

Put fatty lamb cut into pieces into a pot and brown on all sides. Add finely chopped onions and continue cooking until onions are nicely browned. Season meat with salt, ground black pepper, and finely chopped herbs (cilantro, parsley), then add pitted cherry plums.

Lamb Braised With Carrots

Ingredients:
Lamb - 500 g
Lamb tail fat - 50 g

Onions - 4
Potatoes - 3-4
Carrots - 3
Tomatoes - 200 g
Cilantro, parsley, garlic, salt - to taste

Cut lamb into very small pieces and fry 10-15 minutes, then add lamb tail fat passed through a meat grinder or finely chopped, diced onions, potatoes cut into large dice, and 1/2 cup of water, and continue braising.

When potatoes are half-done season contents of the pot with salt, add sliced carrots, peeled and seeded tomatoes, cilantro, parsley, garlic, cover the pot, and continue cooking until completely done.

Lamb Braised with Vegetables (A)

Ingredients:
Lamb - 500 g
Onions - 3
Green beans - 200 g
Tomatoes - 300 g
Sweet bell peppers - 2
Eggplant - 1
Potatoes - 4
Celery, parsley, cilantro, salt - to taste

Cover chopped into pieces fatty lamb (breast), cut green beans, diced onions, bouquet of celery and parsley with boiling water, return to boil and simmer, skimming the foam as it rises to the top.

When meat is half-done add to the pot peeled and diced potatoes, skinned and seeded tomatoes, diced eggplant, sliced sweet bell peppers, and continue cooking until all vegetables are cooked. Just before the end of cooking remove bouquet of herbs from the pot, season the stew with salt, and sprinkle with chopped cilantro.

Lamb Braised with Vegetables (B)

Ingredients:
Lamb - 500 g
Lamb tail fat - 50 g
Onions - 4-5
Sweet bell peppers - 3
Eggplants - 2-3
Tomatoes - 700 g
Garlic, herbs, salt - to taste

Chop lamb (breast) into pieces, season with salt, and, together with chopped onions, fry in rendered lamb tail fat until nicely browned. Transfer lamb with onions to a clean pan, add sliced tomatoes, eggplants, sweet bell peppers, season with salt, and braise until fully cooked. Closer to the end of the cooking add mashed garlic and chopped cilantro and parsley to the pot.

Lamb Braised with Walnuts

Ingredients:
Lamb - 500 g
Onions - 200 g
Wine vinegar - 1-2 tbsp
Shelled walnuts - 200 g
Garlic, cilantro, chili peppers, parsley, scallions, salt - to taste

Wash fatty lamb, cut it into medium-sized pieces, put into a pot and brown on all sides. Drain juice released from cooking into another container and keep it covered.

Clean and wash onions, finely dice them, add to the pot with meat and continue cooking until onions are softened, then add wine vinegar.

In a mortar crush walnuts together with garlic, cilantro, chili peppers. Mix crushed walnuts together with preserved meat juices and add it to the pot with meat. Continue cooking until meat absorbs all the juices.

Just before serving sprinkle the dish with finely chopped parsley and scallions.

Lamb Ragout with Vegetables

Ingredients:
Lamb - 500 g
Onions - 4
Green beans - 300 g
Carrots - 3
Eggplants - 2
Tomatoes - 300-500 g
Parsley - 3-4 sprigs
Ground cinnamon and cloves, chili peppers, garlic, salt - to taste

Cut fatty lamb into pieces and brown together with diced onions.

Blanch string beans. Slice carrots, eggplants, and sauté them in lamb fat together with chopped parsley. Add skinned and chopped tomatoes and continue cooking until vegetables are done, then add lamb and green beans to the pot, season with ground cinnamon and cloves, crushed chili peppers and garlic, and season everything with salt.

Lamb with Dried Dogwood Berries

Ingredients:
Lamb - 500 g

Onions - 3
Dried dogwood berries - 100 g
Salt - to taste

Dice fatty lamb, season it with salt, add finely diced onions, and brown everything together.

Add boiling water to dried (pitted) dogwood berries, simmer them until soft, then mix in lamb with onions and braise 10-15 minutes longer.

Chahohbili with Lamb (A)

Ingredients:
Lamb - 500 g
Onions - 500 g
Tomatoes - 800-1000 g
Herbs, salt - to taste

Cut fatty lamb into pieces, put into a pot and brown on all sides, approximately 20 minutes, then add diced onions, and continue frying until onions are softened. Add cooked and passed through a sieve tomatoes, season with salt, and continue cooking until meat is done.

Shortly before the end of cooking add finely chopped herbs (cilantro, parsley, dill, tarragon, savory, and basil) to taste.

Chahohbili with Lamb (B)

Ingredients:
Lamb - 500 g
Onions - 4
Potatoes - 2-3
Tomatoes - 500 g
Garlic, chili pepper, cilantro, salt - to taste

Cut fatty lamb into pieces, add diced onions and brown everything nicely. Add diced potatoes to the meat and continue cooking.

Put tomatoes into boiling water for 1-2 minutes, skin them, cut in half and remove all seeds. Add prepared tomatoes into the pot with meat and braise 15-20 minutes. Add crushed garlic and chili peppers, finely chopped cilantro, season with salt and simmer 5 minutes longer.

Lamb Braised with Quinces and White Wine

Ingredients:
Lamb - 500 g
Quinces - 400 g
Onions - 2
Lamb tail fat - 50 g
White wine - 1 1/2 cups
Herbs, salt - to taste

Wash lamb (boneless), cut it into medium-sized pieces, put into a pot and brown on all sides. Add passed through a meat grinder lamb tail fat mixed with diced onions and continue cooking until onions are softened. Add white wine and water so it just barely covers the meat, bring to boil, and braise 50 minutes.

Peel and core quinces, cut into thin wedges, add to the pot with lamb, season with salt, and cooking until meat is done. Just before serving sprinkle with finely chopped cilantro or parsley.

Fried Lamb with Pomegranate (A)

Ingredients:
Lamb - 500 g
Onions - 300 g
Pomegranate, black pepper, salt - to taste

Wash fatty lamb, cut into medium-sized pieces, put into a pot and brown. Drain meat juices released during cooking into a different container and keep it covered.

Peel and dice onions, add them to the pot with meat, and continue cooking until onions are browned. Return meat juices back to the pot, season everything with salt and ground black pepper, and continue braising for 10-15 minutes longer.

Meanwhile remove skin from pomegranate and accurately seed it. Add pomegranate seed to the pot with lamb and mix carefully to insure that seeds do not get crushed. Sprinkle with raw diced onions and serve.

This dish can be cooked with beef.

Fried Lamb with Pomegranate (B)

Ingredients:
Lamb - 500 g
Cilantro - 4-5 sprigs
Onions - 2
Pomegranate seeds and salt - to taste

Cut fatty lamb into pieces, put into a pot, season with salt, and fry until cooked through. Add finely chopped cilantro and sweet bell peppers and sauté 2 minutes longer, then remove from heat. Transfer cooked meat to a serving plate and sprinkle with finely diced onions or scallions and pomegranate seeds.

Lamb Meatballs Fried in a Skillet

Ingredients:
Lamb - 500 g
Onions - 2

Dried dogwood berries - 150 g
Vegetable oil - 150 g
Eggs - 2
Cilantro - 1 sprig
Salt and ground black pepper - to taste

Cut boneless lamb into small pieces, and, together with onion (1), cilantro, and softened in water dried dogwood berries (50 g), pass twice through a meat grinder, season with salt and pepper, add beaten eggs and thoroughly mix it. Roll medium-sized meatballs, flatten them with a knife, and fry on all sides in oil in a hot skillet.

Put dried dogwood berries into a hot skillet with oil, and, when it swells, add diced onions, and fry until onions are soft.

Set fried meatballs on a serving plate and garnish with sautéed dogwood berries with onions.

Chanahi (Georgian Lamb Stew) (A)

Ingredients:
Lamb - 500 g
Potatoes - 500 g
Eggplants - 5-6
Lamb tail fat - 30 g
Onions - 4-5
Tomato juice - 1 cup
Tomatoes - 500 g
Ground black pepper, chili pepper, herbs, salt - to taste

Cut fatty lamb into serving-sized pieces and season them with salt. Cut peeled potatoes into large pieces and thinly slice onions. Slice eggplants without cutting all the way through and stuff them with some lamb tail fat mixed with salt and ground black pepper (and some chopped herbs if desired).

Put prepared lamb into an earthenware pot, top with potatoes, then eggplants, onions, whole tomatoes, sprinkle with finely chopped parsley, add a little chili peppers and salt. Pour tomato juice over everything, put into a preheated oven and cook until done.

Serve in the same earthenware pot.

Chanahi (Georgian Lamb Stew) (B)

Ingredients:
Lamb - 500 g
Potatoes - 800-1000 g
Eggplants - 5-6
Lamb tail fat - 30-50 g
Salt and ground black pepper - to taste

Into an earthenware pot put seasoned with salt cut into wedges potatoes, then eggplants stuffed with lamb tail fat mixed with salt and ground black pepper, and top it with a whole piece of lamb, also seasoned with salt. Add one cup of water to the pot and cook until done in a preheated oven. Serve in the same pot it was cooked in.

Chanahi (Georgian Lamb Stew) (C)

Ingredients:
Lamb - 500 g
Lamb tail fat - 30 g
Eggplants - 4-5
Potatoes - 3
Onions - 2-3
Tomatoes - 4-5
Rice - 1/2-3/4 cups
Ground black pepper, herbs, salt - to taste

Put cut and seasoned with salt pieces of fatty lamb on a bottom of an earthenware pot, top meat with eggplants stuffed with lamb tail fat mixed with salt, ground black pepper, and chopped herbs, then add cleaned and sliced onions, add one cup of water and put the pot into a preheated oven. When meat is half-done - add potatoes cut into large dice, whole tomatoes, make a small hollow in the middle and pour rice in. Return pot to the oven and finish cooking. Serve in the same pot.

Roast Lamb

Wash large piece of lamb (ham, shoulder blade, brisket, loin), trim sinews, season with salt, put into a roasting pan and put into a preheated oven.

Baste roasting meat with cooking juices every 10-15 minutes. Add a little broth or hot water if juices are evaporating too fast.

Meanwhile peel and cut potatoes into large pieces. Wash a few eggplants, make a shallow lengthwise cut in each one and stuff it with lamb tail fat mixed with salt and ground black pepper. If desired - add finely chopped herbs (parsley, cilantro, mint).

About 20-30 minutes from the start of cooking add prepared potatoes and eggplants to the roasting pan with meat. Another 10-15 minutes later add washed tomatoes, and continue cooking until meat is cooked through. use larding needle to see if meat is done - if needle goes in easy and clear juices are running - take meat out of the oven.

Take cooked lamb out of the pan, slice across the grain, set on a serving plate and surround meat with pieces of roasted potatoes, eggplants, tomatoes, and drizzle cooking juices from the pan over meat. Sprinkle everything with chopped parsley.

If desired - lamb can be served in the roasting pan it was cooked in. Beef can be used in this recipe instead of lamb.

Roasted Leg of Lamb with Garlic

Thoroughly wash leg of lamb, trim it from sinews and film, season with salt and set it aside for a while. Make shallow cuts in the meaty part of the leg with a tip of a knife and stuff each cut with slivers of garlic. Put prepared leg of lamb into a roasting pan and cook in a preheated to a medium heat oven. From time to time baste meat with pan juices.

Slice cooked leg into serving pieces and serve with a garlic sauce on a side. To make sauce mash 5-6 cloves of garlic with salt and mix it with cold drinking water (1/2-3/4 cup).

Shilaplavi (A)

Ingredients:
Lamb - 500 g
Rice - 1 cup
Onion - 1
Parsley - 1 sprig
Salt and ground black pepper - to taste

Cut fatty lamb into medium-sized pieces, put into a pot, add enough cold water just to cover, and bring to boil. Skim foam as it rises to the top. When the water comes to boil add onion and thoroughly washed rice, season with salt, and cook over low heat for two hours. Add a little ground black pepper to the pot and remove it from heat. Transfer the contents of the pot to a serving bowl and sprinkle the dish with finely chopped parsley.

Shilaplavi (B)

Ingredients:
Lamb - 500 g
Rice - 1 cup
Salt, ground black pepper, cumin - to taste

Cut fatty lamb into medium-sized pieces, season with salt, and set aside in a covered container for 30 minutes.

Meanwhile add water to a pot, bring it to boil, then add meat to the boiling water (water should just barely cover the meat), and cook until meat is half-done. Skim the foam as it rises to the pot. Add picked over and washed rice to the pot and continue cooking until completely done. Season with ground black pepper and cumin just before the end of cooking.

Shilaplavi (C)

Ingredients:
Lamb - 500 g
Onions - 2
Rice - 1 cup
Cilantro - 4-5 sprigs
Parsley - 3 sprigs
Salt - to taste

Cut lamb into medium-sized pieces, put into a pot and brown on all sides. Add finely chopped lamb tail fat, diced onions, chopped cilantro and parsley, and cook until onions are softened. Add soaked in water rice to the pot, season with salt, add enough water just to cover everything, and cook until done.

TOLMA

Tolma with Lamb or Beef (Stuffed Cabbage Leaves)

Ingredients:
Lamb or beef - 500 g
Onions - 200 g
Egg - 1
Cabbage - 700 g
Rice - 1/4 cup
Tomatoes - 800-1000 g
Cilantro, ground black pepper, salt - to taste

Wash boned and trimmed meat (lamb or beef) in cold water, cut into small pieces and pass through a meat grinder together with onions and cilantro. Add raw rice, ground black pepper, salt, beaten egg to the mince and mix everything well.

Blanch whole cabbage leaves in boiling water for 3-5 minutes, take them out of the water and let them cool in a colander. Put some of the stuffing into every cabbage leaf, roll into small packages, and put in tight rows in a shallow pot. Cut peeled and seeded tomatoes into wedges, or cook them separately and pass through a sieve (or just use tomato puree). Add tomatoes to the pot with stuffed cabbage leaves and cook everything in a covered pot over a low heat (1 1/2 - 2 hours).

Transfer cooked tolma to a serving plate and pour the sauce from the pot over.

Tolma with Lamb (A)

Ingredients:
Lamb - 500 g
Onion - 1
Cilantro - 4 sprigs

Basil - 3 sprigs
Tarragon - 1-2 sprigs
Savory - 1 sprig
Rice - 1/2 cup
Cabbage - 800-900 g
Salt and ground black pepper - to taste

Pass fatty lamb meat through a meat grinder together with onion. Add finely chopped cilantro, basil, tarragon, savory, washed rice, salt, ground black pepper and mix everything well.

Scald cabbage leaves with boiling water then cool them. Put some of the stuffing into each leaf, roll into a package and set in tight rows in a pot. Add one cup of water to the pot, cover tolma with a plate, then cover the pot, and cook over a low heat until done (1 1/2 - 2 hours).

Tolma with Lamb (B)

Ingredients:
Lamb - 500-600 g
Onions - 3-4
Cilantro - 6-5 sprigs
Basil - 4 sprigs
Rice - 1/2 cup
Egg - 1
Cabbage - 800-1000 g
Coriander seeds - 1/2 tsp
Tomato juice - 3/4 cup
Hot water - 3/4 cup
Chili pepper, saffron, pomegranate seeds, salt - to taste

Pass fatty lamb together with cilantro (2 sprigs) through a meat grinder, add rice, crushed chili pepper, crushed coriander seeds, saffron, garlic, beaten egg, diced onion (1), and mix everything well.

Accurately roll stuffing in scalded with boiling water and cooled cabbage leaves and set them in tight rows in a pot, alternating with layers of sliced onions, finely chopped herbs (cilantro and basil), and pomegranate seeds, add tomato juice mixed with hot water, cover the pot, and cook until done (1 1/2 - 2 hours).

Summer Tolma

Ingredients:
Lamb - 600 g
Rice - 100 g
Eggplants - 5
Tomatoes - 6 + 500 g
Sweet bell peppers - 6
Apples - 300 g
Onion - 1
Cilantro - 3 sprigs
Basil and parsley - 2 sprigs each
Salt and ground black pepper - to taste

Pass fatty lamb meat through a meat grinder, add finely diced onion, chopped cilantro, basil, and parsley, picked over and thoroughly washed rice, season with salt and ground black pepper and mix everything well.

Wash and cut ripe tomatoes (500 g) into pieces, put into a pot and simmer 8-10 minutes, then pass through a fine sieve.

Make a shallow lengthwise cut in medium-sized eggplants, scoop out the seeds and sprinkle a little salt inside.

Wash sweet bell peppers, cut the tops off and remove all the seeds, scald insides with boiling water and leave to drain in a colander.

Wash medium-sized tomatoes in cold water, cut the tops off and set them aside. Carefully scoop the seeds out making sure to keep tomatoes whole, then season insides with salt.

Wash, peel, and slice apples into thin wedges. Stuff prepared tomatoes, eggplants, and peppers with mince mixture and top tomatoes and peppers with preserved tops.

Set lamb bones on a bottom of a pan, then, in layers, set eggplants, followed by a layer of apple wedges, then stuffed tomatoes and peppers. Add tomato puree to the pot, cover the pot and cook until completely done (1-1 1/2 hours) over a low heat.

Quinces and Apples Tolma Stuffed with Lamb

Ingredients:
Lamb - 500 g
Qunices - 800 g
Apples - 800 g
Rice - 60 g
Onion - 1
Sour plums - 300 g
Cilantro - 3 sprigs
Chili pepper and salt - to taste

Pass fatty lamb through a meat grinder. Make a stock from lamb bones.

Add picked over and washed rice with minced meat, then add finely diced onions, chopped cilantro, crushed chili pepper and salt.

Wash medium-sized apples and quinces in cold water, cut the stem side off and set aside, scoop out some of the flesh together with core. Stuff prepared fruits with meat mixture, cover with sliced tops, and set in a shallow pot. Add pitted sour plums, two cups of lamb stock, cover the pot, and cook over a low heat until done (approximately 1-1 1/2 hours).

Tolma Stuffed with Boiled Beef

Ingredients:
Beef (boiled0 - 200 g
Cabbage - 300-400 g
Onions - 2
Vegetable oil - 50-70 g
Matsoni (yogurt) - 500 g
Salt and ground black pepper - to taste

Pass fatty boiled beef through a meat grinder, add diced and softened in a vegetable oil onions, season with ground black pepper and mix well.

Remove outer leaves from a head of cabbage and core it. Cook prepared cabbage in salted water until half-done. Carefully separate leaves and slightly flatten the stem part of each leaf. Put prepared stuffing into each leaf and wrap into packages, then lightly fry on all sides in a preheated skillet, then transfer tolma into a shallow pot, add a little broth or water and braise over a low heat for 10-15 minutes. Transfer cooked tolma to a serving plate and dress with beaten matsoni.

Lamb Tolma with Apples and Raisins

Ingredients:
Lamb - 500 g
Rice - 50 g
Cabbage - 700 g
Raisins - 50 g
Cilantro and basil - 2 sprigs each
Onions - 250 g
Apples or qunices - 300 g
Salt - to taste

Wash lamb with cold water, cut into pieces and pass it through a meat grinder, add chopped cilantro and basil, picked over and washed raisins, and pass it through a meat grinder again. Add rice to the minced meat, season with salt, and mix well.

Blanch cabbage leaves in boiling water for 5-7 minutes, then remove from the water and let them cool.

Put some of the stuffing into each cabbage leaf and wrap into a parcel. Put tolma into a pot layering them with slices of onions and slices of apples or quinces. Add enough water, or tomatoes passed through the meat grinder, to the pot to cover cabbage leaves, cover the pot, and cook over low heat until done (1 1/2 - 2 hours).

Tolma with Liver

Ingredients:
Liver - 500 g
Onions - 2
Cilantro and tarragon - 3 sprigs each
Ground black pepper, ground dried barberry, salt - to taste

Grill cleaned and washed liver on a skewer over hot coals, then cut into very small pieces, add finely chopped cilantro and tarragon, diced onions, ground black pepper, ground dried barberry, salt, and mix well.

Wash caul fat and cut it into squares. Put some of the prepared stuffing in the middle of each square and wrap it tightly. Put caul fat wraps in a sauté pan, add 1/2-3/4 cups of water or broth, and cook until nicely browned.

Pickled Cabbage and Pork Tolma

Ingredients:
Pickled cabbage - 1 kg
Pork - 300-500 g

Lard - 50 g
Onion - 1
Dried dogwood berries - 3/4 cup
Egg - 1
Salt and ground black pepper - to taste

Blanch a head of pickled cabbage in a pot of boiling water for 5 minutes, then take it out of the pot, let it drain, and separate into leaves. Flatten thick stems with a meat mullet.

Pass pork and lard through a meat grinder, season with salt and ground black pepper, add an egg and finely diced onion and thoroughly mix everything.

Make tolma with stuffing and cabbage leaves, put into a pot, cover with water, and cook in a covered pot.

Put washed pitted dry dogwood berries into a pot with boiling water (1/2 cup), return to boil, and simmer for 10 minutes, then add berries together with cooking liquid to the pot with tolma, and continue cooking until done.

Tolma with Grape Leaves (A)

Ingredients:
Beef or lamb - 500 g
Onions - 200 g
Egg - 1
Grape leaves - as needed
Matsoni (yogurt) - 1 l
Powdered sugar, ground cinnamon, ground black pepper, salt - to taste

Cut boneless fatty beef or lamb into pieces and pass two times through a meat grinder together with onions, then add beaten egg, season with salt and ground black pepper, and mix well.

Cover grape leaves with boiling water and steep for 6-8 minutes, then drain and cool them.

Put a walnut-sized ball of minced meat in the middle of each leaf and fold just like tolma with cabbage. Put stuffed grape leaves into a shallow pot, add enough water to cover, and cook 1 1/2 - 2 hours.

Pour matsoni into a cheese cloth and let it drain. Whip drained matsoni.

Transfer cooked stuffed grape leaves to a serving plate and dress with whipped matsoni, sprinkle with powdered sugar and ground cinnamon.

Tolma with Grape Leaves (B)

Ingredients:
Lamb - 500 g
Rice - 1/4 cup
Onion - 1
Cilantro - 3 sprigs
Basil and savory - 2 sprigs each
Matsoni (yogurt) - 500 g
Garlic, ground black pepper, salt - to taste

Separate meat from bones, cut it into pieces and pass through a meat grinder. Add picked over and washed rice, finely chopped onion, cilantro, basil, and savory to the minced meat, season it with salt, and mix well.

Scald cleaned and washed grape leaves with boiling water, then cool them. Wrap a little of meat stuffing in each grape leaf. Put lamb bones on a bottom of a pan and top them with a layer of stuffed grape leaves. Add water to the pot, cover it, and cook until done (1 1/2 - 2 hours).

Meanwhile mash garlic with salt, put it into matsoni, and beat well to incorporate.

Transfer cooked tolma to a serving plate and dress it with prepared matsoni.

KUPATY AND HINKALI

Kupaty (Homemade Sausage)

Ingredients:
Beef or pork - 1 kg
Lard - 100 g
Onions - 2
Sausage casings - as needed
Ground black pepper, garlic, pomegranate seeds or barberry seeds, salt - to taste

Cut boneless beef or pork (or a mixture - 700 g of pork and 300 g of beef) into small pieces, add lard, onions, and pass everything through a meat grinder. Add salt, ground black pepper (if desired add a little bit of ground cinnamon), mashed garlic, a little of water or broth, and mix everything thoroughly. Add pomegranate or barberry seeds, and carefully mix to avoid breaking them.

Use washed beef or pork intestines for sausage casings. Soak cleaned, washed intestines in water. Stuff prepared casings with minced meat mixture making sure not to stuff them too tight; otherwise the sausage will burst during cooking. Approximate length of individual sausages should be 20-30 cm. Tie the ends of each sausage together and dip into boiling water for 1 minute.

Take sausages out of the water, cool, and store in a cool dry place (up to two weeks). Kupaty should be cooked on all sides in fat in a hot skillet before serving. Serve hot. Kupaty could be cooked without pomegranate or barberry seeds.

Kupaty with Pork Offal

Wash pork intestines under a running water, inside and outside, turn them inside-out and clean them with salt 2-3 times, then wash again, clean intestines with corn flour a couple of times and wash again thoroughly.

Put intestines prepared this way into a pot, cover with cold water, bring to boil, and drain. Add lungs and liver to the pot with intestines, cover everything with boiling water and cook until done. Finely chop cooked offal.

Thoroughly crush chili pepper, garlic, and cilantro with salt, then add crumbled dried savory, crushed coriander seeds, dried suneli, mix, add chopped pork offal and mix everything together. Then add pomegranate seeds and mix again. Stuff sausage casings and cook as described in the previous recipe.

Quickly Cooked Kupaty

Ingredients:
Pork - 500 g
Onions - 2
Ground cloves and cinnamon - 1/2 tsp
Ground black pepper - 1/4 tsp
Garlic - 1 clove
Pomegranate or barberry seeds, chili pepper, salt - to taste

Cut boneless pork into pieces and pass through a meat grinder together with 1 onion. Season mince with salt, ground black pepper, crushed chili pepper, ground cinnamon and cloves, mashed garlic, add a raw egg and thoroughly mix everything. Add pomegranate or barberry seeds and carefully mix to avoid breaking seeds.

Shape minced meat into medium-sized balls, then roll each ball into a cigar shape. Fry prepared meat on all sides in fat in a hot skillet. Transfer cooked meat to a serving plate, sprinkle with diced onion, pomegranate seeds or dried crushed barberry seeds. Serve pomegranate juice (1/4 cup) seasoned with salt and a little of chopped cilantro (2 sprigs) in a sauce boat.

Hinkali

Ingredients:
Meat - 500 g
Onions - 3
Salt and ground black pepper - to taste
Flour - as needed

Cut boneless lamb or pork (or mix - 300 g of beef and 200 g of pork) into pieces and pass them through a meat grinder together with onions. Season minced meat with ground black pepper, salt, add about 1/2 cup of warm water (or as much as chopped meat can incorporate) and mix everything well.

Sift wheat flour onto a wooden board, gather it into a mound, make a well in the middle of the mound, add 1 cup of water and a pinch of salt, and mix a dough. Roll the dough out thinly and cut dessert-plate sized circles out of it. Put a tablespoon of stuffing in the middle of each piece of dough, bring the sides together and twist them at the top.

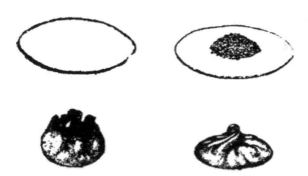

Put prepared hinkali into lightly-salted boiling water and cook at a simmer for 10-15 minutes, until they float to the top. Take cooked hinkali out of the pot with a skimmer and serve hot.

OFFAL DISHES

Braised Beef Offal

Thoroughly wash beef offal (heart, lungs, liver, kidneys, spleen) with cold water; wash intestines outside under a running water, then turn them inside out and wash them again. Twice clean inside part of intestines with salt, then rinse the salt off, clean intestines with corn flour and rinse it off as well.

Put prepared intestines into a pot, cover with cold water, bring to boil, and drain. Add heart, lungs, liver, kidneys, and spleen to the pot with intestines, cover with boiling water and return to boil. Cook over a low heat until done.

Meanwhile, peel and dice onions and nicely brown them in fat in another pot. In a mortar crush chili pepper, cilantro, savory together with salt, then add vinegar to taste and mix well. Cut boiled offal into small pieces while still hot, mix with chopped herbs and add to the pot with browned onions. Cover the pot and braise for 10-15 minutes, then remove from heat. Serve hot.

Braised Pork Offal

Prepare and cook as described above pork intestines, lungs, liver, and kidneys.

Wash, peel, and dice onions, put into a clean pot with some fat and nicely brown them. Cut boiled offal into small pieces while it is still hot, add it to the pot with browned onions, season with salt, crushed chili pepper, crushed coriander seeds, dried savory, garlic, dried suneli, mix and braise 5 minutes. Remove from heat and serve.

Pork Offal with Suneli

Prepared and boiled as described above pork intestines, lungs, liver, spleen cut into very small pieces while still hot, season with salt, add dried suneli (to taste), mix, and serve.

Braised Lamb Heart and Liver with Tarragon

Ingredients:
Heart, liver, caul fat - 1 of each
Onions - 500 g
Tarragon - 7 sprigs
Salt and ground black pepper - to taste
Wash in cold water and cut into pieces heart, liver, and caul fat. Clean, wash, and dice onions, put into a pot together with prepared offal, and cook over low heat. Season contents of the pot with salt and ground black pepper, add finely chopped tarragon, braise for 10 minutes longer, then remove from heat.

Lamb or Pork Heart and Liver with Savory

Ingredients:
Lamb or pork heart and liver with fat - 1 kg
Onions - 4
Dried savory, black pepper, barberry seeds, salt - to taste

Wash lamb or pork heart and liver with cold water, cut into pieces, put into a pot, add finely diced onions, lamb or pork fat, season with salt and cook over low heat until done. Season contents of the pot with crushed dried savory and ground black pepper, transfer cooked offal to a serving plate, sprinkle with barberry seeds and serve.

Fried Lamb or Pork Heart and Liver with Pomegranate

Ingredients:
Lamb or pork heart and liver - 500 g
Lamb fat or pork lard - 100 g
Onions - 4-5
Ground black pepper, herbs (cilantro, savory), pomegranate seeds, salt - to taste

Wash lamb or pork heart and liver, put into a pot, add lamb fat or pork lard and sauté 15 minutes. Add finely diced onions, season with salt, and continue frying until offal is cooked.

Season contents of the pot with ground black pepper, sprinkle with chopped cilantro and savory, sauté 2-3 minutes longer, then take off the heat. Transfer cooked offal to a serving plate and sprinkle with pomegranate seeds.

Liver in Pomegranate Sauce

Ingredients:
Liver - 500 g
Vegetable oil - 2-3 tbsp
Pomegranates - 4-5
Cilantro - 3-4 sprigs
Salt and pepper - to taste

Wash liver, trim it from silver skin and bile ducts, cut into slices 1 cm thick, season with salt and quickly fry in oil in a preheated skillet.

Juice pomegranates, season it with salt, crushed chili peppers, add finely chopped cilantro and mix well.

Transfer cooked liver to a serving plate, pour cooking juices and pomegranate sauce over it and serve.

Liver Braised with Pomegranates

Ingredients:
Liver - 500 g
Fat or vegetable oil - 70-100 g
Onions - 4-5
Ground black pepper, coriander, cilantro, garlic, chili pepper, pomegranate seeds, salt - to taste

Wash and trim liver, cut it into pieces, season with salt, and fry in fat or oil in a preheated skillet, then transfer to a pot.

Peel onions and slice them into rings, lightly fry in the fat left over from liver, then transfer to the pot with fried liver. Add a couple of tablespoons of hot water to the pot and braise liver with onions for 10-15 minutes over a low heat. Season liver with ground black pepper, finely chopped cilantro, crushed coriander seeds, garlic, chili pepper, pomegranate seeds, mix everything, and cook 3-5 minutes longer, then remove from heat.

Transfer cooked liver to a serving plate and sprinkle with diced raw onions and pomegranate seeds.

Braised Liver

Ingredients:
Liver - 500 g
Fat or vegetable oil - 100 g
Onions - 300 g
Salt and ground black pepper - to taste

Cut liver into small pieces, put into a pot over a low heat, and, stirring from time to time, cook until all the liquid evaporates.

In a separate pot brown diced onions with 50 g of fat, then add it to the pot with liver, add remaining 50 g of fat or oil, ground black pepper, salt, and cook until done.

Fried Liver

Ingredients:
Liver - 500 g
Vegetable oil - 3-4 tbsp
Onions - 2
Parsley, pomegranate seeds, salt - to taste

Cut trimmed and washed liver into thin slices, slightly flatten them , season with salt, coat in flour and fry on all sides in vegetable oil.

Transfer cooked liver to a serving plate, and top each slice with onion rings fried in the same skillet as liver. Sprinkle liver with finely chopped parsley and pomegranate seeds and serve.

Spleen with Cilantro and Wine Vinegar

Ingredients:
Spleen - 500 g
Cilantro - 5-6 sprigs
Wine vinegar - 1/2 cup
Salt - to taste

Season trimmed from film and washed in cold water spleen (lamb, veal, or pork) with salt and grill it over a hot coals on a skewer, or cook in a slightly oiled skillet. Cut cooked spleen into pieces, put it on a serving plate and drizzle with wine vinegar mixed with chopped cilantro.

Boiled Tripe with Spicy Sauce

Ingredients:
Tripe - 500 g
Parsley - 1 sprig
Onion - 1
Bay leaf - 1
Red chili peppers - 2-3
Cilantro, savory, basil, dill, garlic, salt - to taste

Wash fresh tripe under a running water, scald it with boiling water, scrub with a knife to remove film and wash in cold water again, then cut into large square pieces, put into a pot together with 5-6 cups of cold water, add onion, bay leaf, salt, parsley, and cook approximately 4-5 hours.

Cover red chili peppers with boiling water and set them aside for a couple of hours. Drain the water, put peppers into a mortar and thoroughly crush it with a small quantity of rock salt, then add to taste cilantro, savory, basil, dill, garlic and mash everything together. Add mixture from the mortar to the 3/4 cups of strained broth.

Cut cooked tripe into smaller pieces and pour the sauce over the tripe. Sprinkle with dried suneli if desired. Serve hot.

This dish can also be cooked cold, in which case mix cut tripe with mixture from the mortar without adding broth, and cool it.

Fried Tripe with Barberry Seeds

Ingredients:
Tripe - 500 g
Vegetable oil - 1 tbsp
Onions - 3
Ground black pepper, scallions, barberry seeds, salt - to taste

Cut prepared and cooked as described above tripe into noodle-sized pieces, season with salt and pepper and fry it in oil in a hot skillet, then mix with dice onions browned in oil, and continue cooking 1-2 minutes longer and remove from heat.

Finely crush dried barberry, mix it with cooked tripe, then sprinkle tripe with finely chopped onions or scallions.

Beef Tongue with Spicy Garnish

Ingredients:
Beef tongue - 500 g
Celery, parsnip, carrot - 1 each
Onion - 1
Bay leaf - 1
Scallions - 2
Cilantro - 4 sprigs
Dill - 6 sprigs
Wine vinegar - 1/4 cup
Chili pepper, horseradish, salt - to taste

Clean beef tongue, remove saliva ducts at the base of the tongue (on both sides), wash it once more, put into a pot with hot water and return water to boil. When tongue is almost cooked take it out of the pot, put into cold water and slightly cool. Remove tough skin from the tongue, return it to the simmering broth and let it simmer for 15 minutes longer, add cleaned and washed roots (celery, parsnip, carrot, onion), bay leaf, salt, and cook until done.

Cut cooked tongue across on a bias into thin slices, set in an elongated dish and serve it with a garnish. To prepare garnish finely chop scallions, chili pepper, herbs (cilantro and dill), grate horseradish on a grater, add wine vinegar, season with salt and thoroughly mix everything.

Tongue can be served hot or cold. If serving cold - let the tongue cool in its broth.

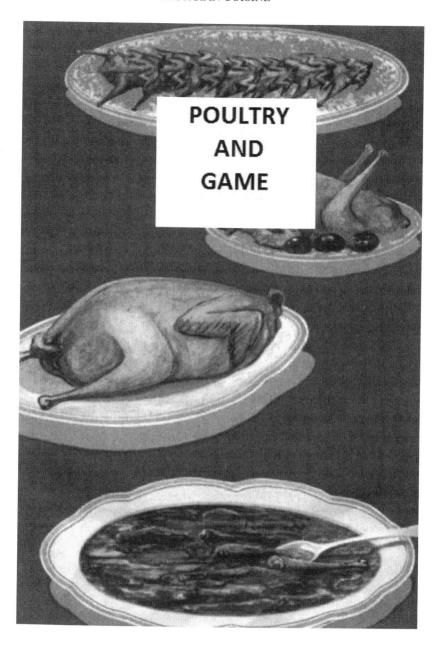

POULTRY
AND
GAME

POULTRY AND GAME

CHICKEN

Boiled Chicken with Garlic Sauce

Ingredients:
Chicken - 1
Broth - 3/4-1 cup
Garlic - 10-12
Salt - to taste

Thoroughly wash whole trimmed chicken in cold water, put into a pot, cover with boiling water, cover the pot, and bring to boil. Skim the foam as it rises to the top. Lower the heat and simmer until chicken is done.

When the chicken is cooked (test it by piercing the chicken leg with a larding needle) take it out of the pot, lightly season with salt, cut into serving pieces, and put into a deep serving bowl.

Mash garlic in a mortar, mix with chicken broth, season with salt, then pour the sauce over the chicken. If desired - serve sauce on a side in a sauce boat.

Boiled Chicken with Walnut Sauce

Ingredients:
Chicken - 1
Shelled walnuts - 2 cups
Garlic - 12-15 cloves
Water - as needed
Coriander seeds and salt - to taste

Cook chicken as described above, then cut it into serving pieces and transfer to a serving bowl.

Pass shelled walnuts through a meat grinder or pound them in a mortar, add crushed garlic and crushed coriander seeds and mix with drinking water to the heavy cream consistency, then pass it through a sieve. Pour the sauce over the chicken and sprinkle the dish with pomegranate seeds.

Braised Chicken with Walnuts (A)

Ingredients:
Chicken - 1
Onions - 3
Crushed shelled walnuts - 1 tbsp
Cilantro and parsley - 2 sprigs each
Cinnamon - 1/2 tsp
Cloves - 3-4
Ground black pepper - 1/4 tsp
Wine vinegar - 3-4 tbsp
Salt - to taste

Cut trimmed and washed carcass of a fatty chicken into serving pieces and nicely brown it with diced onions. Add crushed walnuts, saffron, ground black pepper, ground cinnamon and cloves, finely chopped herbs (cilantro, parsley), add wine vinegar, mix everything, cover the pot and braise 10-15 minutes longer.

Braised Chicken with Walnuts (B)

Ingredients:
Chicken - 1
Shelled walnuts - 200 g
Onion - 1
Cilantro - 4 sprigs
Garlic - 1 clove
Wine vinegar - 1/2 cup
Ground black pepper, ground cinnamon, ground cloves, salt
- to taste

Cut cleaned and washed fatty chicken into serving pieces and brown in a pot.

Thoroughly pound walnuts, garlic, and cilantro, squeeze walnut oil and keep in a separate container.

Mix together crushed walnuts, garlic, ground black pepper, ground cinnamon and cloves, finely chopped cilantro, and wine vinegar, add it to browned chicken and braise 10-15 minutes longer.

Transfer cooked dish to a serving bowl, sprinkle with finely diced raw onion, drizzle with walnut oil and serve.

Chicken with Green Beans

Ingredients:
Chicken - 1
Green beans - 700-800 g
Onions - 3-4
Tomatoes - 500-600 g
Basil - 4-5 sprigs
Chili pepper, salt - to taste

Cut prepared and washed fatty chicken into pieces, put into a pot and brown on all sides for about 15 minutes. Add finely diced onions and continue frying until onions are browned. Add broken into smaller pieces green beans, add boiling water to barely cover the contents of the pot, cover the pot and cook until meat and beans are done (approximately 40-60 minutes).

Meanwhile in a separate pot put braised and passed through a sieve tomatoes and cook them until thickened, then add to the pot with chicken and beans, add finely chopped basil, crushed chili pepper, salt, and cook 10 minutes longer. Remove pot from the heat and transfer to a serving plate.

Chicken with Cherry Plums

Ingredients:
Chicken - 1
Onions - 6-7
Sour cherry plums or tkemali - 1-1 1/2 cups
Coriander seeds - 1/2 tsp
Dill - 10-12 sprigs
Chili pepper and salt - to taste

Cut prepared, washed fatty chicken into pieces, put into a pot, and brown on all sides, then add boiling water coming just half-way up the chicken, and braise over a low heat in a covered pot until the chicken is cooked.

Braise cherry plums or tkemali, then remove pits. About 15 minutes before the chicken is done add onions sliced into thin rings to the pot, season with salt, then, just before the end of cooking, add plums, crushed cilantro and chili pepper and finely chopped dill.

Braised Chicken with Egg

Ingredients:
Chicken - 1
Onions - 3-4
Vegetable oil - 30-50 g
Cilantro - 3-4 tbsp
Parsely - 2 tbsp
Eggs - 3-4
Salt - to taste

Brown finely diced onions in oil. Cut trimmed and washed chicken into medium-sized pieces and brown in a pit, then add browned onions, add enough water just to cover the chicken and cook for a few minutes. Season contents of the pot with salt, add finely chopped cilantro and parsley, break eggs into the pot, and cook until done.

Fried Chicken with Pomegranate

Ingredients:
Chicken - 1
Onions - 4
Cilantro - 6 sprigs
Parsley - 7 sprigs
Basil and savory - 3 sprigs each
Dill - 5 sprigs
Pomegranate seeds, salt - to taste

Cut washed and trimmed fatty chicken into pieces and brown on all sides in a pot. Pour the juice released during the cooking to a clean container. Add thinly sliced onions to the chicken, season with salt, and fry until completely cooked, from time to time adding some of the juice, drained before, back into the pot. Shortly before the end of the cooking add finely chopped herbs (cilantro, parsley, basil, savory, dill), and just before serving sprinkle with pomegranate seeds.

Fried Chicken with Walnuts

Ingredients:
Chicken - 1
Onions - 4
Shelled walnuts - 100-200 g
Egg yolks - 2
Wine vinegar, garlic, chili pepper, mint, salt - to taste

Cut fatty chicken into serving pieces and brown on all side. Drain juices released during cooking into a separate container, add diced onions to the chicken and continue frying until onions are cooked. Add crushed walnuts, garlic, chili pepper, finely chopped mint, and salt to the pot with chicken, and continue cooking 10-15 minutes longer.

Mix egg yolks first - with wine vinegar, then with preserved chicken juice. Gradually pour the egg-yolk mixture into the pot stirring all the time, then remove from heat.

Fried Chicken with Walnuts and Pomegranate

Ingredients:
Chicken - 1
Onions - 4
Shelled walnuts - 100 g
Pomegranate juice - 1 cup
Coriander seeds - 1/2 tsp
Pomegranate seeds, garlic, chili pepper, salt - to taste

Cut fatty chicken into pieces, wash, let it drain, then put

into a pot and brown on all sides. Add diced onions and continue cooking. About 10 minutes before the end of cooking put into the pot with chicken mixed in pomegranate seeds crushed walnuts, mashed garlic, chili pepper, coriander seeds, and salt. Just before serving sprinkle the dish with pomegranate seeds.

Chicken with Tomato-Walnut Sauce

Ingredients:
Chicken - 1
Tomatoes - 1200-1500 g
Shelled walnuts - 1/2-3/4 cup
Garlic - 4-5 cloves
Coriander seeds - 1/2 tsp
Chili pepper and salt - to taste

Put whole trimmed and thoroughly washed whole chicken into a pot with boiling water, cover the pot and cooked until half-done. Then - take it out of the pot, season with salt inside and out, put into a roasting pan, add fat skimmed from the broth, put into a preheated oven and cook in a low heat 30-40 minutes. From time to time baste the chicken with pan juices and fat.

Meanwhile, in a separate pot braise tomatoes in 1/2 cup of water. Pass braised tomatoes through a sieve, strain, together with juices released during cooking into a clean pot, and cook until thickened. About 10 minutes before the end of cooking add crushed walnuts, garlic, chili pepper, coriander seeds, and salt.

Cut nicely browned chicken into serving pieces, put into a deep serving bowl, and top with thick tomato sauce, then sprinkle with finely chopped parsley and serve.

Chicken with Spicy Sauce

Ingredients:
Chicken - 1
Parsnips - 2
Celery - 2 stalks
Garlic - 3 cloves
Onions - 3-4
Bay leaf - 1
Cilantro - 3 sprigs
Parsley - 2 sprigs
Dill - 4 sprigs
Pomegranate seeds, chili pepper, salt - to taste

Put not very fatty trimmed chicken into a pot with boiling water, add parsnips, celery, and garlic, cover the pot, and cook until half-done.

Take parboiled chicken out of the pot, season inside and out with salt, put into a roasting pan, add some fat skimmed from the broth, and put the pan into a preheated oven to brown the chicken.

Cut browned, but not completely cooked chicken, into pieces, put it into a pot, add broth (1-1 1/2 cups) with fat from roasting pan, then add bay leaf, chili pepper, sliced and browned in chicken fat onions, cover the pot, and braise approximately 15-20 minutes. Transfer cooked dish into a serving bowl, remove bay leaf, liberally sprinkle with pomegranate seeds and with finely chopped herbs (cilantro, parsley, and dill).

Boiled Young Chicken with Walnut Sauce

Ingredients:
Chicken - 1
Shelled walnuts - 300 g
Onion - 1

Cilantro and parsley - to taste
Garlic, chili pepper, vinegar or unripe grape juice or
pomegranate juice, salt - to taste

Put prepared young chicken (together with giblets if
desired) into a pot with hot water, add one onion, small
bunch of parsley, and cook until done.

When chicken is done cut it into serving pieces and put
it on a serving plate.

Pound shelled walnuts in a mortar or pass them through
a meat grinder, add mashed together cilantro, garlic, chili
pepper, and salt, then add vinegar or pomegranate juice and
3-4 cups of warm broth. Mix everything well. Pour prepared
sauce over chicken and serve.

Boiled Young Chicken with Pomegranate Sauce

Ingredients:
Chicken - 1
Pomegranate juice - 3/4 cup
Drinking water - 1/2-3/4 cup
Garlic - 4-5 cloves
Coriander seeds - 1/2 tsp
Chili pepper, scallions, pomegranate seeds, salt - to taste

Cook young chicken as indicated in the previous recipe,
cut into serving pieces and put into a serving bowl.

Mix pomegranate juice with drinking water, then add
garlic mashed with chili pepper and coriander seeds. Pour
the sauce over chicken, sprinkle chicken with finely chopped
scallions and pomegranate seeds, and serve.

Chahohbili with Young Chicken

Ingredients:
Chicken - 1
Onions - 3-4

Vegetable oil - 2 tbsp
Tomatoes - 700-800 g
Cilantro - 4-5 sprigs
Basil - 2-3 sprigs
Black or chili pepper, salt - to taste

Cut washed young chicken into medium-sized pieces. Slice onions, put them into a pot together with vegetable oil and sauté over a low heat until onions are caramelized. Put chicken into the pot with onions, season it with ground black pepper or crushed chili pepper and salt, add finely chopped cilantro and basil, tomatoes cut into wedges, and braise until chicken is cooked.

Young Chicken with Tarragon

Ingredients:
Chicken - 1
Butter - 50-70 g
Wine vinegar - 1/4 cup
Tarragon - 8-10 sprigs
Egg yolks - 2
Salt - to taste

Cut trimmed and thoroughly washed young chicken into serving pieces, put into a pot, brown for 10 minutes, then add butter and continue cooking 15-20 minutes longer. Pour the juice released during the cooking into a clean container. Add enough water to the pot to cover the chicken and cook until meat is done.

About 10 minutes before the end of cooking add wine vinegar to the pot, then add finely chopped tarragon, salt, egg yolks mixed with juice from cooking, and mix everything well. Continue cooking without letting contents of the pot to boil.

Young Chicken with Tomatoes and Eggs

Ingredients:
Chicken - 1
Tomatoes - 3
Vegetable oil - 70-100 g
Onions - 2
Scallions - 1
Eggs - 2-3
Salt - to taste

Cut trimmed and washed young chicken into pieces, put into a pot, and brown for 10 minutes. Add vegetable oil and onions to the pot and continue cooking until onions are nicely browned, then add cut into wedges potatoes and braise until thickened.

Beat eggs, season them with salt, add finely chopped scallion, mix well, then pour it into the pot with chicken. Continue cooking until eggs are set. If desired - sprinkle finished dish with chopped cilantro.

Young Chicken with Walnuts and Eggs

Ingredients:
Chicken - 1
Shelled walnuts - 1 cup
Onions - 2
Wine vinegar - 1/4-1/2 cup
Dill - 4-5 sprigs
Cilantro - 2 sprigs
Eggs - 2
Pomegranate seeds, scallions, chili pepper, tarragon, salt - to taste

Boil or fry washed and trimmed chicken until cooked, then cut it into servings.

Pass walnuts through a meat grinder, add finely chopped onions, chili pepper, dill, pomegranate seeds, wine vinegar mix with water, season everything with salt, and pour the sauce over chicken. Transfer the dish to a serving bowl, sprinkle with finely chopped herbs (tarragon and cilantro), scallions and pomegranate seeds, and decorate with sliced hard-boiled eggs.

Young Chicken with Walnut Sauce

Ingredients:
Chicken - 1
Shelled walnuts - 200 g
Vegetable oil - 2 tbsp
Onions - 200 g
Corn flour - 1 tbsp
Ground cinnamon and cloves - 3/4 tsp
Cilantro, garlic, vinegar, chili pepper, salt - to taste

Brown washed and trimmed young chicken just like "Chicken Tabaka". Dice onions, add it to a pot together with vegetable oil, and sauté until nicely browned.

Pass shelled walnuts through a meat grinder together with a sprig of cilantro and some salt. Squeeze walnut oil from the crushed nuts and store it in a covered container.

Pound cilantro, garlic, and chili pepper in a mortar, add crushed walnuts, corn flour, mix with 4-5 cup of boiling water, mix well, and pour it into the pot with onions. Simmer for 10-15 minutes.

While the mixture is cooking add to it wine vinegar, or pomegranate juice, or juice from unripe grapes, and season it with ground cinnamon and cloves.

Cut fried chicken into medium-sized pieces, put into hot walnut sauce, return the sauce to boil and remove from heat.

Just before serving transfer the dish to a serving bowl and drizzle walnut oil over chicken. Serve warm or cold.

SPRING CHICKEN

Chahohbili with Spring Chicken (A)

Ingredients:
Spring chicken - 1
Onions - 300 g
Vegetable oil - 100-150 g
Potatoes - 3-4
Salt and ground black pepper - to taste

Wash spring chicken, cut it into pieces, and wash once more. Put chicken into a pot and cook over a low heat. Pour the juice released during cooking into a separate container and keep it covered.

Meanwhile - chop onions, add it to the pot with chicken, add vegetable oil, and brown onions stirring from time to time to avoid burning. Pour juices from the step 1 back into the pot, add cut into large pieces potatoes, and braise everything together until potatoes are completely cooked.

About 5 minutes before the end of cooking season chicken with salt and ground black pepper and mix well.

Chahohbili with Spring Chicken (B)

This dish is cooked as described above; however, without potatoes and ground black pepper. Instead about 10 minutes before the end of cooking add crushed chili pepper, and, to taste, chopped herbs (parsley, cilantro, dill, basil, savory, tarragon, a little of mint).

Chahohbili with Spring Chicken and Tomatoes

Ingredients:
Chicken - 1
Onions - 300-400 g

Vegetable oil - 100 g
Tomatoes - 800-1000 g
Salt - to taste

Thoroughly wash spring chicken, cut it into pieces, then wash again and let it drain in a colander. Put chicken into a pot, cover the pot, and braise stirring from time to time to prevent burning.

Dice onions and add them and vegetable oil to the pot with chicken. Continue cooking until meat is done.

Cut tomatoes into pieces, simmer them, then pass through a sieve, put into a clean pot and simmer until they thicken. Transfer tomato sauce into the pot with chicken and cook 10-15 minutes longer.

If desired - potatoes can be added to the chicken. Dish can be seasoned to taste with crushed chili pepper and finely chopped herbs.

Tomato puree (3/4 cup) mixed with water (1/2 cup) can replace fresh tomatoes.

Chicken-Tabaka (Fried Spring Chicken)

Wash spring chicken, cut it along its breast, and flatten the chicken on a board, season on both sides with salt and put into a preheated skillet with clarified butter or vegetable oil. Set cleaned and prepared giblets around the chicken.

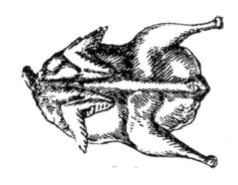

Top the chicken with a plate, and put a weight atop the plate, to insure that chicken is flattened against the surface of the skillet. Fry over a medium heat for 40-60 minutes.

When one side of the chicken is cooked, i.e. a nice brown crust form on it, flip the chicken over and fry it on the other side.

Fried chicken can be served without garnish, or garnished with fried potatoes, tomatoes, cooked rice, cucumbers and so on. If desired - serve with a sauce (walnut, tomato) on a side.

Fried Breaded Chicken with Pomegranate

Ingredients:
Spring chicken - 1
Butter - 50-70 g
Pomegranate juice - 1/4 cup
Garlic - 2 cloves
Egg - 1
Crushed breadcrumbs - as needed
Pomegranate seeds, salt - to taste

Wash prepared spring chicken, cut into four parts, thoroughly dry, season with salt and coat in flour, then dip in beaten egg, coat in crushed breadcrumbs in fry each piece in butter in a preheated skillet on both sides until nicely crusted. Set fried pieces of chicken on a serving plate to resemble a whole bird, drizzle with pomegranate juice, sprinkle with grated garlic and pomegranate seeds, decorate with salad greens and serve.

Fried Spring Chicken with Garlic-Walnut Sauce

Ingredients:
Spring chicken - 1
Shelled walnuts - 1 1/2-2 cups
Garlic - 7-10 cloves
Salt - to taste

Fry prepared spring chicken in a skillet, over hot coals on a skewer, in a rotisserie, or roast it in a preheated oven, then cut into serving pieces and set on a serving plate.

Crush shelled walnuts in a mortar or pass them through a meat grinder, season to taste with salt and mashed garlic, mix it with 1 1/2-2 cups of drinking water. Pour prepared sauce over the chicken and serve.

Fried Spring Chicken with Garlic Sauce

Ingredients:
Spring chicken - 1
Butter or vegetable oil - 30-50 g
Garlic - 5-6 cloves
Salt - to taste

Fry prepared and seasoned with salt chicken in hot butter or vegetable oil, cut into pieces and put into a pot.

Add one cup of hot water to the skillet used to fry chicken, let is simmer 2-3 minutes, then pour it into the pot with chicken. Cover the pot and braise chicken for 10 minutes over a low heat. Add mashed garlic to the pot, mix everything and remove from heat.

Fried Spring Chicken Stuffed with Giblets

Ingredients:
Spring chicken - 1
Scallions - 1
Tarragon - 2 sprigs

Parsley - 3 sprigs
Basil - 2 sprigs
Clarified butter - 2 tbsp
Ground cinnamon - 1/4 tsp
Salt - to taste

Boil cleaned and washed stomach and liver of a spring chicken, finely chop them, add chopped scallions, tarragon, parsley, and basil. Put this mixture into a skillet, add a little clarified butter, ground cinnamon, salt, mix, and sauté for 5-8 minutes.

Stuff spring chicken with prepared stuffing. Put chicken into a skillet with remaining clarified butter, cover the skillet and fry the bird, basting it with melted fat from time to time. Stuffed chicken can also be roasted in an oven.

Take the stuffing out of the cooked chicken, cut chicken into pieces, set it on a serving plate together with stuffing and decorate with parsley sprigs.

TURKEY, GOOSE, DUCK

Boiled Turkey

Put trimmed, cleaned, and thoroughly washed turkey into a pot, cover with boiling water, cover the pot and cook until done. Skim the foam as it rises to the top.

Approximately 30 minutes before the end of cooking add parsnip, celery, and mashed garlic to the pot.

Season cooked turkey with salt while it is still hot (inside and outside), cut into pieces, set them on a serving plate and decorate with parsley sprigs or salad leaves. Serve garlic sauce, tkemali sauce, or walnut sauce on a side in a sauce boat.

Turkey can be served hot or cold.

Goose with Eggs

Ingredients:
Goose - 1
Onions - 400-500 g
Eggs - 3-4
Salt - to taste

Gut and wash a goose, cut it into serving-size pieces and fry in a shallow sauté pan. When goose renders its fat, add finely chopped onions to the pan and cook it together with the bird until nicely browned, then add enough water to cover the meat and cook until meat is cooked. Season contents of the pan with salt and break egg into the pan. Continue cooking until eggs are set.

Goose with Sour Fruit Leather

Ingredients:
Goose - 1
Onions - 300-400 g
Sour fruit leather - 100 g
Cilantro - 6-7 sprigs
Garlic - 3 cloves
Chili pepper and salt - to taste

Wash prepared fatty goose and cut it into pieces, put into a pan and nicely brown it. Add finely diced onions and sauté it together with the goose until the meat is almost cooked. Season contents of the pan, add sour fruit leather soaked in hot water (1-1 1/2 cups) and passed through a sieve together with soaking liquid, and continue braising 10-15 minutes longer. Just before the end of cooking add chopped cilantro, whole garlic cloves and chili peppers.

Roasted Goose with Dried Dogberries

Put trimmed and thoroughly washed goose into a pit, cover with water, and cook until half-done. Add parsnip, celery, and mashed garlic to the water during cooking.

Take goose out of the broth, season with salt, and set it in a roasting pan, breast-side down, add a little broth to the pan and put it into a preheated oven.

Baste goose from time to time with the juices and fat from the pan, and turn it to so that it browns on all sides evenly. If juices from the pan evaporate too fast - add a little more broth.

Cook dried pitted dogberries in some broth. While the goose is roasting add to the pan potatoes, sliced into rings onions, and cooked dried dogberries together with their cooking liquid. Cook until done.

Roast Duck with Dogberry Sauce

Season thoroughly cleaned and washed duck with salt inside and outside, put into a roasting pan breast-side up, add hot water to the pan, put the pan into a preheated oven and roast until done.

Peel large potatoes, cut into smaller pieces, wash them in cold water, and season with salt. When duck is half-done , add potatoes to the roasting pan and continue cooking.

Turn duck over from time to time, and baste it with fat and juices released during cooking. Brown finely diced onions (3-4) in some of the duck fat, add dried dogberries and hot water to the pan with onions (1-1 1/2 cups of water to 1 cup of dried dogberries) and braise until berries are cooked. Season with salt when the sauce is ready.

Cut cooked duck into serving pieces, set it on an oblong serving plate together with oven-roasted potatoes, drizzle the pan juices and decorate with parsley sprigs. Serve sauce on a side in a sauce boat.

Poultry Braised in Walnut Sauce

Ingredients:
Chicken, turkey, duck, or goose - 1
Shelled walnuts - 400 g
Onions - 300 g
Garlic - 1 clove
Ground black pepper - 1/4 tsp
Cilantro - 3-4 sprigs
Wine vinegar, chili pepper, cinnamon, cloves, salt - to taste

Cut prepared turkey, chicken, goose, or duck into pieces, wash with cold water, leave in a colander, and, when all the water is drained, put them into a pot together with diced onions, and brown over a medium heat.

Pass shelled walnuts through a meat grinder twice, add mashed garlic, chopped cilantro, crushed chili pepper, ground cinnamon and cloves, season with salt, and dilute with boiling water (6-8 cups). Pour the sauce over browned bird and simmer for 20 minutes. If desired - season with dried suneli (to taste).

About 5-10 minutes before the end of cooking season contents of the pot with ground black pepper, add a little wine vinegar or pomegranate juice, return to boil, remove from heat, transfer to a serving bowl, and let it cool.

This dish can also be cooked a bit differently: pass shelled walnuts through a meat grinder and pound them in a mortar and squeeze oil out of them. Add pounded together cilantro, garlic, chili pepper, salt, ground cinnamon and cloves to the crushed walnuts and mix everything well. Add boiling water to the walnut mixture (7-8 cups) and pour the sauce over the browned bird, then cook for 20 minutes.

Just before the end of cooking add juice from a few pomegranates and instantly remove from heat. Transfer the dish into appropriate serving container and cool. Just before serving sprinkle with whole pomegranate seeds and drizzle with walnut oil.

Cooked Poultry with Satsebeli-Bazha Sauce

Ingredients:
Chicken, turkey, duck, or goose - 1
Shelled walnuts - 200-300 g
Garlic - 4-5 cloves
Wine vinegar, pomegranate juice, verjuice, blackberry juice, or mixture of verjuice and blackberry juice - to taste
Chili peppers, cilantro, coriander seeds, saffron, salt - to taste

Cook prepared turkey, chicken, goose, or duck in water, fry or roast it. Cut cooked bird into serving pieces and set on a serving plate.

Pound shelled walnuts together with cilantro and coriander seeds, garlic, chili pepper, saffron, and salt in a mortar, gradually squeezing oil into a separate container (if desired).

Mix crushed walnuts with two-three cups of drinking water or poultry broth, add to taste wine vinegar or pomegranate juice or verjuice or blackberry juice or a mixture of verjuice and blackberry juice, then pour the sauce over the prepared poultry and drizzle squeezed walnut oil over the dish. If the sauce is made with pomegranate juice - sprinkle the dish with pomegranate seeds.

Roast Turkey or Chicken with Garo Sauce

Ingredients:
Turkey or chicken - 1
Shelled walnuts - 200 g
Onions - 2
Cilantro - 4 sprigs
Wine vinegar - 1/2 cup
Egg yolks - 2
Salt - to taste

Season well trimmed and thoroughly washed young fatty turkey or chicken with salt, put into a roasting pan, add two-three tablespoons of water and roast in a preheated oven until done.

Make a stock from giblets, necks and wings of the bird. Pound walnuts together with cilantro, garlic, and salt in a mortar, gradually add wine vinegar and stock from the step 2 (2 cups), mixing to incorporate. Add diced onions to walnut mixture, bring it to boil in a pot, let it simmer for 1o minutes, then remove from heat.

Beat egg yolks, temper them with a small quantity of lightly cooled walnut sauce, then gradually add remaining sauce, mixing all the time to prevent yolks from curdling.

Cut roasted turkey or chicken into serving pieces, set it on a plate, and decorate with parsley sprigs. Serve the sauce over on a side in a sauce boat.

GIBLETS

Chahohbili with Giblets

Ingredients:
Giblets - From 1 bird
Onions - 200 g
Vegetable oil - 50-70 g
Salt and ground black pepper - to taste

Put washed giblets into a pot, add a little vegetable oil, and sauté them.

Dice onions and soften them in oil in a separate pot, then add to the pot with giblets, and continue cooking until giblets are done. Season giblets with salt and ground black pepper, mix, and braise for 5-10 minutes longer.

Chahohbili with Giblets and Tomatoes

Ingredients:
Giblets - From 1 bird
Onions - 300 g
Vegetable oil - 70 g
Tomatoes - 500 g
Parsley, salt - to taste

Wash giblets in cold water. Dice onions and soften it in some vegetable oil. About 5-7 minutes from the start of the cooking add giblets and more vegetable oil to the pot with onions, mix everything and continue cooking mixing from time to time.

Chop tomatoes, add them to the pot with giblets and onions and cook 20-25 minutes longer. Season everything with salt, finely chopped parsley, and, if desired, chili pepper.

SATSIVI

SATSIVI WITH MEAT AND POULTRY

Satsivi with Poultry (A)

Ingredients:
Poultry - 1 bird
Onions - 300-400 g
Shelled walnuts - 400-500 g
Cilantro - 3-4 sprigs
Coriander seeds - 1 tsp
Ground cinnamon, cloves, chili pepper, saffron, suneli - to taste
Wine vinegar, salt - to taste

Put whole prepared turkey, chicken, goose, or duck into a pot, cover with water, bring to boil and cook until half-done. Transfer the bird to a roasting pan, breast-side down, season with salt, add a little broth from the pot, and put into a preheated oven.

Baste the bird from time to time with pan juices and turn it over to insure even browning on all sides.

Meanwhile, skim some of the fat from the broth, put it into a skillet, and brown diced or passed through a meat grinder onions in it. Add more skimmed fat to the skillet as needed. Pound shelled walnuts or pass them through a meat grinder, then mix crushed walnuts with mashed garlic, chopped cilantro, crushed chili pepper, saffron, and salt.

Add broth to the walnut mixture (6-8 cups), add to the skillet with browned onions and simmer for 15-20 minutes. About 5-10 minutes before the end of cooking add wine vinegar, ground cinnamon and cloves, crushed coriander seeds, dried suneli (if using).

If using less walnuts than suggested by the recipe - add 2-3 tbsp of corn flour.

Cut cooked bird into serving pieces, transfer into a serving bowl, pour hot satsivi over, let it cool, then serve.

Satsivi with Poultry (B)

Ingredients:
Poultry - 1 bird
Onions - 400 g
Shelled walnuts - 300-400 g
Corn flour - 1 tbsp
Cilantro - 3-4 sprigs
Ground cinnamon and cloves - 1/2 tsp
Wine vinegar, chili pepper, garlic, salt - to taste

Put prepared turkey, chicken, goose, or duck into a pot, cover with water, bring to boil, and simmer for 15 minutes.

Transfer the bird into a roasting pan, season with salt, and cook in a preheated oven.

Pass shelled walnuts, garlic, and cilantro through a meat grinder. Squeeze oil from walnuts and store it into a clean, covered container.

Add corn flour, crushed chili pepper, and ground cinnamon and cloves to the walnut mixture and mix well. Put this mixture into a clean pot together with 6 cups of broth and cook for 10 minutes. Add vinegar to taste and simmer 5 minutes longer.

Meanwhile dice onions or pass them through a meat grinder, sauté them in walnut oil, then add to the pot with walnut mixture and cook 5 minutes more. Add cooked bird cut into pieces to the pot with the sauce, return it to boil and remove the pot from heat. Transfer contents of the pot to a serving bowl and let it cool before serving.

Satsivi with Poultry (C)

Ingredients:
Poultry - 1 bird
Shelled walnuts - 400-500 g
Onions - 300 g
Cilantro - 3 sprigs
Garlic, ground black pepper, chili pepper, wine vinegar, cinnamon, cloves, salt - to taste

Boil prepared turkey, chicken, goose, or duck until half-done, then finish cooking by roasting it in a preheated oven.

Pound shelled walnuts in a mortar or pass them through a meat grinder, squeeze oil from crushed walnuts and store it in a clean, covered container.

Pound cilantro together with garlic, salt, and chili pepper. Mix these ingredients with crushed walnuts and 7-8 cups of the broth, bring to boil, and simmer for 10 minutes. Season contents of the pot with ground black pepper, ground cloves and cinnamon, add wine vinegar and cook 5-10 minutes longer.

Cut roasted bird into serving pieces, put into a serving bowl, sprinkle with finely diced raw onions, then pour hot satsivi over it, let the dish cool, then, before serving, drizzle it with walnut oil.

Satsivi with Poultry (D)

Ingredients:
Poultry - 1 bird
Shelled walnuts - 200-300 g
Onions - 300 g
Coriander seeds - 1 tsp
Dried suneli - 1 tsp
Ground black pepper - 1/2 tsp
Ground cinnamon and cloves - 1 tsp
Egg yolks - 2
Wine vinegar or pomegranate juice - to taste
Chili pepper, garlic, saffron, salt - to taste

Put prepared whole turkey, chicken, goose, or duck into a pot with boiling water and cook until half-done. Transfer the bird to a roasting pan breast-side down, lightly season with salt, add a little broth to the pan and put it into a preheated oven.

From time to time baste the bird with fat and pan juices. Strain broth to a clean pot, add finely diced onions and bring it to boil.

Pound shelled walnuts together with garlic, salt, and chili pepper in a mortar, then add ground black pepper, ground cinnamon and cloves, crushed coriander seeds, crushed saffron to the walnut mixture and thin it with a little bit of broth, then pour it to the pot with broth and simmer for 15 minutes.

Season broth with dried suneli, wine vinegar or pomegranate juice, let it simmer for 5 minutes longer, then remove from heat. Mix two-three egg yolks with some of the cooled satsivi sauce, then gradually pour it into pot with hot sauce constantly stirring.

Cut cooked bird into serving pieces, put into a serving bowl, pour prepared hot satsivi over it, let it cool, then serve.

Satsivi with Turkey or Chicken

Ingredients:
Turkey or chicken - 1
Shelled walnuts - 100-200 g
Onions - 300-400 g
Wheat flour - 1 1/2-2 tbsp
Garlic, chili pepper, saffron, vinegar or pomegranate juice, cilantro, salt - to taste

Put whole prepared turkey or chicken into a pot, cover with water, bring to boil, and cook until half-done, then transfer to a roasting pan and finish cooking in a preheated oven.

Thoroughly pound shelled walnuts together with garlic, salt, chili pepper, saffron, and cilantro in a mortar, then mix with broth (6-8 cups), season with wine vinegar or pomegranate juice and simmer 15-20 minutes.

Sauté diced onions in fat skimmed from the broth for 5-8 minutes, then add flour and sauté a bit longer. Add softened onions to the simmering sauce.

Cut cooked turkey or chicken into serving pieces, put into a serving bowl and pour hot sauce over it.

Satsivi with Chicken

Ingredients:
Chicken - 1

Shelled walnuts - 100-200 g
Corn flour - 1-1 1/2 tbsp
Onions - 4-5
Wine vinegar, cilantro, pepper (chili and black) cinnamon,
saffron, garlic, dried suneli, salt - to taste

Cut prepared fatty chicken into pieces, season with salt,
put into a pot and brown on all sides.

Pass onions together with chicken fat through a meat
grinder, then add it to the pot with chicken, and sauté until
softened.

Pound shelled walnuts together with salt, add corn
flour, mashed garlic, cilantro, crushed coriander, chili
pepper, mix it with boiling water (5-6 cups) and wine
vinegar. Pour prepared mixture to the pot with chicken and
cook 15-20 minutes.

About 5-10 minutes before the end of cooking season
chicken with ground black pepper and cinnamon, crushed
saffron, and, if using, dried suneli.

Satsivi with Chicken

Ingredients:
Chicken - 1
Shelled walnuts - 100-200 g
Corn flour - 1-1 1/2 tbsp
Onions - 4-5
Wine vinegar, cilantro, pepper (chili and black) cinnamon,
saffron, garlic, dried suneli, salt - to taste

Cut prepared fatty chicken into pieces, season with salt,
put into a pot and brown on all sides.

Pass onions together with chicken fat through a meat
grinder, then add it to the pot with chicken, and sauté until
softened.

Pound shelled walnuts together with salt, add corn flour, mashed garlic, cilantro, crushed coriander, chili pepper, mix it with boiling water (5-6 cups) and wine vinegar. Pour prepared mixture to the pot with chicken and cook 15-20 minutes.

About 5-10 minutes before the end of cooking season chicken with ground black pepper and cinnamon, crushed saffron, and, if using, dried suneli.

Satsivi with Turkey Roasted on a Spit

Ingredients:
Turkey - 1
Shelled walnuts - 200 g
Egg yolks - 3
Onions - 5
Wine vinegar, cinnamon, cloves, chili and black pepper, saffron, garlic, cilantro, salt - to taste

Cook trimmed and washed whole turkey in a pot of boiling water until half-done, remove from the broth, season with salt, set it on a spit, and cook over glowing coals constantly turning, and basting with walnut oil from time to time.

Thoroughly crush shelled walnuts with garlic, salt, and chili pepper and squeeze walnut oil (which is used to baste the bird) from this mixture.

Add finely chopped cilantro, crushed coriander seeds, crumbled saffron, ground cinnamon and cloves, ground black pepper, onions passed through a meat grinder, and wine vinegar to the walnut mixture. Put everything into a clean pot together with turkey broth and simmer 10-15 minutes.

Bean egg yolks with a small quantity of the sauce, then gradually pour it into the pot with the sauce stirring all the time. Remove from heat.

Cut roasted turkey into serving pieces, put into a serving bowl, top with hot satsivi, and drizzle with remaining walnut oil. Let the dish cool before serving.

Satsivi with Giblets (A)

Ingredients:
Giblets - From 1 bird
Onions - 2
Wheat flour - 1 tbsp
Vegetable oil - 1 tbsp
Shelled walnuts - 1-1 1/2 cups
Cilantro - 2-3 sprigs
Wine vinegar, garlic, chili pepper, cloves, cinnamon, salt - to taste
Put thoroughly washed and trimmed giblets into a pot, add finely diced onions and sauté for 8-10 minutes, then add vegetable oil, and 2 minutes later - add flour, and continue cooking a little longer.

Pound shelled walnuts together with garlic, chili pepper, and salt in a mortar. Add chopped cilantro, ground cinnamon and cloves, 4-5 cups of water, mix everything well and add to the pot with giblets. Simmer for 10-15 minutes, then add vinegar, return to boil and remove from heat.

Satsivi with Giblets (B)

Ingredients:
Giblets - From 1 bird
Onions - 3-4
Corn flour - 1 tbsp
Shelled walnuts - 3/4 cup
Coriander seeds - 1/3 tsp
Ground cloves and cinnamon - 1 tsp
Garlic - 2 cloves
Saffron, chili and black pepper, wine vinegar, salt - to taste

Put thoroughly trimmed and washed giblets together with fat into a pot and cook over medium heat.

Meanwhile finely dice onions, put it into a clean pot, add some fat from the pot with giblets and sauté until softened. Add corn flour and fry 5 minutes longer, then add to the pot with browned giblets.

Pound shelled walnuts with garlic, and chili pepper, mix walnut mixture with 3-4 cups of water and add it to the pot with giblets. About 10 minutes after liquid came to boil add crushed coriander seeds, saffron, ground cinnamon and cloves, ground black pepper, wine vinegar, and salt, simmer 5-8 minutes longer, then remove from heat.

Satsivi with Beef

Ingredients:
Beef - 500 g
Shelled walnuts - 1 1/2 cups
Onions - 5
Bay leaves - 2
Celery - 1 stalk
Parsley - 1 sprig
Corn flour - 1 tbsp
Wine vinegar or pomegranate juice - to taste
Cilantro, chili pepper, garlic, whole black pepper, salt - to taste

Cut fatty beef into pieces, put into a pot with boiling water, add whole onion, celery stalk, and parsley sprig and cook until meat is half-done. Skim the foam as it rises to the top. Add whole black peppers and bay leaves to the broth during cooking.

Brown diced onions and half-cooked beef in the fat skimmed from the top of the broth.

Pound shelled walnuts together with chili peppers, cilantro, garlic, and salt in a mortar, add corn flour to the walnut mixture, mix, then add strained broth (6 cups), add to the pot with meat, return to boil, and simmer 10-15 minutes.

About 5 minutes before the end of cooking season the dish with wine vinegar or pomegranate juice.

Satsivi with Pork

Ingredients:
Pork - 500 g
Onions - 300 g
Shelled walnuts - 200 g
Cilantro - 3 sprigs
Garlic - 1-2 cloves
Corn flour - 1-1 1/2 tbsp
Coriander seeds - 1 tsp
Dried suneli - 1 tsp
Chili pepper, wine vinegar, cinnamon, cloves, salt - to taste

Cut fatty pork into pieces, put into a pot and brown it together with diced onions.

Crush shelled walnuts in a mortar or pass them through a meat grinder, add pounded together cilantro, garlic, salt, and chili pepper. Then add corn flour, mix it with 6 cups of water, add to the pot with pork, bring to boil, and simmer 20-25 minutes.

About 5 minutes before the end of cooking add crushed coriander seeds, dried suneli, ground cinnamon and cloves, wine vinegar, and salt. Is using pomegranate juice instead of wine vinegar - add it to the finished dish.

Cool cooked dish, transfer it to a serving plate, and serve.

VEGETARIAN SATSIVI

Satsivi with Eggs

Ingredients:
Shelled walnuts - 200 g
Onions - 4
Cilantro - 3 sprigs
Ground cinnamon and cloves - 1/2 tsp
Water - 4 cups
Eggs - 5-6
Chili pepper, garlic, vinegar, salt - to taste

Pound shelled walnuts together with salt, cilantro, and garlic in a mortar, squeeze walnut oil into a clean pot, add finely diced or passed through a meat grinder onions and nicely brown them.

Add crushed chili pepper, ground cinnamon and cloves, and wine vinegar to the crushed walnuts, mix everything well, then dilute the mixture with boiling water, pour it into a pan with onions, return to boil and simmer 10-15 minutes.

Break eggs and carefully add them into the pot with the sauce one after the other, and cook until eggs are done. Remove from heat and cool before serving.

If it was not possible to squeeze walnut oil, use 30-50 g of unsalted butter instead.

Satsivi with Eggplants

Ingredients:
Eggplants - 5-6
Vegetable oil - 30-50 g
Onions - 200 g
Cilantro and parsley - 2 sprigs each
Celery - 2 stalks
Shelled walnuts - 200 g

Ground cinnamon and cloves - 1/2 tsp
Wine vinegar or pomegranate juice - to taste
Chili pepper, garlic, saffron, salt - to taste

Wash eggplants, cut them across into slices 1-1 1/2 cm thick, season with salt, cover with a clean kitchen towel and set aside for 40-60 minutes, then carefully squeeze juice out of eggplant slices by lightly pressing with hand making sure that slices do not lose their shape. Brown prepared eggplants in a hot skillet with vegetable oil, one layer at a time. As eggplant slices are cooked - transfer them to a serving plate and sprinkle them with finely diced raw onions, chopped parsley, basil, and celery leaves.

Prepare satsivi sauce - thoroughly pound shelled walnuts together with salt, garlic, cilantro, and chili peppers, then add crumbled saffron, ground cinnamon and cloves, wine vinegar, mix everything well, add to the pot with 3-4 cups of water, bring to boil, and simmer 15-20 minutes. Pour boiling sauce over prepared eggplants, let it cool, then serve. If desired - sprinkle finished dish with pomegranate seeds.

Satsivi with Green Beans

Ingredients:
Green beans - 500 g
Onions - 2
Vegetable oil - 30-50 g
Cilantro - 4 sprigs
Shelled walnuts - 3/4-1 cup
Wine vinegar, chili pepper, garlic, cinnamon, cloves, salt - to taste

Trim pods of green beans with breaking them, wash in cold water, put into a pot with boiling water (5 cups) and cook 50-60 minutes. Drain cooked beans in a colander preserving some of the cooking liquid.

Peel onions, finely dice them, put into a clean pot, and brown them in vegetable oil.

Pound shelled walnuts together with cilantro, garlic, chili pepper, and salt, mix with preserved cooking liquid (2-3 cups), add to taste wine vinegar, ground cinnamon and cloves, pour this mixture into the pot with onions, return it to boil and cook 15-20 minutes. Before the end of cooking add cooked beans into the pot, let them simmer for about 1 minute, then remove the pot from heat. Serve cold or warm.

Satsivi with Beans

Ingredients:
Beans - 500 g
Shelled walnuts - 300 g
Onions - 3
Wine vinegar, chili pepper, cilantro, parsley, garlic, cinnamon, cloves, saffron, salt - to taste

Cook beans until done in 5-6 cups of water (beans should be completely cooked but still retain their shape). Strain cooking liquid into a separate pot and keep it covered.

Meanwhile pound (or pass through a meat grinder) shelled walnuts together with cilantro, garlic, and salt, and squeeze oil from the mixture.

Pour walnut oil into a clean pot and brown diced or passed through a meat grinder onions in it.

Add ground cinnamon and cloves, crushed chili peppers, and crumbled saffron to the walnut mixture, mix everything well, dilute with 5-6 cups of preserved cooking liquid, pour into the pot with browned onions, bring to boil, and simmer 10-15 minutes. Add cooked beans to the pot with the sauce, bring it to boil and immediately remove from heat. Transfer cooked dish to a serving bowl, sprinkle with chopped parsley and let it cool.

Annotation to Satsivi Recipes

Satsivi can be thickened with egg yolks. When the dish is almost cooked 3-4 beaten egg yolks are tempered with a little bit of sauce and then gradually added to the pot with the sauce while the sauce is being stirred. Once all the egg yolks are incorporated - the sauce should be instantly removed from heat.

If egg yolks are used to thicken the sauce - the quantity of walnuts should be decreased or the quantity of broth used in a recipe should be increased.

While satsivi is cooking it could be seasoned with bay leaf.

Only half of the satsivi sauce can be served with a protein, and the other half can be served with fried potatoes or other garnish.

Satsivi is good when served with chadi (corn-flour bread) or gomi, presented on small plates for every diner.

COOKING
ON
SKEWERS

COOKING ON SKEWERS

Cooking of meat or vegetables on a skewer or a spit is done directly over glowing wooden charcoals. Thread products onto a spit or a skewer, place it over the charcoals, and cook until done, frequently turning them over. Charcoals should not be burning or smoking before the food is placed over them. Control the heat by controlling the distance between charcoals and food.

Suckling Pig on a Spit

Ingredients:
Suckling pig - 1
Pomegranate juice - 1 cup
Water - 1/4-1/2 cup
Shelled walnuts - 100-150 g
Garlic - 5 cloves
Cilantro - 3-4 sprigs
Chili pepper and salt - to taste

Season whole gutted and washed suckling pig (with head and feet) with salt, inside and outside, put it on a spit and cook over glowing charcoal until completely done, frequently turning it over. From time to time brush the pig with oil. To check if the pig is cooked through - prick it with larding needle. If meat is cooked - the needle goes in easily and the juices run clear. Pig on a spit should be cooked directly before serving. Stuffed suckling pig can also be cooked following these instructions.

While the suckling pig is cooking it could be brushed with a walnut paste. To make the paste pound walnuts together with salt, garlic, cilantro, and coriander seeds in a mortar, then squeeze oil from this mixture.

Cover chili peppers with a small quantity of boiling water and leave to soak for 2 hours, then pound peppers together with salt and mix them with walnut oil.

A wonderful accompaniment to roasted suckling pig is a sauce made from walnuts pounded together with garlic, salt, and cilantro, them mixed with pomegranate juice and water, and seasoned with crushed chili peppers.

Lamb on a Spit

Thoroughly wash whole carcass of a lamb. Boil lamb's offal (heart, kidneys, liver, lungs) until half-done, then cut into pieces, season with salt and ground black pepper, add chopped cilantro and tarragon, and mix well. Stuff lamb with offal mixture and sew the opening with a coarse thread.

Put prepared lamb into a wooden spit and cook over wood charcoal until done, periodically basting with salted water or fat drippings.

Lamb Offal on a Skewer

Season lamb offal (liver, lungs, kidneys, heart) with salt, thread it on a skewer, wrap in lamb's caul fat, season with salt again, tie the ends of the caul fat with coarse thread, and grill over glowing coals frequently turning the skewer.

Shashlik with Tenderloin

Trim tenderloin from all silver skin and sinew, thread it on skewer whole, and tie to a skewer with a coarse thread.
Grill this tenderloin over glowing coals until fully cooked. Rotate the skewer frequently.

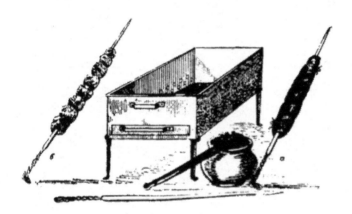

Cooked shashlik can be served directly on a skewer - the thread should be removed before serving. It can also be sliced across the grain into fairly thin slices, set on a serving plate, decorated with parsley, and garnished with cucumbers, tomatoes, and onions,
Serve sauces tkemali, masharabi on a side. Grilled tomatoes are wonderful to serve with shashlik - just grill tomatoes on a skewer over glowing coals until done, then remove from skewers, peel the skins off the tomatoes, cut each on in half and season with salt and ground black

pepper. Sprinkle grilled tomatoes with chopped onions or scallions and herbs.

Tenderloin Shashlik-Basturma

Trim tenderloin from silver skin and sinew, cut into uniform medium-sized pieces, put into a ceramic or enameled container, season with ground black pepper and salt, sprinkle with chopped onions (if desired - add chopped herbs and bay leaves), cover the container and leave it to marinate in a cool place. If a little of wine vinegar is add - the meat can keep for 3-4 days in a cool place, or, if vinegar was boiled and cooled down - the meat can keep 10-15 days.

Thread marinated tenderloin onto a skewer and grill over glowing coals until done frequently turning skewers over.

Take cooked shashlik off the skewer, set on a serving plate, decorate with scallions and parsley. If desired - serve shashlik on a skewer.

Lamb or Pork Shashlik-Basturma

Cut fatty lamb or pork (loin or leg (ham)) into uniform medium-sized pieces, put into a ceramic or enameled pot, season with salt and ground black pepper, add chopped onions, a little wine vinegar, mix well, cover the pot and leave in cool place for 2-3 hours.

Prepared this way meat can be kept 3-4 days in a cool place.

Finish cooking following instructions of the previous recipe.

Lamb or Pork Shashlik with Eggplants

Cut fatty lamb or pork into medium-sized pieces, season with salt, thread on a skewer and grill until done over glowing coal, rotating the skewer frequently.

Prepared meat can be threaded onto the skewers alternating with pieces of onions or kidneys (cut in half). Serve cooked shashlik on a skewer or take it off the skewers and serve it on a plate decorated with parsley and scallions. Lamb shashlik can be served together with grilled eggplants.

To grill eggplants - thoroughly wash small eggplants, make a shallow lengthwise cut in the middle of eggplant, put a little bit of salt and pepper together with a small piece of lamb tail fat, and - if desired - some herbs (parsley, cilantro, mint). Thread prepared eggplants onto a skewer and grill over glowing coals, first on a side of the cut, then on the other side of the eggplants, until they become soft.

Shashlik Fried in a Skillet

Prepared as described above lamb or pork can also be cooked in fat on a hot skillet. Transfer cooked meat to a serving plate and serve with a garnish of scallions or onions, fresh tomatoes cut into wedges, or tomatoes fried in a skillet.

Shashlik-Chahohbili

Put chopped onions into a clean enameled pot, put pieces of cooked shashlik on top of onions, cover the pot and cook over high heat.

Take the pot off the heat in 5-10 minutes, transfer shashlik and cooked onions to a serving plate, decorate with parsley leaves and serve.

Kebabi

Ingredients:
Lamb - 500 g
Lamb tail fat - 75 g
Egg - 1
Ground black pepper - 1/4 tsp
Onions, barberry, salt - to taste

Pass boneless lamb together with onions, lamb fat tail, and small quantity of barberries through a meat grinder twice, season mixture with salt and ground black pepper, add beaten egg and thoroughly mix.

Heat up small skewers over glowing coals. Carefully wrap prepared portions of lamb mince around the skewers, and grill over the same coals until cooked through, frequently rotating the skewers.

Take cooked kebabi off the skewers, roll each one in lavash (flat bread). In a separate bowl serve sliced onions or scallions. Kebabi can also be served on a plate, sprinkled with finely chopped onions or scallions and crushed barberries.

Meatballs on a Skewer

Ingredients:
Lamb or beef - 500 g
Ground black pepper - 1/4 tsp
Ground cinnamon and cloves - 1/2 tsp
Onions - 3-4
Salt - to taste

Cut fatty lamb or beef into pieces, then pass through a meat grinder together with 1 onion. Season minced meat with ground black pepper, cinnamon, cloves, and salt.

Heat up small skewers over a glowing coals. Roll meatballs with hands dipped in water, then thread these meatballs onto the preheated skewers and grill over same coals until done.

Remove cooked meatballs from the skewers, put into a sautee pan, sprinkle with chopped onions, cover the pan and cook on a stove for 5-7 minutes.

Spring Chicken or Young Chicken on a Skewer

Wash young chicken or a spring chicken, cut it long the breast, unfold and flatten the bird, season with salt on both side, thread on a skewer and cook over glowing charcoal until fully cooked.

Chicken can also be cooked differently. Season whole young or spring chicken with salt inside and outside, put giblets and feet inside the chicken and sew the chicken closed with coarse thread. Put prepared chicken onto a skewer and grill until done over glowing charcoals.

Chickens can be stuffed with different stuffing before cooking.

Stuffing I

Mix cooked rice, soaked dried pitted dogberries, prunes, barberries, and clarified butter, or cooked rice, soaked dried pitted dogberries, and softened in butter onions. Season with salt. Ingredients for one young or spring chicken: rice — 50-70 g, dried pitted dogberries — 30-50 g, pitted prunes — 30-50 g, dried barberries — 10-15 g, clarified butter — 50-70 g, salt — to taste.

Stuffing II

Pass onions, pitted prunes, and seedless raisins through a meat grinder. Add vegetable oil or clarified butter to this mixture and sauté until onions are softened. Remove from heat and add pomegranate seeds and carefully mix to avoid breaking the seeds. Ingredients for one 300 g chicken: prunes — 50 g, seedless raisins — 50 g, onions — 50 g, oil or butter — 50 g, pomegranate seeds and salt — to taste.

Stuffing III

Finely chop suluguni cheese (cheese closely resembling salted mozzarella cheese). If desired - add pomegranate seeds to this stuffing.

Stuffing IV

Pound shelled walnuts together with garlic, chili pepper, and salt, then squeeze oil from this mixture. Add finely chopped cilantro, onions, pomegranate seeds or barberries to the crushed walnuts and mix thoroughly. Chicken stuffed with this stuffing can be from time to time brushed with squeezed walnut oil. Also, chicken stuffed with walnut stuffing can be cooked in a covered oval Dutch oven.

Kidneys Cooked on a Skewer with Pomegranate Sauce

Wash kidneys, cut into smaller pieces but do not remove the fat, season with salt, thread on a metal skewer and cook over glowing coals until done.

Take cooked kidneys off the skewer, put into a small pot, add finely chopped onions and sauté 2-3 minutes, then add pomegranate juice to the pot.

To make pomegranate sauce squeeze juice from a few pomegranates, add (to taste) garlic crushed together with chili peppers, cilantro, and salt to the juice and mix well.

Tongue on a Skewer

Wash and dry thoroughly cleaned tongue, thread it on a skewer and cook until done over glowing charcoals. From time to time baste the tongue with lightly-salted water.

Cooked tongue should be served instantly on a warm plate, decorated with sliced tomatoes and scallions.

Basturma with Fish

Ingredients:
Fish - 500 g
Onions - 2
Lemon - 1/2
Salt and pepper - to taste

Put cleaned, washed, and cut into pieces fish (sturgeon, stellate sturgeon, salmon) into a ceramic or enameled pot, season with salt and pepper, add finely chopped onions, slices of lemons, mix, cover the pot, and leave in a cold place for a couple of hours (fish can be stored in cold like this for one or two days).

Thread pieces of marinated fish onto skewers and grill over glowing coals.

Take cooked fish off the skewers, transfer to a serving plate, garnish with onions or scallions and slices of lemons.

Salmon, Sturgeon, or Stellate Sturgeon on a Skewer

Ingredients:
Fish - 1 kg
Shelled walnuts - 1/4 cup
Pomegranate juice - 1/2-3/4 cup
Cilantro - 2-3 sprigs
Parsley, dill - to taste
Ground black pepper, ground bay leaf, onions or scallions, salt - to taste

Season cleaned, washed, and cut into pieces fish with salt, ground black pepper, ground bay leaf. Thread fish on skewers and grill over glowing coals until done.

Take cooked fish off the skewers, transfer to a serving plate, decorate with parsley and serve.

Serve sauce in a sauce boat on a side. To make sauce thoroughly crush shelled walnuts together with salt, then add pomegranate juice, finely chopped cilantro, parsley, and dill, chopped onions or scallions and thoroughly mix.

Chahohbili with Salmon on a Skewer

Ingredients:
Salmon - 1 kg
Onions - 2
Wine vinegar - 1/2-3/4 cup
Water - 1/4-1/2 cup
Salt - to taste

Cut cleaned and washed salmon into small pieces, season with salt, thread on a skewer and cook over glowing coals until done.

Finely chop onions, add to the pot with vinegar and water, and simmer it until onions are soft.

Take cooked fish off the skewer, transfer into the pot with vinegar and onions, summer 2-3 minutes longer, then remove from heat.

Trout Grilled on a Skewer

Carefully gut trout from side of the head so that the fish appears to be whole, wash, season with salt, thread on a skewer and grill over glowing coals.

Take cooked fish off the skewers and transfer to a serving plate, drizzle with pomegranate or lemon juice and sprinkle with finely chopped onions.

Suluguni Cheese on a Skewer

Thread small round of suluguni (similar to halloumi) cheese and grill over glowing coals. When one side of the cheese is cooked - nice brown crust forms on the side - rotate the skewer and grill the other side. Serve cooked cheese hot.

If desired - the cheese can be cooked in a skillet. Put round of cheese into a preheated skillet with oil, cover the skillet and fry until nicely browned. Turn the cheese to the other side and continue frying without covering the skillet. Cheese can also be sliced into thin strips before frying.

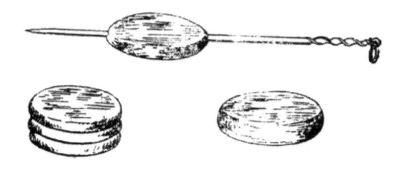

Serve fried suluguni hot, decorated with parsley, tarragon, or meat.

Garnishes for Grilled Dishes

Dishes grilled on a skewer should be served with the following garnishes: onions and scallions (onions should be sliced into rings), slices of lemon, fresh tomatoes, fresh cucumbers or pickles, tomatoes grilled on a skewer, eggplants stuffed with lamb tail fat, salt, pepper, and herbs.

Dishes should be decorated with parsley sprig, celery leaves, or salad leaves.

On a side serve sauces tkemali, tomato, masharabi, or pomegranate.

VEGETABLES
AND
MUSHROOMS

VEGETABLE DISHES

POTATOES

Boiled Potatoes with Walnuts

Ingredients:
Potatoes - 500 g
Onion - 1
Shelled walnuts - 3/4 cup
Garlic - 1-2 cloves
Cilantro - 2 sprigs
Parsley or dill, wine vinegar, chili pepper, salt - to taste

Cook thoroughly washed potatoes in their skins, then peel and cut them into cubes.

Pound shelled walnuts together with garlic, chili peppers, cilantro, and salt in a mortar. Add to taste wine vinegar and diced onion to the walnut mixture, then mix it with potatoes, set in a mound on a serving plate and sprinkle with chopped parsley or dill.

Kaurma with Potatoes

Ingredients:

Potatoes - 500 g
Onions - 4
Cilantro - 2-3 sprigs
Eggs - 2
Clarified butter - 2 tbsp
Salt - to taste

Dice washed and peeled onions, but into a pot with clarified butter and nicely brown them. Add peeled, washed, and cut into wedges potatoes to the pot, add enough water to cover potatoes and bring to boil. Season potatoes with salt and add finely chopped cilantro while they are cooking. When potatoes are soft and cooked through add beaten eggs to the pot, and remove pot from the heat when the eggs are cooked.

Potato Balls (A)

Ingredients:
Potatoes - 500 g
Onion - 1
Shelled walnuts - 1/2 cup
Wine vinegar - 2-3 tbsp
Water - 1 tbsp
Garlic - 1-2 cloves
Cilantro - 2 sprigs
Cilantro and dill - 1/2 cup finely chopped
Crushed saffron, chili pepper, salt - to taste

Boil potatoes, then thoroughly mash them. Pound shelled walnuts with garlic, cilantro, chili pepper, and salt in a mortar. Squeeze oil from walnut mixture and store in another container. Mix walnuts with vinegar and water, then add very finely chopped onion, chopped cilantro and dill, crushed saffron, mashed potatoes, and mix everything well.

Roll egg-sized balls from the potato mixture and carefully set them on a serving plate. Make small indentations in every ball and add some walnut oil to each.

Potato Balls (B) (Croquette)

Ingredients:
Potatoes - 500 g
Onions - 1-2
Egg - 1
Shelled walnuts - 1/4-1/2 cup
Garlic - 1-2 cloves
Coriander seeds - 1/2 tsp
Vegetable oil - 2-3 tbsp
Breadcrumbs - as needed
Salt - to taste

Steam peeled potatoes or cook them in a very small quantity of water. Mash potatoes while they are still hot to insure a smooth puree without any clumps. Add raw egg to the mashed potatoes, mix in softened in vegetable oil finely diced onions, crushed walnuts, coriander seeds, and garlic, then season with salt, mix well and roll into walnut-sized balls. Coat prepared balls in flour or breadcrumbs and fry in oil in a preheated skillet. Transfer cooked croquettes to a serving plate, drizzle with hot oil, sprinkle with chopped parsley or dill.

CABBAGE

White Cabbage with Walnuts (A)

Ingredients:
White cabbage - 500 g
Shelled walnuts - 3/4 cups

Garlic - 1 clove
Cilantro - 2 sprigs
Dried suneli - 1 tsp
Wine vinegar, chili pepper, salt - to taste

Remove dirty and spoiled outer leaves from a head of cabbage, core the cabbage, cut it in half, and cook in a pot with a small quantity of boiling water (1 cup) for about 30-40 minutes. Transfer cooked cabbage to a colander and let it drain. When cabbage is cool enough to handle squeeze any excess liquid with your hand, and shred it on a cutting board.

Pound shelled walnuts together with salt, garlic, chili peppers, and cilantro on a mortar. Add wine vinegar to the walnut mixture. Transfer shredded cabbage to a serving bowl, then pour walnut dressing over it.

White Cabbage with Walnuts (B)

Ingredients:
White cabbage - 500 g
Shelled walnuts - 1/2-3/4 cup
Garlic - 1-2 cloves
Onions - 2
Coriander seeds - 1/2 tsp
Dried suneli - 1 tsp
Cilantro - 2-3 sprigs
Parsley - 2 sprigs
Dill - 4 tbsp
Wine vinegar, chili pepper, salt - to taste

Cook and shred white cabbage following instructions of the previous recipe.

Thoroughly pound shelled walnuts together with salt, garlic, and chili pepper. Add finely diced onions, herbs (cilantro, parsley, dill), dried suneli, crushed coriander seeds, and wine vinegar and mix well. Combine shredded cabbage with the walnut mixture, then transfer to a serving plate and sprinkle with chopped dill.

White Cabbage with Walnuts (C)

Ingredients:
White cabbage - 500 g
Shelled walnuts - 1/2 cup
Garlic - 1-2 cloves
Onions - 2
Cilantro - 3 sprigs
Wine vinegar, chili pepper, saffron, salt - to taste

Remove wilted outer leaves from a head of cabbage, cut it into two or four pieces, remove the core, and then finely shred. Transfer shredded cabbage to a pot, mix it with salt, cover the pot and set it aside for 15-20 minutes. Rub cabbage between palms of your hands to soften it, and squeeze slightly.

Thinly slices peeled onions, sprinkle it with salt, set it aside for 30-40 minutes, then squeeze.

Mix pounded together shelled walnuts, cilantro, chili peppers, garlic, saffron, and salt with prepared onions and wine vinegar. Add walnut mixture to prepared cabbage and transfer it to a serving plate.

Sour Cabbage with Walnuts

Ingredients:
Sour cabbage - 500 g
Shelled walnuts - 1/4 cup
Garlic - 1-2 cloves
Coriander seeds - 1 tsp
Dried suneli - 1/2 tsp
Dill - to taste

Chop sour cabbage on a cutting board, then squeeze it dry. Transfer squeezed juice to a mixing bowl, add crushed walnuts, mashed garlic, coriander seeds, dried suneli, chopped cabbage, chopped dill, and mix everything well.

Cauliflower with Walnuts

Ingredients:
Cauliflower - 500 g
Shelled walnuts - 1/4-1/2 cup
Wine vinegar - 1/4 cup
Coriander seeds - 1 tsp
Salt - to taste

Cook cleaned and washed cauliflower in a pot of boiling water, then separate it into florets when it is cool enough to handle.

Pound shelled walnuts with garlic and salt, add crushed coriander seeds, mix with wine vinegar, add prepared cauliflower florets and mix carefully to avoid breaking the florets.

Cauliflower with Butter and Eggs

Ingredients:
Cauliflower - 500 g
Onion - 1
Butter - 70-100 g
Eggs - 2-3
Herbs and salt - to taste

Cook cauliflower in a pot with salted boiling water until half-done, cool and separate it into florets.

Melt butter in a sauté pan and soften finely diced onion in it. Add prepared cauliflower florets to the pan, season with salt, cover the pan, and sauté cauliflower for 10 minutes. Add finely chopped cilantro, parsley, dill, mix, then pour in beaten eggs mixed with finely chopped dill and seasoned with salt, cover the pan and continue cooking until eggs are set. Serve hot in the pan it was cooked in.

BEETS

Beets with Walnuts

Ingredients:
Beets - 500 g
Shelled walnuts - 3/4 cup
Garlic - 2-3 cloves
Wine vinegar - 1/4 cup
Cilantro - 2 sprigs
Chopped parsley and dill, chili peppers, salt - to taste

Cooked washed beets in boiling water or roast them in an oven. Peel cooked beets and cut them into small dice.

Thoroughly pound shelled walnuts, salt, cilantro, and garlic in a mortar, or pass everything through a meat grinder, add crushed chili peppers, mix it with wine vinegar and add this mixture to diced beets. Transfer dressed beets to a serving plate and sprinkle with finely chopped parsley.

If desired - squeeze oil from walnuts and drizzle the finished dish with it.

Beets with Dogberries – Chogi

Ingredients:
Beets - 500 g
Dried dogberries - 1/2 cup
Onions - 2

Cilantro - 3 sprigs
Parsley - 2 sprigs
Salt - to taste

Boil or roast washed beets until done. Peel and slice cooked beets.

Boil dried dogberries until soft, then pass it together with cooking liquid through a sieve - the puree should not be too thin or too thick. Add finely diced onions, chopped herbs (cilantro and parsley), salt, and sliced beets to the berry puree, mix everything well and transfer to a serving plate.

Pickled Beets with Walnuts

Ingredients:
Pickled beets - 500 g
Shelled walnuts - 1/2-3/4 cup
Garlic - 2 cloves
Coriander seeds - 1 tsp
Chili peppers and salt - to taste

Cut pickled beets into small dice. Pound shelled walnuts together with garlic and chili peppers in a mortar, add crushed coriander seeds, mix with 1-2 tbsp of pickling liquid, then add prepared beets and mix well.

TOMATOES AND PEPPERS

Tomatoes with Walnut Sauce

Ingredients:
Tomatoes - 8-10
Onions - 300 g
Butter - 30 g

Cilantro - 6 sprigs
Garlic - 2 cloves
Shelled walnuts - 1 cup
Wine vinegar, salt - to taste

Put diced onions into a pot with butter and sauté until softened.

Pound shelled walnuts together with garlic, cilantro (2 sprigs), and salt in a mortar, then squeeze walnut oil from the mixture.

Crush 2 sprigs of cilantro together with chili peppers and salt, add wine vinegar to taste, crushed walnuts, and mix together with 1 1/2 cups of water. Add prepared mixture to the softened onions and simmer for 10 minutes.

Wash ripe, medium-sized tomatoes, cut out the stem side of each tomato and extract seeds through the opening.

Crush 1/2 cup of walnuts with garlic, chili peppers, remaining cilantro, and salt. Stuff prepared tomatoes with this mixture. Put stuffed tomatoes into the pot with sauce, let it cook for 2 minutes, then remove the pot from heat. Drizzle finished dish with walnut oil before serving.

Braised Tomatoes with Walnuts

Ingredients:
Tomatoes - 500 g
Shelled walnuts - 1/4 cup
Vegetable oil - 1/2 tbsp
Onion - 1
Garlic - 1-2 cloves
Coriander seeds - 1/2 tsp
Chili pepper, parsley, salt - to taste

Put ripe, whole tomatoes into a skillet, roast them, then peel tomatoes and cut each one into 4 parts.

Lightly brown diced onion in vegetable oil, add prepared tomatoes and cook for 10 minutes, then let it cool. Add walnuts pounded together with coriander seeds, garlic, chili peppers, and salt in a mortar to cooked tomatoes and mix well. Sprinkle with chopped parsley just before serving.

Tomatoes and Eggs Salad with Walnut Dressing

Ingredients:
Tomatoes - 300 g
Eggs - 3-4
Onion - 1
Shelled walnuts - 1/2 cup
Garlic - 1 clove
Cilantro - 1 sprig
Parsley and dill - 2-3 sprigs each
Wine vinegar, chili pepper, salt - to taste

Wash and slice ripe tomatoes into thin round. Cook eggs to hard-boiled stage, peel them, and slice them into thin round as well.

Pound shelled walnuts, sprig of cilantro, garlic, chili pepper, and salt into a mortar, then mix it with 1/2 cup of water and wine vinegar (to taste).

Set sliced tomatoes and eggs in a salad bowl, pour walnut dressing over, then sprinkle with chopped onions or scallions, and chopped parsley and dill.

Tomato and Walnut Salad

Ingredients:
Tomatoes - 500 g
Onions or scallons - 100 g
Shelled walnuts - 3/4 cup
Garlic - 1-2 cloves
Crushed saffron - pinch

Coriander seeds - 1 tsp
Chili pepper, herbs, salt - to taste

Wash and slice ripe, unblemished tomatoes into rounds and put into a bowl. Add finely chopped onion or scallion, sprinkle with chopped parsley and dill. Pound together walnuts, garlic, chili peppers, saffron, coriander seeds, and salt in a mortar. Add walnut mixture to the tomatoes, mix everything well, transfer to a serving plate and sprinkle with chopped basil and savory.

Green Tomatoes with Walnuts (A)

Ingredients:
Green tomatoes - 500 g
Shelled walnuts - 3/4 cup
Herbs - 6-8 sprigs each
Garlic - 2-3 cloves
Chili pepper, wine vinegar, salt - to taste

Wash green tomatoes and make a cut each tomato across making sure not to cut all the way through.

Finely chop herbs (parsley, cilantro, celery leaves, basil, dill), mix them with mashed garlic, crushed chili peppers, season with salt and mix everything well. Stuff tomatoes with prepared herb mixture, set them in a skillet in a single layer, cover the skillet and roast until done.

Meanwhile pound shelled walnuts together with salt, garlic, cilantro (1 sprig), and chili pepper in a mortar. Add wine vinegar to the walnut mixture to taste. Transfer cooked tomatoes to a serving plate and put walnut mixture over them.

If desired - squeeze oil from walnuts and drizzle finished dish with this oil.

Green Tomatoes with Walnuts (B)

Ingredients:
Green tomatoes - 500 g
Shelled walnuts - 1/2 cup
Coriander seeds - 1/2 tsp
Imereti saffron - 1 tsp
Dried suneli - 1 tsp
Garlic - 2-3 cloves
Onions - 2
Chili pepper, wine vinegar, salt - to taste

Cut washed green tomatoes into 4 parts, remove seeds, cover with boiling water and set aside for 3-5 minutes. Then squeeze tomatoes dry and finely chop them

Pound walnuts together with coriander seeds, Imereti saffron, dried suneli, garlic, and chili peppers, add finely chopped herbs (parsley, cilantro, dill), chopped onion, and mix with wine vinegar. Add prepared green tomatoes to the walnuts, mix everything thoroughly, and transfer to a serving plate.

Green Tomatoes with Carrots and Garlic

Ingredients:
Green tomatoes - 500 g
Onions - 2
Celery leaves - 2 sprigs
Parsley - 3 sprigs
Carrots - 3
Vegetable oil - 2-3 tbsp
Garlic - 4-5 cloves
Salt - to taste

Put finely chopped onions on a bottom of a pan. Set washed and cut tomatoes on top of the onions, top with finely chopped parsley and celery, peeled, washed, and sliced carrots, season with salt and pepper, add vegetable oil to the pot, cover the pot, and cook for 20-30 minutes.

Add mashed garlic to the tomatoes when they are cooked, transfer to a serving plate, and let it cool before serving.

Green Tomatoes with Vegetable Oil

Ingredients:
Green tomatoes - 500 g
Onions - 200 g
Parsley, cilantro, dill, basil, celery - 3 sprigs each
Vegetable oil - 2-3 tbsp
Chili peppers, salt - to taste

Cut washed green tomatoes into wedges, put into a pot, add finely chopped herbs (parsley, celery, cilantro, dill, basil), chopped onions, chili peppers, and vegetable oil, season with salt, cover the pot and cook 30-40 minutes.

Sweet Bell Peppers with Walnuts

Ingredients:
Sweet bell peppers - 500 g
Cilantro - 4-5 sprigs
Shelled walnuts - 3/4 cup
Onions - 2-3
Wine vinegar, garlic, salt - to taste

Pick sweet bell peppers over, wash, put into a pot with boiling water (1 cup), and cook until done, approximately 20-25 minutes, then drain in a colander, and squeeze excess liquid when cool enough to handle.

Pound shelled walnuts together with salt and garlic, add finely chopped cilantro, diced onions, wine vinegar, prepared peppers, mix everything well and transfer to a serving plate.

ASPARAGUS

Asparagus with Walnuts

Ingredients:
Asparagus - 500 g
Shelled walnuts - 3/4 cup
Onions - 2
Garlic - 1-2 cloves
Cilantro - 4 sprigs
Parsley - 6 sprigs
Dill - 4-5 sprigs
Wine vinegar, chili pepper, salt - to taste

Peel asparagus, remove hard parts making sure not to break heads, break spears into smaller pieces, add to a pot with a small quantity of boiling water, cover the pot and cook until asparagus is cooked. Make sure that asparagus does not become overcooked - otherwise it loses its flavor and turns watery. When heads become soft - asparagus is ready. All water should evaporate from the pot by the time asparagus is cooked.

Pound shelled walnuts, together with salt, chili peppers, garlic, cilantro stems in a mortar. Add finely chopped onions, cilantro, parsley, and dill, mix with wine vinegar, and to cooked asparagus, mix well and transfer to a serving plate.

Asparagus with Butter and Eggs

Ingredients:
Asparagus - 500 g
Butter - 100-120 g
Eggs - 2
Salt - to taste

Cook asparagus as described in the previous recipe, add butter, season with salt and sauté slightly. Add one beaten egg, mix everything, then pour in the second beaten egg, smooth the top , cover the pot, and cook until the eggs are set.

Asparagus Salad

Ingredients:
Asparagus - 300 g
Garlic - 1 clove
Verjuice - 1/4 cup
Cilantro - 3-4 sprigs
Chili pepper, salt - to taste

Cook asparagus in salted water, then drain in a colander.

Meanwhile mix verjuice with mashed garlic, crushed chili pepper, and chopped cilantro and mix well.

Transfer cooked asparagus to a salad bowl and dress with prepared dressing.

LEEKS, RAMPS

Leeks with Walnuts (A)

Ingredients:
Leeks - 500 g
Shelled walnuts - 1 cup
Garlic - 1-2 cloves
Cilantro - 2 sprigs
Chili pepper, wine vinegar, salt - to taste

Put cleaned and washed leeks (whole) into a pot with boiling water (2 cups) and cook until done, 30-40 minutes, then drain in a colander, cool, carefully squeeze excess water making sure not to break stalks. Wrap outer leaves around the stalks - shaping small packages.

Pound shelled walnuts , cilantro, salt, garlic, chili pepper in a mortar, mix it with wine vinegar or pomegranate juice. Roll leeks in the walnut mixture and set on a serving plate.

If desired - squeeze walnut oil and drizzle finished leeks with it.

Leeks with Walnuts (B)

Ingredients:
Leeks - 500 g
Shelled walnuts - 1/2 cup
Garlic - 1-2 cloves
Coriander - 1/2 tsp
Imereti saffron - 1 tsp
Dried suneli - 1/2 tsp
Wine vinegar or pomegranate juice - to taste
Chili pepper and salt - to taste

Cook leeks as described in the previous recipe, transfer to a cutting board and finely chop them.

Thoroughly pound shelled walnuts, coriander seeds, garlic, chili pepper, salt, Imereti saffron in a mortar, add dried suneli and mix everything with wine vinegar or pomegranate juice. Add prepared leeks to the walnut mixture, transfer to a serving plate, and sprinkle with pomegranate seeds or cilantro.

Ramps

Ingredients:
Ramps - 500 g
Vegetable oil, salt - to taste

Pick ramps over, remove roots, wash in cold water, put into a pot with 2 cups of boiling water and cook 5 minutes, then drain in a colander, rinse with cold water and leave in cold water for 1 hour. Drain again in a colander, season with salt and vegetable oil.

SPINACH

Spinach with Walnuts

Ingredients:
Spinach - 500 g
Onions - 200 g
Shelled walnuts - 1 cup
Garlic - 2 cloves
Cilantro - 12 sprigs
Parsley - 3 sprigs
Wine vinegar or pomegranate juice - to taste
Chili pepper, salt - to taste

Pick spinach over, remove tough stems and wilted or spoiled leaves, thoroughly wash in cold water, put into a pot together with 10 sprigs of cilantro, add 1 cup of boiling water to the pot, cover the pot and cook over high heat 15-20 minutes.

Drain spinach in a colander (cooking liquid can be used in some other dishes), and, when it is cool enough to handle - squeeze all excess liquid and chop it finely with a knife.

Pound shelled walnuts together with garlic, cilantro (2 sprigs), and chili pepper in a mortar, mix it with wine vinegar or pomegranate juice, add finely diced onions and chopped cilantro and parsley, and mix everything together with prepared spinach. Sprinkle finished dish with pomegranate seeds if using pomegranate juice. Pomegranate seeds can also be added to the spinach, but in this case mix salad taking care not to break the seeds.

Spinach with Butter and Eggs (A)

Ingredients:
Spinach - 500 g
Clarified butter - 2 tbsp

Eggs - 2
Salt - to taste

Pick spinach over, cook, and squeeze it as described in the previous recipe, chop it on cutting board, then sauté it in a skillet in clarified butter. Add one beaten egg to the spinach, mix it well, top spinach with another beaten egg, smooth the top, cover the skillet, and cook until eggs are done.

Spinach with Butter and Eggs (B)

Ingredients:
Spinach - 500 g
Clarified butter - 3-4 tbsp
Onion - 1
Eggs - 3-4
Herbs, salt - to taste

Cook and chop spinach as described in the previous recipe.

Sauté finely diced onion in some clarified butter until softened, add spinach and sauté a bit longer. Add more clarified butter and chopped herbs (cilantro, parsley, dill), season with salt, mix, and add beaten eggs mixed with finely chopped dill. Smooth the top of the mixture and make indentations to let egg to reach the bottom of the pan. Remove from heat when eggs are cooked.

Spinach Braised in Vegetable Oil

Ingredients:
Spinach - 500 g
Vegetable oil - 2 tbsp
Onions - 200 g

Salt - to taste

Pick spinach over, cook, squeeze, and chop on a clean cutting board.

Dice onions, put into a skillet with 1 tbsp of vegetable oil and soften them, then add prepared spinach and remaining vegetable oil and sauté until warmed through.

Spinach with Matsoni (Yogurt)

Ingredients:
Spinach - 500 g
Cilantro - 4 sprigs
Garlic - 2 cloves
Matsoni (yogurt) - 2 cups
Chili peppers, salt - to taste

Cook spinach, let it cook, squeeze and chop on a cutting board. Pound cilantro, garlic, chili pepper, and salt in a mortar, add beaten matron, mix it with squeezed and chopped spinach and serve.

Borani with Spinach

Ingredients:
Spinach - 500 g
Clarified butter - 1/2 cup
Onions - 150 g
Parsley and dill - 3 sprigs each
Cilantro - 4 sprigs
Chicken - 1
Ground cinnamon - 1/2 tsp
Powdered sugar - 2 tbsp
Salt - to taste

Cook spinach, squeeze it with hands, chop on a cutting board, add finely chopped herbs (parsley, dill, cilantro) and mix well.

Add 1/4 cup of a clarified butter to a skillet and brown chopped onions in it. Add prepared spinach to the onions and remaining 1/4 cup of clarified butter
and sauté everything together.

Separate prepared spinach into two parts, put half of the spinach on a bottom of a serving plate. Put pieces of fried chicken on top of the spinach. Cover the chicken with remaining spinach. Pour drained and beaten matsoni, sprinkle with powdered sugar and ground cinnamon. This dish can also be served without a chicken.

SARSAPARILLA

Sarsaparilla with Walnuts

Ingredients:
Sarsaparilla - 500 g
Shelled walnuts - 3/4 cup
Garlic - 2-3 cloves
Cilantro - 4 sprigs
Wine vinegar, finely chopped dill, pennyroyal, cilantro leaves, crushed chili pepper, salt - to taste

Clean sarsaparilla, remove all hard parts and wilted leaves, put into a pot, cover with boiling water and cook until done - about 1 hour. Drain, cover with cold water and leave for 40-60 minutes. Take sarsaparilla out and squeeze water.

Pound shelled walnuts together with cilantro leaves, garlic, chili pepper, and salt in a mortar. Add finely chopped dill, pennyroyal, cilantro leaves, wine vinegar, squeezed sarsaparilla, mix everything well, transfer to a serving plate, and sprinkle with chopped dill.

If desired - squeeze oil from crushed walnuts and drizzle finished dish.

Verjuice can be used instead of wine vinegar in this recipe.

Sarsaparilla with Tkemali

Ingredients:
Sarsaparilla - 500 g
Tkemali - 3/4 cup
Cilantro - 3-4 sprigs
Dill - 8-10 sprigs
Pennyroyal - 5 sprigs
Garlic - 2-3 cloves
Chili pepper and salt - to taste

Cook and squeeze sarsaparilla as described in the previous recipe.

Cook tkemali plums in water, pit the plums, add finely chopped herbs (cilantro, dill, pennyroyal), mashed garlic, and salt. Mix in prepared sarsaparilla, transfer to a serving plate, and sprinkle with chopped dill.

NETTLE, LATHYRUS, MALLOW, PURSLANE

Nettle with Walnuts

Ingredients:
Nettle - 500 g
Onions - 2-3
Shelled walnuts - 3/4 cup
Cilantro - 3-4 sprigs
Salt - to taste

Cook picked over and cleaned nettle in salted boiling

water and drain in a colander. Pound shelled walnuts together with salt, add finely chopped onions, cilantro, cooked nettle, mix everything well and transfer to a serving plate.

Nettle with Butter and Eggs

Ingredients:
Nettles - 500 g
Clarified butter - 3-4 tbsp
Onions - 3
Cilantro - 3-4 sprigs
Eggs - 2
Salt - to taste

Cook nettles in salted boiling water, drain and lightly squeeze it. Put 2 tbsp of clarified butter into a skillet, add finely diced onions and cook until softened. Add cooked nettles, finely chopped cilantro, salt, remaining clarified butter, mix and cook everything together, then add beaten eggs, smooth the tope and continue cooking until the eggs are done.

Lathyrus with Walnuts

Ingredients:
Lathyrus - 500 g
Shelled walnuts - 1 cup
Cilantro - 4-5 sprigs
Salt - to taste

Pick leaves off the lathyrus and trim dried ends of the stalks. Cut prepared lathyrus into large pieces, wash, put into a pot with boiling water, lightly salted water, and cook until done. When lathyrus is cooked add crushed walnuts and chopped cilantro. Remove from heat when all the liquid has evaporated.

Lathyrus with Butter and Eggs

Ingredients:
Lathyrus - 500 g
Butter - 100-150 g
Onions - 200 g
Eggs - 2
Salt - to taste

Cook lathyrus as described in the previous recipe, and squeeze any excess water.

Soften diced onions in a skillet in butter, add prepared lathyrus and cook a bit longer, then add beaten eggs to the skillet and continue cooking until eggs are set.

Mallow

Ingredients:
Mallow - 500 g
Garlic - 5-6 cloves
Parsley and cilantro - 4 sprigs each
Dill - 2 sprigs
Wine vinegar, salt - to taste

Put picked over mallow into a pot with a small quantity of boiling water, cook and drain in a colander. Squeeze excess liquid, transfer mallow to a cutting board and chop it. Add mashed garlic, chopped parsley, cilantro, and dill, season with salt, and dress with wine vinegar. Mix everything well and transfer to a serving plate.

Purslane with Vinegar

Ingredients:
Purslane - 500 g
Garlic, vinegar, salt - to taste

Pick purslane over, wash in cold water, put into a pot with boiling salted water (1 cup) and cook until done (15-20 minutes). Drain purslane in a colander, squeeze excess liquid when it is cool enough to handle. Transfer purslane to a salad bowl, sprinkle with chopped garlic and dress with vinegar.

EGGPLANTS

Eggplants with Walnuts (A)

Ingredients:
Eggplants - 1 kg
Shelled walnuts - 3/4-1 cup
Onions - 2
Garlic - 2 cloves
Cilantro and basil leaves - 1 cup, finely chopped
Parsley and celery leaves - 3/4 cup, finely chopped
Savory - 1/4 cup, finely chopped
Chili pepper, wine vinegar, salt - to taste

Wash and peel (if desired) eggplants. Cut eggplants lengthwise, put into a pot, add 1 cup of boiling water, and cook 20-30 minutes. Drain cooked eggplants in a colander, let them cool, and squeeze with your hand.

Pound shelled walnuts with garlic and salt in a mortar. If desired - squeeze oil from walnuts. Add chili peppers pounded with cilantro leaves, add finely chopped parsley, celery, cilantro, savory, basil, wine vinegar or pomegranate juice. Put this mixture into a bowl with eggplants, thoroughly mix, then transfer to a serving plate. Sprinkle finished dish with pomegranate seeds or drizzle it with walnut oil.

Eggplants with Walnuts (B)

Ingredients:
Eggplants - 1 kg
Shelled walnuts - 1 cup
Garlic - 1-2 cloves
Coriander seeds - 1 tsp
Imereti saffron - 1 tsp
Parsley and cilantro - 1 cup, finely chopped
Celery leaves - 1/2 cup, finely chopped
Basil - 1/4 cup, finely chopped
Wine vinegar or pomegranate juice - to taste
Chili pepper and salt - to taste

Thoroughly wash eggplants with cold water, make a lengthwise slice in every eggplant without cutting it all the way through. Put eggplants into a pot with boiling water, with enough water to reach just half-way up of the eggplants, return to boil, and cook approximately 20-30 minutes, making sure that eggplants do not overcook.

Take cooked eggplants out of the pot, set on a cutting board, cover with another board and put some weight on top - to squeeze as much liquid as possible.

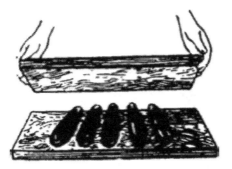

Thoroughly pound shelled walnuts together with salt and garlic in a mortar, or pass them through a meat grinder, and, if desired, squeeze oil from the mixture. Add crushed chili peppers, diced onions, finely chopped parsley, cilantro, basil, celery, crushed coriander seeds, Imereti saffron, wine vinegar or pomegranate juice to the walnuts and mix well.

Stuff prepared eggplants with walnut mixture and spread some of the mixture on the skin of eggplants. Just before serving drizzle eggplants with walnut oil and sprinkle with pomegranate seeds.

If desired - add ground cinnamon and cloves to the walnut stuffing.

Eggplants Fried in Vegetable Oil and Stuffed with Walnuts

Ingredients:
Eggplants - 1 kg
Shelled walnuts - 1 cup
Celery stalks - same qty as number of eggplants
Vegetable oil - 3-4 tbsp
Garlic - 1-2 cloves
Onions - 2
Herbs - 1 1/4-1 1/2 cups, finely chopped
Ground cinnamon and cloves - 1/2 tsp
Wine vinegar or pomegranate juice - to taste
Chili pepper and salt - to taste

Thoroughly wash eggplants with cold water, make a cut along each eggplant, put into a pot together with celery stalks, add boiling water to reach half-way up the eggplants, cover the pot, and cook until eggplants are half-done.

Meanwhile, finely chop onions, sprinkle them with salt, set aside for 30-40 minutes, then squeeze thoroughly. Put half-cooked eggplants on a board, cover with another board and top with some weight. Leave them for 1 hour to let all the liquid to drain.

Add vegetable oil to a preheated skillet, put eggplants in one layer on a skillet and fry until cooked on all sides.

Thoroughly pound shelled walnuts together with salt, garlic, and chili peppers in a mortar. Add prepared onions, finely chopped cilantro, parsley, celery, dill, ground cinnamon and cloves, pour in wine vinegar or pomegranate juice and mix well.

Stuff fried eggplants with prepared walnut stuffing, wrap it with boiled celery stalks, set on a serving plate, and spread some of the walnut stuffing on the skin of the eggplants. Sprinkle finished dish with pomegranate seeds or finely chopped parsley and serve.

Roasted Eggplants with Walnuts

Ingredients:
Eggplants - 500 g
Onion - 1
Shelled walnuts - 1/2 cup
Garlic - 1-2 cloves
Dried suneli - 1/2 tsp
Coriander seeds - 1/2 tsp
Imereti saffron - 1/2 tsp
Cilantro and celery leaves - 1/2 cup, finely chopped
Parsley and dill - 1/4 cup, finely chopped
Wine vinegar, chili pepper, salt - to taste

Roast eggplants in an oven or on a grill, peel them, cut flesh lengthwise into pieces, add finely diced onion, walnuts pounded together with chili pepper, garlic, coriander seeds, dried suneli, Imereti saffron, finely chopped cilantro, parsley, celery, dill, season with salt, add wine vinegar, mix everything well, transfer to a serving plate and sprinkle with chopped dill.

Roasted Eggplants with Walnuts and Pomegranates

Ingredients:
Eggplants - 500 g
Onion - 1
Shelled walnuts - 1/4 cup
Pomegranate seeds - 1/2 cup
Ground black pepper, salt - to taste

Roast eggplants in an oven or over a grill, peel them, chop eggplant flesh, season with salt and ground black pepper, add finely diced onion, crushed walnuts, and pomegranate seeds. Carefully mix everything taking care not to break pomegranate seeds, transfer to a serving plate and serve.

Pickled Eggplants with Walnuts

Ingredients:
Eggplants, pickled - 4-5
Shelled walnuts - 1/2 cup
Garlic - 2 cloves
Onion - 1
Herbs - 1-1 1/2 cups, finely chopped
Pomegranate juice - 1/4 cup
Chili pepper, pomegranate seeds, salt - to taste

Take pickled, whole eggplants out of the pickling liquid, cut each one into quarters lengthwise, then finely chop them, scald with boiling water and squeeze.

Add shelled walnuts pounded with garlic, chili peppers, salt, mixed with finely chopped cilantro, dill, parsley, and celery leaves, diced onion, and pomegranate juice. Add the walnut and herb mixture to the chopped eggplants and mix well. Transfer finished dish to a serving plate and sprinkle with pomegranate seeds.

Eggplants Stuffed with Lamb Tail Fat

Ingredients:
Eggplants - 8
Lamb tail fat - 50 g
Onions - 3-4
Ground pepper, herbs, salt - to taste

Wash lamb tail fat and cut it into 8 pieces, season with salt and ground black pepper. Mix with finely chopped herbs.

Wash eggplants, make a lengthwise cut 3-4 cm long in each eggplant. Sprinkle a little bit of salt into the slash then stuff a piece of lamb tail fat together with some herbs inside the eggplant. Set eggplants cut-side down on a skillet, cover the skillet and put it on a stove. When one side of the eggplant is cooked - turn it over and cook on the other side. Serve hot.

Stuffing can also be prepared as follows: cut lamb tail fat (50 g), dice onions (3-4), and sauté onions in rendered fat. Season with salt, ground black pepper, add finely chopped herbs, mix well, and use the mixture to stuff eggplant. Cook as described above.

Fried Eggplants with Walnut Stuffing

Ingredients:
Eggplants - 6-8
Shelled walnuts - 1/2 cup
Cilantro - 1 sprig
Garlic - 2 cloves
Cooking fat - 50-80 g
Herbs (savory, basil, cilantro) - 3 sprigs each
Parsley and celery leaves - 2 sprigs each
Chili peppers and salt - to taste

Prepare eggplants as described in the previous recipe. Thoroughly pound shelled walnuts together with salt, chili peppers, cilantro, and garlic, add finely diced herbs (parsley, basil, celery, savory) and mix well. Stuff eggplants with prepared stuffing, put into a hot skillet with cooking fat, cover the skillet, and cook on all sides.

Eggplants with Sweet Bell Peppers

Ingredients:
Eggplants - 10
Sweet bell peppers - 6
Tomatoes - 800 g
Onions - 2-3
Vegetable oil - 1/2-3/4 cup
Herbs (savory, cilantro, parsley, basil, celery leaves) - to taste
Garlic, chili pepper, salt - to taste

Wash eggplants, make a lengthwise slash and scrape seeds out with a tea spoon.

Wash sweet bell peppers, julienne them, add finely chopped herbs, mashed garlic and crushed chili peppers, peeled and diced tomatoes, diced onions, season everything with salt and mix well. Stuff eggplants with prepared stuffing, put into a pot, add vegetable oil, and cook over low heat until eggplants are cooked.

Fried Eggplants with Garlic-Vinegar Sauce

Ingredients:
Eggplants - 6
Vegetable oil - 1/4 cup
Onions - 4
Garlic - 5-6
Wine vinegar, salt - to taste

Wash eggplants with cold water, cut each one lengthwise into 4-5 slices, sprinkle them with salt, cover with a clean towel and set aside for 10-15 minutes. Carefully squeeze eggplant slices making sure to not to break them.

Add vegetable oil to a hot skillet, put prepared eggplants in one layer and fry on both sides.

Dice onions and soften them in vegetable oil, then mix them with cooked eggplants, transfer to a serving plate and pour garlic-vinegar sauce over eggplants.

To make sauce pound 5-6 cloves of garlic and mix it with wine vinegar to taste.

Braised Eggplants

Ingredients:
Eggplants - 6
Onions - 3
Clarified butter or vegetable oil - 2-3 tbsp
Salt - to taste

Wash and peel eggplants, cut into wedges, sprinkle with salt, cover with clean towel and set aside for 15-20 minutes, then squeeze any liquid and cut each wedge lengthwise.

Soften diced onions in clarified butter or vegetable oil, add prepared eggplants to the skillet, add more oil and 1-2 tbsp of wine vinegar, mix well and cook everything together until done.

Eggplants with Walnut Sauce

Ingredients:
Eggplants - 8
Shelled walnuts - 1-1 1/2 cups
Cooking fat - 30-50 g
Cilantro - 2 sprigs
Chili pepper, garlic, wine vinegar or pomegranate juice, salt - to taste

Cut washed eggplants lengthwise into slices 1/2-2 cm thick, sprinkle with salt, put into a hot frying pan with cooking fat in one layer and fry on both sides until nicely browned.

Pound shelled walnuts with garlic and salt in a mortar, add chopped cilantro, crushed chili pepper, wine vinegar or pomegranate juice, mix well and dilute with two cups of water.

Transfer cooked eggplants to a serving plate and pour walnut sauce over.

Eggplants with Cheese and Matsoni (Yogurt)

Ingredients:
Eggplants - 300 g
Cheese (fresh, low-salt) - 150 g
Eggs - 2
Clarified butter - 100-150 g

Matsoni (yogurt) - 300 g

With a tip of a small knife remove (scoop) seeds from young eggplants. Put eggplants into a roasting pan, put into a preheated oven, and cook until half-done.

Peel hard-boiled eggs, finely chop them, mix with chopped cheese, and mix in clarified butter. Stuff eggplants with prepared cheese stuffing, then put into an oiled ovenproof skillet, return to the oven, and cook until done.

Transfer cooked eggplants to a serving plate and pour beaten yogurt over.

Fried Eggplants with Tomato Sauce

Ingredients:
Eggplants - 4-5
Onions - 2
Wheat flour - 1 tbsp
Butter - 2-3 tbsp
Tomatoes - 500-600 g
Garlic - 2 cloves
Basil, parsley, chili pepper, salt - to taste

Scald eggplants, cut into thin slices, season with salt, and brown in oil or butter.

Brown finely diced onions in oil in a skillet, sprinkle with flour, mix well, and fry a bit longer. Add tomatoes cooked until half-done then passed through a sieve to the skillet and cook 10-15 minutes from the moment tomatoes come to boil.

About 5 minutes before the end of cooking season sauce with crushed chili pepper and mashed garlic. Remove skillet from the heat and add chopped basil and parsley to the sauce. Pour the sauce over cooked eggplants.

Fried Eggplants with Garlic and Herbs

Ingredients:
Eggplants - 500 g
Vegetable oil - 2-3 tbsp
Wine vinegar - 1/4-1/2 cup
Garlic - 6-7 cloves
Basil - 3 sprigs
Cilantro and parsley - 1 sprig each
Dill - 2 sprigs
Onion - 1
Salt - to taste

Wash eggplants, cut them across, sprinkle with salt, cover with clean towel, and set aside for 30 minutes, then carefully squeeze with your hand.

Put prepared eggplants in one layer into an oiled hot skillet and nicely brown on both sides.

Meanwhile pound garlic together with rock salt. Deglaze skillet with wine vinegar, strain it and add to the mashed garlic.

Transfer cooked eggplants to a serving plate, pour prepared sauce over, then sprinkle with finely chopped leaves of basil, cilantro, dill, and parsley, and with diced onion or scallions.

Fried Eggplants with Rice and Tomatoes

Ingredients:
Eggplants - 8-10
Tomatoes - 600-700 g
Onions - 4-5
Rice - 3 tbsp
Butter or vegetable oil - 70-100
Savory - 2 sprigs

Wash young eggplants and make 3-4 cm long lengthwise slash in each.

Cook rice in salted water until half-done, season it with ground black pepper, mix well and stuff eggplants with rice. Put eggplants in one layer, slash side down, into an oiled hot skillet and fry on all sides.

Transfer cooked eggplants into a shallow pot, add fried in vegetable oil onions, finely chopped savory, top with thinly sliced tomatoes, add vegetable oil, cover the pot and cook approximately 20-30 minutes.

Eggplant Caviar (A) (Eggplant Spread)

Ingredients:
Eggplants - 500 g
Sweet bell peppers - 3-4
Garlic - 2 cloves
Coriander seeds - 1 tsp
Vegetable oil - 1-2 tbsp
Tomatoes - 2-3
Salt and ground black pepper - to taste

Bake washed eggplants. Wash sweet bell peppers in cold water, dice them and sauté in vegetable oil.

Finely dice peeled onions, sprinkle with salt, set aside for 1 hour, then squeeze with hand.

Peel baked eggplants, finely chop the flesh, season with salt, ground black pepper, crushed garlic, sautéed sweet bell peppers, prepared onions, juice squeezed from tomatoes, crushed coriander seeds, mix everything well, transfer to a serving plate, and serve.

Eggplant Caviar (B) (Eggplant Spread)

Ingredients:
Eggplants - 300 g

Onions - 1-2
Parsley - 1 sprig
Basil - 2 sprigs
Scallions - 1
Salt and ground black pepper - to taste

Bake washed eggplants in a preheated oven, peel, finely chop eggplant flesh, season with salt and ground black pepper, add finely chopped onions, chopped parsley and basil, and mix well. Transfer eggplant spread to a serving plate and sprinkle with finely chopped scallions.

Eggplant Caviar with Pomegranates

Ingredients:
Eggplants - 300 g
Onions - 2
Pomegranates - 2
Garlic - 2 cloves
Cilantro - 2 sprigs
Chili peppers and salt - to taste

Squeeze juice from one pomegranate and mix it with garlic and cilantro pounded with salt in a mortar.

Bake eggplants in a preheated oven, peel them, chop eggplant flesh, add pomegranate sauce and thinly slices chili pepper. Mix everything well, transfer to a serving plate, and sprinkle with finely chopped onions and pomegranate seeds.

Eggplants with Eggs

Ingredients:
Eggplants - 500 g
Vegetable oil - 100 g
Eggs - 3

Salt - to taste

Finely chop peeled eggplants, sprinkle with salt, and set aside for 15-20 minutes. Squeeze eggplants with your hand, put into a pot, season with salt, add vegetable oil, and braise until done. Add beaten eggs to eggplants, mix well, and cook until eggs are done.

Eggplants Grilled on a Skewer with Garlic

Grill whole eggplants on a skewer over glowing-hot coals, then peel them, chop eggplant flesh and season it with mashed garlic and salt to taste.

Eggplants Fried in Lamb Tail Fat

Ingredients:
Eggplants - 300 g
Lamb tail fat - 100 g
Onions - 2-3
Chili pepper and salt - to taste

Bake eggplants in a preheated oven, peel them, and finely chop eggplant flesh.
Cut lamb tail fat into long, thin slices, mix with salt, put into a skillet together with diced onions and sauté until nicely browned. Add chopped eggplants, season with thinly sliced chili pepper, and cook 5 minutes longer.

Eggplants with Meat

Ingredients:
Eggplants - 6-7
Boiled meat - 300 g
Tomatoes - 1 kg

Onions - 3
Butter - 70-100 g
Herbs, ground black pepper, garlic, salt - to taste

Cut the top of medium-sized eggplants off, wash them, cut in half lengthwise, sprinkle with salt and set aside for 30 minutes to get rid of moisture and bitterness. Squeeze eggplants with hand and fry in a skillet with butter.

Meanwhile, cook tomatoes, then pass them through a sieve.

Pass boiled meat through a meat grinder, brown it in butter together with finely chopped onions, season with salt and ground black pepper, and mix well.

Set a layer of fried eggplants on a bottom of a shallow pan and cover them with a layer of chopped herbs (parsley, celery leaves, basil, savory, dill, and cilantro). Put browned meat on top of herbs, and top layer of meat with another layer of eggplants, then sprinkle everything again with chopped herbs. Pour tomato sauce over, season with salt, cover the pot, and braise over a low heat approximately 10-15 minutes.

Borani with Eggplants

Ingredients:
Eggplants - 8
Spring chicken - 1
Clarified butter - 100-150 g
Onions - 200 g
Salt - 1 tbsp
Matsoni (yogurt) - 1 l
Cilantro, mint, basil - 3 sprigs each
Powdered sugar - 2 tbsp
Cinnamon - 1/2 tsp
Salt - to taste

Pour matsoni into a cheesecloth a hang to drain (or just cover it with a cheesecloth and squeeze a couple of time it as it absorbs whey). Add 1/2 cup of cold water to the strained yogurt and beat well.

Wash and peel eggplants, cut them into thin slices lengthwise, sprinkle with salt, cover with a clean towel and set aside for 15-20 minutes, then squeeze with your hand.

Put diced onions and prepared eggplants into a preheated skillet with clarified butter and cook until nicely browned. Add chopped herbs to the skillet while eggplants are cooking.

Set some of the cooked eggplants in a layer on a serving plate. Top with pieces of fried spring chicken, then cover chicken with remaining eggplants. Pour beaten matsoni over eggplants and sprinkle with powdered sugar and ground cinnamon.

YOUNG GREENS OF BEETS, RADISHES AND CAULIFLOWER

Young Beet Greens with Walnuts

Ingredients:
Young beet greens - 500 g
Shelled walnuts - 1/2-3/4 cup
Cilantro - 2 sprigs
Garlic - 1-2 cloves
Onions - 200-300 g
Dill - 3 sprigs
Wine vinegar, chili peppers, salt - to taste

Put picked over and washed young beet greens into a pit, add 1 cup of boiling water, bring it to boil, and cook 30-40 minutes. Drain cooked greens in a colander, squeeze excess liquid when it is cool enough to handle.

Pound shelled walnuts in a mortar, then add pounded together cilantro, chili peppers, garlic, and salt, mix in diced onions and chopped dill, then add wine vinegar and prepared beet greens. Transfer dressed beet greens to a serving plate.

Radish Greens with Walnuts

Ingredients:
Radish greens - 500 g
Shelled walnuts - 3/4-1 cup
Onions - 2-3
Garlic - 2 cloves
Cilantro, chili peppers, wine vinegar, salt - to taste

Put picked over, cleaned and washed radish greens into a pot with boiling water (1 cup) and cook 20-25 minutes. Drain cooked greens in a colander, and squeeze excess liquid when it is cool enough to handle.

Pound shelled walnuts or pass them through a meat grinder, squeeze oil from crushed walnuts and set it aside.

Pound garlic, salt, chili pepper together, add chopped cilantro and crushed walnuts, wine vinegar, prepared radish greens, thoroughly mix everything, transfer to a serving plate and drizzle with walnut oil.

Cauliflower Leaves with Walnuts

Ingredients:
Cauliflower leaves - 500 g
Shelled walnuts - 1/2 cup
Garlic - 3 cloves
Cilantro, wine reasons, chili pepper, salt - to taste

Put picked over and washed cauliflower leaves into a pot with boiling water (1 cup) and cook 25-30 minutes. Drain and cool leaves in a colander, squeeze excess liquid, transfer to a cutting board and chop into pieces.

Thoroughly pound garlic, cilantro, and chili peppers together with salt in a mortar, add crushed walnuts, wine vinegar, prepared cauliflower leaves, mix everything well and transfer to a serving plate.

If desired - squeeze oil from crushed walnuts and use it to drizzle the finished dish.

MIXED VEGETABLE DISHES

Adzhapsandali (A)

Ingredients:
Eggplants - 500 g
Onions - 3-4
Garlic - 1-2 cloves
Sweet bell peppers - 2
Vegetable oil - 1-2 tbsp
Tomatoes - 800 g
Herbs, salt - to taste

Bake medium-sized eggplants making sure that they do not burn. When eggplants are cooked - carefully peel them while they are still hot and separate flesh into long strands.

Peel onions, finely dice them and sauté them in vegetable oil until softened.

Cut and cook tomatoes in a pot, then pass them through a sieve. Put tomato puree into a pot, add softened onions, crushed garlic, scalded, peeled, and diced sweet bell peppers, and cook everything together until the sauce is thickened. Add prepared eggplants to the pot, finely chopped herbs (parsley, cilantro, basil, savory, dill) season with salt, let it simmer 2-3 minutes longer and remove from heat. Serve cold.

Adzhapsandali (B)

Ingredients:
Eggplants – 500g
Onions - 3
Potatoes - 2-3
Tomatoes - 500 g
Garlic - 1-2 cloves
Vegetable oil - 2 tbsp
Herbs, chili peppers, salt - to taste

Cut medium-sized eggplants across into rounds 1/2 cm thick, sprinkle with salt, set aside for 30-40 minutes, then lightly squeeze with hand.

Sauté finely diced onions in vegetable oil in a skillet until softened. Add prepared eggplants, more vegetable oil, potatoes cut into large pieces, and cook until potatoes are done. Add peeled tomatoes and continue cooking until the sauce thickens.

About 5-10 minutes before the end of cooking - add crushed garlic, chili peppers, finely chopped herbs to the skillet and season everything with salt.

Adzhapsandali (C)

Ingredients:
Eggplants - 5
Potatoes - 2-3
Onions - 300 g
Tomatoes - 500-700 g
Herbs (cilantro, parsley, basil, savory, mint, dill) - 3-4 sprigs each
Butter or vegetable oil - 2 tbsp
Chili peppers, salt - to taste

Cut unpeeled, washed eggplants across into 1.2-2 cm thick slices.

Peel potatoes and cut them into large pieces. Peel, wash, and thinly slice onions. Finley chop herbs (cilantro, parsley, basil, savory, mint, dill).

Set sliced onions on a bottom of a pan, top onions with slices of eggplants, followed by a layer of potatoes, then herbs, season with salt and crushed (or sliced fresh) chili peppers, top with layer of tomatoes and put butter or pour vegetable oil over the contents of the pot. Cover the pot and put it on a stove over low heat. Cook for 1 hours.

Adzhapsandali (D)

Ingredients:
Eggplants - 5
Sweet bell peppers - 2-3
Onions - 400 g
Potatoes - 2-3
Tomatoes - 700 g
Butter or vegetable oil - 100-150 g
Herbs, salt - to taste

Soften diced onions in a pot in vegetable oil. Add more vegetable oil and eggplants sliced across into rounds.

After 10-15 minutes of cooking add potatoes, sweet bell peppers, season with salt, add chopped herbs, then pour in tomatoes passed through a meat grinder, cover the pot and cook until done, about 1 hour.

Vegetables in Brine

Dice boiled potatoes, carrots, and baked beets. Add diced onions or scallions to taste, cauliflower, chopped herbs, ground black pepper, salt, and mix everything carefully. Dress vegetables with brine from sour cabbage and vegetable oil, decorate with onion rings, slices of beets and hard-boiled eggs.

Vegetarian Chahohbili

Ingredients:
Tomatoes - 700 g
Onions - 4-5
Potatoes - 2
Butter - 50 g
Whole chili peppers, herbs, salt - to taste

Cut washed ripe tomatoes into pieces, put into a pot and cook until tomatoes are cooked through, then pass them through a sieve.

Peel onions, dice them, put into a pot with 30 g of butter, and sauté until softened. Add potatoes cut into pieces together with remaining butter, pour in tomato puree, add whole chili peppers, season with salt. Cook until potatoes are done, remove from heat, add finely chopped herbs, mix and serve.

PUMPKIN AND ZUCCINI DISHES

Boiled Pumpkin

Remove seeds from a pumpkin, cut it into wedges together with its skin, put into a pot, add hot water to come up half way up the pumpkin, cover the pot and cook 20-25 minutes.

Cooked pumpkin should be set in one layer on a serving plate and serve hot. If desired - sprinkle with powdered sugar or drizzle with honey.

Pumpkin with Dogberries and Walnuts

Ingredients:
Pumpkin - 500 g
Dried dogberries - 1/3 cup
Crushed shelled walnuts - 2 tbsp
Onnions - 2
Salt - to taste

Peel pumpkin and remove seeds, cut into pieces, put into a pod with boiling salted water to reach half-way up the pumpkin, and cook until done. Cool cooked pumpkin, cut into smaller pieces, add chopped pitted dried dogberries, diced onions, crushed walnuts, put everything into a pot, sauté for a short time, then remove from heat.

Pumpkin with Walnuts and Sugar

Ingredients:
Pumpkin - 500-700 g
Shelled walnuts - 1 cup
Honey - 2 tbsp
Granulated sugar - 1/3-3/4 cup

Cook pumpkin following instructions of the previous recipe. Thoroughly pound shelled walnuts and mix them with powdered sugar.
Dissolve honey and granulated sugar in hot water (3/4 cup). Cut cooked pumpkin into smaller pieces and carefully mix with crushed walnuts and syrup. Serve cooled.

Pumpkin Braised with Rice and Raisins

Ingredients:
Pumpkin - 500 g

Milk - 1/3 cup
Granulated sugar - 3/4 cup
Rice - 1 cup
Butter - 100 g
Raisins - 70 g

Peel pumpkin and remove seeds. Cut prepared
pumpkin into small pieces, put into a pot, add 1/2 cup of
hot water, cover the pot, and braise pumpkin for 15 minutes.
Add milk, cooked rice, butter (30 g), sugar, and cook 15-20
minutes longer, stirring from time to time.

Put seedless raisins into a hot skillet with remaining
butter, and, when raisins swell, transfer them to the pot with
pumpkin, mix, and 2-3 minutes later remove from heat.
Serve hot.

Baked Pumpkin

Cut pumpkin in half, remove seeds, and put into a
preheated oven in a roasting pan.

Remove cooked pumpkin from the oven, cut pumpkin
into serving pieces, transfer to a serving plate, and serve hot.

Fried Zucchini with Matsoni (Yogurt)

Ingredients:
Zucchini - 500 g
Butter or vegetable oil - 50-80 g
Matsoni (yogurt) - 2 cups
Powdered sugar - 1 tbsp
Salt - to taste

Peel zucchini, cut them into slices 1-1 1/2 cm thick. Put
prepared zucchini in one layer into a hot skillet with butter
and fry on both sides until nicely browned. Just before

serving pour drained and beaten matsoni over zucchini and sprinkle with powdered sugar.

DISHES WITH BEANS

Green Beans with Butter and Eggs (A)

Ingredients:
Green beans - 1 kg
Onions - 3-4
Clarified butter - 150-200 g
Eggs - 2-3
Parsley, tarragon, savory, mint, dill - 4 sprigs each
Basil - 6 sprigs
Salt - to taste

Clean green beans, break into pieces, wash with cold water, put into a pot with 2 cups of boiling water, cover the pot and cook until done (from 1 to 2 hours). Add diced onions to the pot while beans are cooking.

When beans are cooked and all the water is boiled out, season beans with salt, add finely chopped leaves of parsley, basil, savory, tarragon, mint, dill, butter and sauté for 10 minutes. Add beaten eggs to the pot, smooth the top, making holes in some places to let eggs sip into beans, cover the pot and cook until eggs are set.

Green Beans with Butter and Eggs (B)

Ingredients:
Green beans - 1 kg
Butter - 150 g
Eggs - 3
Salt - to taste

Clean green beans, break them into pieces, wash in cold water, put into a pot with boiling water (2 cups), cover the pot and cook until beans are done (from 1 to 2 hours).

When beans are cooked and all the water has evaporated, season beans with salt, add butter and sauté 10 minutes, Add one beaten eggs , mix everything well, pour remaining beaten eggs, smooth the top, cover the pot and cook until the eggs are set.

Green Beans with Caramelized Onions and Eggs

Ingredients:
Green beans - 1 kg
Onions - 300 g
Butter - 150-200 g
Eggs - 3
Parsley, savory, mint, dill, basil, salt - to taste

Clean green beans, break them into pieces, wash with cold water, put into a pot with 2 cups of boiling water, add a bouquet of herbs (cilantro, parsley, basil, savory), cover the pot and cook until beans are cooked (from 1 to 2 hours).

Caramelize thinly sliced onions in 50 g of butter in a sauté pan.

When beans are cooked - remove bouquet of herbs out of the pot, season beans with salt, add caramelized onions, finely chopped leaves of parsley, basil, savory, mint, dill, butter, mix well, and sauté for 15-20 minutes. Pour beaten eggs over beans, smooth the top, making wholes in some places to let eggs to sip into beans, cover the pot and cook until eggs are set.

Borani with Green Beans

Ingredients:
Green beans - 1 kg

Spring chicken - 1
Butter - 200-250 g
Scallions - 2-3
Savory, dill, tarragon, cilantro - 6 sprigs each
Matsoni (yogurt) - 500 g
Ground cinnamon and cloves, granulated sugar, salt - to taste

Clean green beans, break them into pieces, wash with cold water and cook as described in previous recipe. Add finely chopped scallions, chopped leaves of basil, savory, tarragon, parsley, cilantro and dill, season with salt, ground cinnamon and cloves, mix everything well, add clarified butter and sauté 10-15 minutes,

Meanwhile fry spring chicken until completely done, then cut it into serving pieces.

Put matsoni into a cheesecloth, tie the ends of the cheesecloth up, and hang it to drain. Once the yogurt is drained -- whip it up, then mix in half a cup of drinking water.

Set half of the cooked beans on a serving plate, top it with pieces of fried chicken, cover the chicken with remaining beans. Pour matsoni over the beans, sprinkle with granulated sugar and ground cinnamon.

Green Beans with Walnuts (A)

Ingredients:
Green beans - 500 g
Shelled walnuts - 1/2-3/4 cup
Onions - 2-3
Garlic - 1-2 cloves
Cilantro and savory - 4 sprigs each
Basil - 3 sprigs
Dill, salt - to taste

Break green beans into pieces, cook, drain in a colander, let it cool, then squeeze excess liquid.

Pound shelled walnuts together with salt, garlic, and one sprig of cilantro in a mortar, and thin walnut mixture with 1-2 tbsp of bean cooking liquid. Add finely chopped onions, chopped leaves of basil, savory, and cilantro, and mix well. Add squeezed beans to the walnut mixture, mix everything well, transfer to a serving plate and sprinkle with chopped dill.

Green Beans with Walnuts (B)

Ingredients:
Green beans - 500 g
Shelled walnuts - 3/4 cup
Garlic - 2-3 cloves
Onions - 2-3
Cilantro - 3-4 sprigs
Salt - to taste

Break and cook green beans until done, drain in a colander and squeeze excess liquid.

Pound shelled walnuts with salt and garlic in a mortar, squeeze walnut oil and set it aside.

Mix 1/4 cup of bean cooking liquid with crushed walnuts, then add squeezed green beans, add finely diced onions and mix again. Transfer the dish to a serving plate or a bowl, smooth the top and make a small hole in the middle of the beans and pour preserved walnut oil into it.

Green Beans with Walnuts and Vinegar

Ingredients:
Green beans - 300 g
Shelled walnuts - 1/2-1 cup
Onions - 2-3

Garlic - 1-2 cloves
Basil, savory, parsley, dill, cilantro - 3-4 sprigs each
Wine vinegar, pomegranate juice, or tkemali - to taste
Chili pepper, scallions, pomegranate seeds, salt - to taste

Break green beans, cook, drain in a colander, cool, and squeeze excess liquid.

Pound shelled walnuts together with salt, garlic, chili peppers, and cilantro leaves, mix in wine vinegar (or use pomegranate juice or tkemali sauce instead of vinegar), diced onions or scallions, finely chopped leaves of basil, savory, parsley, cilantro, dill, and mix everything together with squeezed beans.

Transfer the dish to a serving plate, sprinkle with chopped herbs and pomegranate seeds (to taste).

Green Beans with Tomatoes and Walnuts

Ingredients:
Green beans - 500 g
Tomatoes - 600 g
Shelled walnuts - 1/2 cup
Onions - 2
Cilantro - 1 sprig
Parsley and basil - 3 sprigs each
Garlic - 1 clove
Chili peppers, salt - to taste

Cut tomatoes, put into a pot, set the pot on the stove, bring tomatoes to boil and let it boil 1-2 minutes, then remove from heat and pass tomatoes through a sieve.

Break green beans into smaller pieces, cook, add to a pot with browned onions and tomato puree, bring to boil, then add walnuts pounded together with salt, chili peppers, garlic, and cilantro in a mortar, and chopped parsley and basil leaves, and cook 5-10 minutes longer.

Green Beans with Matsoni (Yogurt)

Ingredients:
Green beans - 500 g
Matsoni (yogurt) - 500 g
Basil, cilantro, and parsley leaves - 3 sprigs each
Garlic - 3-4 cloves
Mint - 2-3 sprigs
Chili peppers, salt - to taste

Break green beans into pieces, cook them, drain in a colander, cool, and squeeze excess liquid.

Beat matsoni, add squeezed beans, finely chopped leaves of basil, parsley, mint, cilantro, salt, crushed chili peppers, garlic, mix everything well and transfer to a serving plate.

Green Beans Salad

Ingredients:
Green beans - 300 g
Wine vinegar - 2 tbsp
Onion - 1
Dill - 4 sprigs
Chili peppers, salt - to taste

Clean green beans, cut into pieces, cook in boiling salted water, drain in a colander. Season green beans with salt, crushed chili peppers, add wine vinegar, finely diced onion, and mix everything well. Sprinkle salad with finely chopped dill.

Green Beans with Tkemali

Ingredients:

Green beans - 500 g
Tkemali plums - 1 cup
Onions - 1-2
Garlic - 1 clove
Cilantro, pennyroyal - 2 sprigs each
Dill, basil - 4 sprigs each
Chili peppers, salt - to taste

Scald ripe Tkemali plums, pit them and pass through a sieve. Add chili peppers crushed together with pennyroyal, cilantro leaves, and garlic, then add finely chopped dill and mix well.

Clean green beans, break each pod in half, put into a pot, add a little boiling salted water and cook until done. Add chopped onion to the pot while beans are cooking.

When beans are cooked and all the water has evaporated, add prepared tkemali puree, let it simmer for 1-2 minutes, then remove from heat. Transfer the dish into a serving bowl, cool, and sprinkle with finely chopped basil leaves.

Sautéed Green Beans

Ingredients:
Green beans - 500 g
Onions - 250 g
Cooking fat - 100-150 g
Basil - 3 sprigs
Savory, mint, parsley, tarragon - 2 sprigs
Chili peppers, salt - to taste

Prepare and cook green beans until done, drain in a colander.

Peel onions, wash and finely dice them. Sauté onions in a pot with cooking fat until softened. Add cooked beans to the pot with softened onions, add more cooking fat and continue cooking 5 more minutes. Add crushed chili peppers, finely chopped leaves of basil, mint, savory, parsley, tarragon, a little more fat and continue cooking 10 minutes longer, then remove from heat.

Beans with Butter and Eggs

Ingredients:
Beans (fresh) - 500 g
Green beans - 500 g
Onions - 3
Clarified butter or pork fat - 100-150 g
Eggs - 3-4
Cilantro, parsley, savory, salt - to taste

Pick out fresh beans from ripe (yellow) pods, and cook until half-done in a small quantity of water.

Remove strings from green beans, cut them into pieces, add to a pot with 3/4 cup of boiling water and cook until done (1-1 1/2 hours). All liquid has to evaporate during cooking.

Into a pot with half-cooked beans add diced onions, clarified butter or pork fat, and cook until beans are done. Add cooked beans to the pot, put more cooking fat, then add chopped leaves of cilantro, parsley, and savory, season to taste with salt, mix well, pour in beaten eggs and make a few holes to let egg to sip in. Remove from heat when eggs are set.

Boiled Beans with Herbs

Ingredients:
Beans - 500 g
Onions - 2
Cilantro - 4 sprigs
Garlic - 2 cloves

Parsley - 3 sprigs
Savory and mint - 3 sprigs
Chili peppers and salt - to taste

Put picked over and washed beans into a pot, cover with water, and bring to boil. Add more boiling water if necessary during cooking.

Add crushed garlic and diced onions into the pot while the beans are cooking.

When beans are cooked mash them with a spoon, preferably wooden, season with salt, crushed chili peppers, finely chopped leaves of parsley, cilantro, savory, and mint, let it simmer 1-2 minutes longer, then remove from heat.

If desired, while the beans are cooking you can add to the pot 2-3 tbsp of crushed walnuts, and, to taste, sour fruit leather, tkemali, or wine vinegar. Finished dish should have a consistency of thin porridge.

Beans with Celery and Scallions

Ingredients:
Beans - 300 g
Celery - 5-6 stalks
Scallions - 1-2
Chili peppers, salt - to taste

Cook beans until done, add finely diced celery and scallions to the pot with beans, season everything with salt and crushed chili peppers, let it simmer 1-2 minutes longer, remove from heat. Finished dish should have a consistency of a thin porridge.

Beans with Vegetable Oil, Cinnamon, and Cloves

Ingredients:

Beans - 500 g
Onions - 200-300 g
Vegetable oil - 1/4 cup
Ground cloves and cinnamon - 1 1/2 tsp
Cilantro - 4 sprigs
Chili pepper, Imereti saffron, salt - to taste

Put picked over and washed beans into a pot, cover with water, and bring to boil.

When beans are cooked, drain them preserving the cooking liquid and keep beans in a covered pot.

In another pot sauté diced onions in vegetable oil until softened. Add cooked beans to the pot with onions and sauté 5-10 minutes longer.

Season cooking liquid with salt, crushed Imereti saffron, crushed chili peppers, ground cloves and cinnamon, then pour it into the pot with beans and onions.

Let everything simmer together for 1-2 minutes, mash beans with a spoon, add finely chopped cilantro and remove from heat.

Beans with Vegetable Oil

Ingredients:
Beans - 200 g
Onions - 1
Vegetable oil, cilantro and parsley leaves, salt - to taste

Cook beans until done, then drain. Season cooked beans with salt, transfer to a serving boil, drizzle with vegetable oil, sprinkle with finely diced onion and chopped cilantro and parsley leaves.

Beans with Wine Vinegar and Vegetable Oil

Ingredients:
Beans - 500 g
Vegetable oil - 1/2 cup
Onions - 3
Wine vinegar - 1/2 cup
Salt and ground black pepper - to taste

Cook beans until done, drain them and preserve cooking liquid. Pour vegetable oil into a skillet, and soften finely diced onions in it. Season onions with salt, ground black pepper, and wine vinegar, mix it well and sauté 2-3 minutes longer. Add beans to the skillet with onions, pour 1 cup of cooking liquid, let it simmer 1-2 minutes and remove from heat.

Beans Sautéed in Vegetable Oil

Ingredients:
Beans - 500 g
Onions - 2
Vegetable oil - 1/4 cup
Salt - to taste

Cook beans making sure that beans retain their shape, drain, and season beans with salt.
Pour some of the vegetable oil into a skillet, add finely diced onions and sauté until softened. Add beans to the skillet with remaining vegetable oil, sauté until desired doneness, then remove from heat.

Beans with Clarified Butter and Eggs

Ingredients:

Beans - 500 g
Onions - 2
Clarified butter - 1/4 cup
Eggs - 2
Salt - to taste

Cook beans until beans are cooked and all the water has evaporated, season beans with salt. Soften onions in a hot skillet with clarified butter. Add cooked beans to the skillet with onions, add more clarified butter and sauté until beans are heated through. Pour beaten eggs over beans, poke holes in some places to let eggs to sip though, cover the skillet and cook until eggs are set.

Bean Croquettes

Ingredients:
Beans - 500 g
Shelled walnuts - 1 cup
Garlic - 1 clove
Onions - 2
Cilantro - 2 sprigs
Ground cinnamon and cloves - 1/2 tsp
Chili peppers, ground black peppers, salt - to taste

Cook beans until done and drain in a colander. Pound shelled walnuts together with salt and garlic in a mortar, squeeze oil and set it aside. Add crushed chili peppers, chopped cilantro, ground black pepper, ground cloves and cinnamon, and finely diced onions to the crushed walnuts. Add beans to the walnut mixture, mix everything well, then shape egg-sized croquettes. Set bean croquettes on a serving plate, sprinkle with finely chopped parsley and drizzle with walnut oil.

Beans with Walnuts

Ingredients:
Beans - 300 g
Shelled walnuts - 1/3-3/4 cup
Garlic - 2-3 cloves
Cilantro - 3-4 sprigs
Onions - 2
Salt - to taste

Cook beans until done, making sure that beans preserve their shape.

Pound shelled walnuts together with garlic and cilantro, add cooked beans and finely diced onions, carefully mix everything.

Transfer finished dish to a serving plate, decorate with thin slices of onions.

Beans with Walnuts and Pomegranate

Ingredients:
Beans - 500 g
Onions - 2
Shelled walnuts - 3/4-1 cup
Cilantro - 4 sprigs
Garlic - 2 cloves
Imereti saffron - 1 tsp
Pomegranate juice - 1/2 cup
Pomegranate seeds - from 1/2 of pomegranate
Chili peppers, ground cinnamon, cloves, salt - to taste

Pick beans over, wash, cook in water, and drain in a colander.

Pound shelled walnuts in a mortar. Add diced onions, crushed chili peppers, mashed garlic, chopped cilantro, crushed Imereti saffron, and salt to the crushed walnuts, mix it with pomegranate juice and ground cloves and cinnamon, then add cooked beans to the walnut mixture and mix everything well. Transfer the dish to a serving plate and sprinkle it with pomegranate seeds.

If desired - squeeze oil from crashed walnuts and drizzle the finished dish with it.

Beans with Walnuts and Wine Vinegar (A)

Ingredients:
Beans - 500 g
Wine vinegar - 1/3-1/2 cup
Shelled walnuts - 1/2 cup
Cilantro - 4 sprigs
Onions - 2
Scallion - 1
Garlic - 1 clove
Parsley - 2 sprigs
Chili peppers, salt - to taste

Cook beans in water until done. Pound shelled walnuts together with cilantro, garlic, chili peppers, and salt in a mortar, mix with vinegar, add diced onions , chopped scallion and parsley. Add walnut mixture to the pot with beans, simmer 10-15 minutes longer, then remove from heat and let it cool.

Beans with Walnuts and Wine Vinegar (B)

Ingredients:
Beans - 500 g
Shelled walnuts - 3/4-1 cup
Garlic - 1-2 cloves
Dried suneli - 1/2 tsp
Coriander seeds - 1/2 tsp
Parsley and dill - 6-8 sprigs each

Onion – 1
Wine vinegar, chili peppers, salt - to taste

Cook beans in water. Pound shelled walnuts together with cilantro, garlic, chili peppers, and salt in a mortar, add dried suneli and crushed coriander seeds, chopped parsley and dill, and mix with wine vinegar. Add cooked beans to the walnut mixture, combine everything, and transfer to a serving plate. Sprinkle with finely chopped onions.

MUSHROOM DISHES

Mushrooms Cooked with Eggs

Ingredients:
Mushrooms - 500 g
Onions - 200 g
Eggs – 3
Butter - 1-2 tbsp
Parsley - 2 sprigs
Salt - to taste

Cook fresh mushrooms in boiling salted water (1-1 1/2 liters), drain in a colander, and rinse with hot water. When all the water is drained, transfer to a cutting board, chop them, then fry in a hot skillet with butter.

Soften diced onions in butter and mix with sautéed mushrooms.

Beat eggs, mix with finely chopped parsley, pour beaten eggs to a skillet with mushrooms, and cook until eggs are set.

Mushrooms in Cream

Ingredients:
Mushrooms - 500 g

Butter - 50 g
Cream - 1-1 1/2 cup
Bay leaf – 1
Parsley and dill - 3 sprigs each
Black peppercorn – 1
Cinnamon, cloves, salt - to taste

Wash picked over fresh mushrooms, pour boiling water over them to cover and leave for 2-3 minutes. Take mushrooms out of the water, cut into pieces, put into a pot with butter, sauté for 10 minutes, then add boiling cream to the pot.

Tie parsley and dill into a bundle, and put it into the pot with mushrooms, together with cinnamon, cloves, black peppercorn, and bay leaf. Season to taste with salt. Cover the pot and simmer for approximately 1 hour. Remove bundle of herbs and spices from the dish before serving.

Champignons with Butter and Eggs

Ingredients:
Mushrooms - 500 g
Onion – 1
Clarified butter - 2-3
Eggs – 3
Herbs, salt - to taste

Wash clean fresh champignons in cold water, then finely chop them

Melt butter in a skillet, then fry mushrooms in butter until browned. Add finely diced onion to the skillet with mushrooms, add more butter, season with salt and continue frying until onions are softened.

Beat whole eggs, season with salt, mix with finely chopped parsley and dill. Pour beaten eggs over mushrooms and cook until eggs are set.

Fried Champignons

Ingredients:
Mushrooms - 500 g
Onions - 1-5
Clarified butter - 2-3 tbsp
Wine vinegar - 1-2 tbsp
Cilantro, salt - to taste

Finely chop prepared champignons, put into a skillet with melted butter and fry until half-done, then add finely diced onions, season with salt, add more butter, mix well and continue cooking until mushrooms are nicely browned. Transfer cooked mushrooms to a serving plate, drizzle with wine vinegar and sprinkle with finely chopped cilantro.

Sautéed Champignons with Walnuts

Ingredients:
Mushrooms - 500 g
Vegetable oil - 2 tbsp
Shelled walnuts - 1/2 cup
Garlic - 1-2 cloves
Wine vinegar - 1/4 cup
Cilantro - 4 sprigs
Dill, salt - to taste

Thoroughly wash cleaned fresh champignons, slice them, and put into a sauté pot with vegetable oil. Season mushrooms with salt and cook until done.

Pound shelled walnuts together with garlic, salt, cilantro leaves in a mortar and mix with wine vinegar. Add walnut mixture to the pan with mushrooms, mix well, and cook 5 minutes longer. Sprinkle with chopped dill before serving.

Honey Mushrooms with Walnuts

Ingredients:
Mushrooms - 500 g
Onions - 2-3
Crushed shelled walnuts - 1-2 tbsp
Garlic - 1-2 cloves
Cilantro - 3 sprigs
Salt - to taste

Slice fresh mushrooms, put into a pot, cover with cold water so it just barely covers mushrooms, bring to boil, and cook until half-done. Take mushrooms out with a skimmer, lightly cool, squeeze excess liquid, finely chop them, and put into a clean pot together with diced onions. Pour strained mushroom cooking liquid over mushrooms and cook until done. Add crushed walnuts, salt, garlic, Imereti saffron, finely chopped cilantro, simmer 3-5 minutes longer, then remove from heat.

Mushrooms Baked in Ketsi

(ed. note — Ketsi is a shallow ceramic cooking pan.)
Pick large, unblemished mushroom caps, was and dry them, and season with salt.
Heat ketsi up, set prepared mushrooms in it, top with another hot ketsi. Put glowing coals into the top ketsi and cook until mushrooms are done.

Grilled Mushrooms with Walnut Sauce

Ingredients:
Mushrooms - 500 g
Shelled walnuts - 1/2 cup
Garlic - 1-2 cloves

Cilantro - 3-4 sprigs
Wine vinegar, chili pepper, salt - to taste

Set a clean iron grill over glowing coals. Put large mushroom caps, washed, dried, and seasoned with salt, on a grill and cook until done.

Pound shelled walnuts together with garlic, chili peppers, cilantro, and salt in a mortar, add wine vinegar and cold drinking water.

Transfer cooked mushrooms to a serving plate, pour prepared walnut sauce over, and serve.

SAUCES

SAUCES

Tkemali Sauce (A)

Sauce for meat and fish dishes.

Ingredients:
Tkemali plums - 2 cups
Cilantro and dill - 2 sprigs each
Pennyroyal - 1 sprig
Garlic - 1 clove
Chili peppers, salt - to taste

Put picked over and washed tkemali plums into a pot, add enough water to cover, and bring to boil.

Take the pot off heat when tkemali are cooked and soft, pass plums though a sieve together with cooking liquid. Add pounded in a mortar cilantro leaves, chili peppers, salt, garlic, dill, and pennyroyal to the tkemali puree and mix well.

Tkemali Sauce (B)

Ingredients:
Tkemali plums - 2 cups
Cilantro - 1 sprig
Dill - 2 sprigs
Garlic - 1 clove
Chili peppers, salt - to taste

Put picked over and washed tkemali plums into a pot, add enough water to cover, bring to boil, and cook until done.

Remove pot from heat when plums are soft, pit the plums, and return to pot to the stove. Add pounded together cilantro (with seeds - if desired), dill, garlic, and chili peppers. Let it simmer 1 minute longer, then pass everything through a sieve and pour the sauce into a sauce boat. The sauce should have consistency of a thin sour cream.

Tkemali Sauce (C)

Ingredients:
Tkemali plums - 500 g
Water - 2 cups
Garlic - 2-3 cloves
Cilantro - 3 sprigs
Dill - 4-5 sprigs
Pennyroyal, chili peppers, salt - to taste

Put picked over and washed tkemali or sour cherry plums into a pot, add 2 cups of boiling water and cook 10-15 minutes. Remove pot from heat, pit the plums, cool, add garlic, salt, herbs (cilantro, dill, pennyroyal), chili peppers and mix everything well, then pass the mixture through a sieve, pour into a sauce boat and serve.

Tkemali Sauce (D)

Ingredients:
Tkemali plums - 500 g
Garlic - 2-3 cloves
Scallions - 1-2
Cilantro - 3-4 sprigs
Dill - 5-6 sprigs
Parsley - 2 sprigs
Pepper, salt - to taste

Cook tkemali plums as described in previous recipes and pass through a sieve together with cooking liquid. Add mashed garlic, ground chili peppers, finely chopped leaves of cilantro, dill, and parsley, chopped scallions, season with salt and mix everything well.

Sauce from Unripe Grapes (A)

This sauce is served with fried fish, pork, or poultry.

Ingredients:
Unripe grapes - 500 g
Cilantro - 3-4 sprigs
Garlic - 1 clove
Salt - to taste

Mash unripe grapes with a wooden spoon, squeeze juice from mashed grapes, strain it and pour into a clean container. Add mashed together with salt cilantro leaves and garlic, mix everything well. If desired - add crushed chili peppers

Sauce from Unripe Grapes (B)

Ingredients:
Juice from unripe grapes - 1/2 cup
Water - 1/2 cup
Cilantro - 3-4 sprigs
Parsley - 2 sprigs
Dill - 4 sprigs
Chopped tarragon leaves - 2 tsp
Garlic - 1-2 cloves
Salt - to taste

Squeeze juice from unripe grapes, add cool drinking water, chopped leaves of cilantro, parsley, tarragon and dill, garlic mashed with salt, and mix everything well.

Sauce from Unripe Grapes with Walnuts

This sauce is served with fried or boiled poultry.

Ingredients:
Unripe grapes - 500 g
Shelled walnuts - 1/2-3/4 cup
Garlic - 1 clove
Cilantro - 3 sprigs
Pennyroyal - 1 sprig
Chili pepper, salt - to taste

Mash unripe grapes and juice them, gradually adding water (1 cup). Add crushed walnuts and pounded together with salt chili peppers, cilantro leaves, garlic, pennyroyal, and mix everything well.

Sauce from Blackberry Juice and Unripe Grapes

Ingredients:
Blackberries - 500 g
Unripe grapes - 300 g
Cilantro - 3 sprigs
Dill - 1 sprig
Garlic - 1 clove
Chili peppers, salt - to taste

Mash blackberries with a wooden spoon and squeeze all the juice from mashed berries. Mash unripe grapes as well and also juice them.

Mix blackberry juice with juice from unripe grapes and season it with pounded together cilantro, dill, garlic, chili peppers, and salt.

Sauce from Blackberry Juice and Unripe Grapes with Walnuts

Serve this sauce with fried poultry or fish.

Ingredients:
Blackberry juice - 3/4 cup
Juice from unripe grapes - 3/4 cup
Shelled walnuts - 1/2 cup
Garlic - 1 clove
Cilantro - 2 sprigs
Chili pepper, salt - to taste

Mix blackberry juice with the juice from unripe grapes and 1/3-1/2 cup of water. Add walnuts pounded together with cilantro, garlic, chili peppers, and salt, mix everything well and pour into a sauce boat.

If the sauce is served with fish, fried or poached, add to it finely diced onions.

Blackberry Juice Sauce

Ingredients:
Blackberry juice - 1 cup
Garlic - 4 cloves
Coriander seeds - 1 tsp
Salt - to taste

Juice blackberries, add garlic and coriander seeds crushed with salt, mix everything well and pour into a sauce boat.

Blackberry Juice and Walnut Sauce

Ingredients:
Blackberry juice - 1 cup

Shelled walnuts - 1/2 cup
Garlic - 3 cloves
Coriander seeds - 1 tsp
Chili peppers, salt - to taste

Make the sauce as described in the previous recipe, but add crushed walnuts and chili peppers to it.

Pomegranate Sauce (A)

This sauce is served with meat and fish dishes.

Ingredients:
Pomegranate juice - 1/2 cup
Water - 1/2 cup
Cilantro - 1-2 sprigs
Garlic - 1-2 cloves
Chili peppers, salt - to taste

Squeeze juice from pomegranate, add to it cilantro, chili peppers, and garlic pounded with salt, dilute with water and mix everything well.

Pomegranate Sauce (B)

Serve with dishes with fried or poached fish.

Ingredients:
Pomegranate juice - 1 cup
Cilantro - 2 sprigs
Savory, dill - 1 sprig each
Garlic - 1-2 cloves
Onion - 1
Salt - to taste

Squeeze juice from pomegranate. Pound together leaves of cilantro, savory, and dill with garlic and salt, mix with pomegranate juice, then add diced onion.

Pomegranate Sauce (C)

Squeeze juice from a pomegranate, mix it to taste with garlic mashed with salt.

Pomegranate Juice and Walnuts Sauce (A)

Serve with meat and fish dishes

Ingredients:
Pomegranate juice - 1 cup
Shelled walnuts - 1/3 cup
Cilantro - 2-3 sprigs
Garlic - 1 clove
Chili peppers, salt - to taste

Juice pomegranates. Thoroughly pound together shelled walnuts, cilantro, garlic, chili peppers, and salt, add pomegranate juices, water (1/2 cup) and mix well. If serving this sauce with meat dishes - add to it finely diced onions or scallions.

Pomegranate Juice and Walnuts Sauce (B)

Ingredients:
Pomegranate juice - 1 cup
Shelled walnuts - 1/4 cup
Coriander seeds - 1 tsp
Salt - to taste

Squeeze juice from pomegranates and add to it shelled

walnuts pounded together with coriander seeds and salt. Mix everything well.

Tomato Sauce (A)

Wash ripe tomatoes, cut them, put into a pot and bring to boil. When tomatoes thicken, pass them through a sieve. Season tomato puree with mashed cilantro leaves, crushed chili peppers, garlic, and mix everything well.

Tomato Sauce (B)

Ingredients:
Tomatoes - 500 g
Water - 1/2 cup
Garlic - 3-4 cloves
Cilantro - 3-4 sprigs
Parsley, dill - 3 sprigs each
Onion - 1
Chili peppers, dried suneli, salt - to taste

Wash ripe tomatoes, cut into wedges, put into a pot and cook 10 minutes, then remove from heat, pass tomatoes through a sieve, thinning the mixture with water. Add mashed garlic to the tomato puree, season with salt, bring to boil and simmer for 10 minutes. Add crushed chili peppers, dried suneli, chopped herbs (cilantro, parsley, dill), diced onions, and mix everything well.

Tomato and Walnut Sauce

Serve the sauce with fried poultry dishes.

Ingredients:
Tomatoes - 500 g

Shelled walnuts - 1/4 cup
Carlic - 1/2-1 clove
Chili peppers, cilantro, salt - to taste

Cook tomatoes, pass them through a sieve, pour tomato puree into a pot and bring to boil. About 5 minutes from the start of boiling add shelled walnuts pounded together with garlic, cook 5 minutes longer, then add crushed chili peppers, cilantro, and salt, and cook 5 more minutes.

Tomato Juice Sauce

Ingredients:
Tomato juice - 1 cup
Coriander seeds - 1/2 tsp
Garlic - 1-2 cloves
Ground red pepper, salt - to taste

Juice very ripe tomatoes, add crushed coriander seeds and garlic, season with ground red chili pepper, salt, and mix everything.

Tomato Juice and Walnuts Sauce

Ingredients:
Tomato juice - 1 1/2 cups
Shelled walnuts - 1/4-1/2 cup
Cilantro - 4 sprigs
Onion - 1
Dill, pennyroyal, chili peppers, salt - to taste

Juice very ripe tomatoes. Thoroughly pound shelled walnuts together with garlic, chili peppers, cilantro, dill, pennyroyal, and salt in a mortar, mix with tomato juice and finely diced onions or scallions.

Blackthorn Plum Sauce

Ingredients:
Blackthorn plums - 500 g
Cilantro and dill - 3-4 sprigs each
Garlic - 1 clove
Chili peppers, salt - to taste

Put picked over and washed blackthorn plums into a pot, add enough water just to cover, and bring to boil. When plums are soft and are falling apart take the pot off the heat, remove pits from the pot, and pass contents of the pot through a sieve. Add pounded together with salt chili peppers, garlic, cilantro and dill leaves to the blackthorn puree and mix well.

Blackthorn Plum and Tkemali Plum Sauce

Ingredients:
Blackthorn plums - 300 g
Tkemali plums - 300 g
Garlic - 1-2 cloves
Coriander seeds - 1 tsp
Red chili pepper, salt - to taste

Put picked over and washed blackthorn plums and tkemali plums into a pot, add enough water just to cover, bring to boil and cook for 15 minutes. Remove the pot from heat and pass its contents of the pan through a sieve. Mix into the plum puree pounded together salt, garlic, coriander seeds, red chili peppers.

Dogberry Sauce (A)

Ingredients:
Dogberries - 700 g
Water - 1/2 cup
Coriander seeds - 1/2 tsp
Garlic - 1-2 cloves
Dried suneli - 1/2 tsp
Chili peppers, herbs, salt - to taste

Pass ripe dogberries through a sieve, add drinking water, crushed coriander seeds, chili peppers, garlic mashed with salt, dried suneli, chopped herbs (cilantro, dill) and mix everything well.

Dogberry Sauce (B)

Ingredients:
Dogberries - 500 g
Garlic - 1-2 cloves
Cilantro - 3-4 sprigs
Chili peppers, salt - to taste

Put picked over and washed dogberries into a pot, add enough water to cover, bring to boil, and cook 10-15 minutes, then pass them through a sieve. Add thoroughly pounded cilantro, chili peppers, garlic, and salt to the dogberry puree and mix everything well.

Barberries Sauce

Ingredients:
Barberries - 1 cup
Garlic - 1-2 cloves
Cilantro - 4 sprigs

Parsley - 3 sprigs
Dill - 5 sprigs
Scallions - 1-2
Paprika, salt - to taste

Put picked over, cleaned, and washed barberries into a pot, add enough water to cover, bring to boil, and cook 15-20 minutes, then remove from heat and pass through a sieve together with cooking liquid. Add finely chopped herbs (cilantro, dill, parsley), paprika, scallions (green part only), season with salt and mix well.

Sauce with Sour Fruit Leather (Tklapi)

Ingredients:
Sour fruit leather - 100 g
Cilantro, garlic, chili pepper, salt - to taste

Cut sour fruit leather (from tkemali plums, blackthorn plums, dogberries, or plums) into small pieces, put into a ceramic or enameled pot, add boiling water to cover, cover the pot and let it soften for a few hours. Mash sour fruit leather then pass it through a sieve, add mashed cilantro leaves, crushed chili peppers, salt, and garlic. Mix everything well.

Walnut Sauce (A)

Ingredients:
Shelled walnuts - 3/4 cup
Water - 1 cup
Coriander seeds - 1 tsp
Imereti saffron - 1/2 tsp, crushed
Wine vinegar, cilantro, garlic, chili pepper, salt - to taste

Thoroughly pound walnuts together with garlic, and cilantro leaves in a mortar, then add crushed chili peppers, Imereti saffron, crushed coriander seeds, mix everything with wine vinegar and water.

Walnut Sauce (B)

Ingredients:
Shelled walnuts - 1 cup
Pomegranate juice - 1/2 cup
Water - 3/4-1 cup
Garlic - 1-2 cloves
Imereti saffron, coriander seeds, dried suneli - 1/2 tsp each
Cilantro - 2-3 sprigs
Chili peppers, salt - to taste

Thoroughly pound together shelled walnuts, garlic, salt, and cilantro in a mortar, squeeze walnut oil from the mixture and set it aside. Add crushed coriander seeds, crushed Imereti saffron, chopped cilantro, ground dried suneli to the walnut mixture and mix everything well. Thin the mixture with pomegranate juice and water to the desired consistency. Pour the sauce into a sauce boat, sprinkle it with pomegranate seeds and drizzle with walnut oil.

Garlic Sauce (A)

Ingredients:
Garlic - 6-8 cloves
Water or stock - 1/2-3/4 cup
Salt - to taste

Lightly season garlic with salt and pound in a mortar until it is completely mashed. Transfer mashed garlic to a sauce boat, add stock or water and mix well. Serve this sauce with cold dishes, boiled or fried turkey, chickens, spring chickens, fish, or with boiled lamb.

Garlic Sauce (B)

Ingredients:
Garlic - 8 cloves
Coriander seeds - 1/2 tsp
Wine vinegar - 1/4 cup
Water - 1/2-3/4 cup
Salt - to taste

Add crushed coriander seeds to the garlic thoroughly pounded with some salt in a mortar, then mix it with wine vinegar diluted with water. Serve is a sauce boat.

DISHES WITH EGGS, DAIRY AND FLOUR

Hard-Boiled Eggs with Walnut Sauce

Ingredients:
Eggs - 6
Shelled walnuts - 1 cup
Garlic - 1 clove
Cilantro - 1 sprig
Wine vinegar or pomegranate juice - to taste
Chili pepper, Imereti saffron - to taste

Cook eggs until hard-boiled stage, cool and peel them cut each in half lengthwise and set on a serving plate.

Pound shelled walnuts together with garlic, chili peppers, Imereti saffron, and salt in a mortar. Mix in 1 cup of water and add to taste wine vinegar or pomegranate juice. Pour sauce over prepared eggs.

Eggs with Green Beans

Ingredients:
Eggs - 3
Green beans - 100 g
Cooking fat - 1 tbsp
Salt - to taste

Clean, wash, and break green beans into smaller pieces. Put prepared beans into a boiling salted water and cook over high heat for 15-20 minutes, then drain in a colander. Transfer drained beans into a hot skillet with cooking fat and sauté for a while, the pour in beaten eggs and cook until eggs are set.

Omelette with Walnuts

Ingredients:
Eggs - 2
Butter - 10-15 g
Shelled walnuts - 30 g
Lemon, salt - to taste

Beat eggs, season them with salt, add crushed walnuts, mix everything well and pout into a hot skillet with butter. Cook until eggs are set.

Omelette with Eggplants

Peel eggplants and thinly slice them across into rounds, put in one layer on a well-oiled hot skillet, fry on both sides. Season eggplants with salt, then pour eggs beaten with finely chopped parsley and basil leaves, and continue cooking until eggs are done.

Omelette with Suluguni Cheese

Ingredients:
Suluguni cheese - 50 g
Eggs - 3
Butter - 10 g

Cut young suluguni cheese into thin strips, put in one layer on a hot skillet with butter. In 2-3 minutes pour beaten eggs into the skillet over the cheese and cook until eggs are set.

Omelette with Tomatoes

Ingredients:
Tomatoes - 2
Eggs - 3
Butter - 10
Ground black pepper, salt - to taste

Wash tomatoes, cut them into pieces, put into a hot skillet with butter, season with salt and pepper. When all tomato juice evaporates add butter and beaten eggs and cook until eggs are set. Serve in the same skillet it was cooked.

Omelette with Scallions

Ingredients:
Eggs - 3
Scallion - 1
Cooking fat - 15 g
Salt - to taste

Finely chop cleaned and washed scallion, season with salt, put into a hot oiled skillet and cook until softened. Smooth the layer of scallion in the skillet and pour beaten eggs over. Cook until eggs are set.

Omelette with Walnuts and Pomegranates

Ingredients:
Eggs - 4
Shelled walnuts - 1 cup
Onion - 1
Butter - 1 tbsp
Pomegranate seeds, chili peppers, salt - to taste

Thoroughly pound shelled walnuts. Finely dice onion and soften it in butter.

Beat eggs, add crushed walnuts, softened onions, salt, crushed chili peppers, mix well, then add pomegranate seeds and carefully mix again. Put egg mixture into a hot buttered skillet, cover the skillet, and cook until eggs are done.

Matsoni

Pour boiled and cooled until lukewarm milk into a half-quart jar, add one teaspoon of starter culture, mix well and cover the jar. Wrap the jar with a blanket to keep it warm and set it aside until done - approximately 5-7 hours.

Eggs Poached in Milk

Ingredients:
Milk - 3 cups
Eggs - 4
Salt - to taste

Add whole eggs, one after another, into a pot with boiling milk, and cook until eggs are done. Eggs should keep their shape. Season with salt to taste and serve hot.

Noodles with Walnuts

Ingredients:
Wheat flour - 500 g
Shelled walnuts - 300 g
Onions - 3
Salt - to taste

Sift wheat flour to a clean work surface, make a well in the middle of the mound, and adding salted water little by little, make a stiff dough.

Roll the dough out thinly on a board dusted with flour, cut it into strips, and then cut each strip into noodles.

Thoroughly pound shelled walnuts and mix them with water.

Dice onions, put them into a pot with boiling water, add mix with water crushed walnuts and let it simmer for a while. Add noodles to the pot and cook until noodles are done.

If desired - add mashed garlic to the noodles.

Gomi (A)

Ingredients:
Italian millet - 1 cup
Water - 3 cups

Pick over Italian millet, wash in cold water, put into a pot, cover with warm water, and bring to boil. Skim the foam as it rises to the top and stir and mash contents of the pot from time to time. When millet is cooked through, mix and mash it for about 10 minutes, then cover the pot and keep over a low heat for a couple of minutes to let the grain to dry a bit.

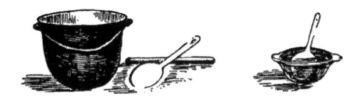

Cooked gomi should have a consistency of a medium-thickness porridge. Thoroughly mix it once more, then transfer into serving plates with a moistened wooden spoon. Serve hot.

Gomi (B)

Ingredients:
Italian millet - 1 cup
Water - 4 cups
Corn flour - 2-3 tbsp

Pick Italian millet over, wash in cold water, put into a pot, cover with warm water and bring to boil. Skim the foam as it rises to the top, and periodically stir and mash millet in the pot. When millet is cooked add corn flour to the pot and mix it in finely, cover the pot and continue cooking over low heat until done.

Once more mix everything well mashing it in the process, then transfer to serving plates with a moistened in cold water wooden spoon. Serve hot.

Gomi from Coarsely Ground Corn

Ingredients:
Coarsely ground corn - 1 cup
Water - 3 1/2-4 cups
Corn flour - 3-4 tbsp

Put coarsely ground corn into a pot, add water, bring to boil and cook until it is done. Add corn flour to the pot, mix everything well, and continue cooking and mixing over low heat until the flour loses its smell and taste of raw flour.

Gomi with Corn Flour (A)

Ingredients:
Corn flour - 2 cups
Water - 3 cups

Pour water into a pot, add sifted corn flour, mix everything well to break clumps, and bring to boil, mixing from time to time and breaking clumps agains the walls of the pot. Stop cooking when all the water evaporates and gomi thickens and loses taste of raw flour.

Transfer hot gomi into serving plates and serve. It should be served with kharcho, satsivi, or beans.

Gomi with Corn Flour (B)

Ingredients:
Corn flour - 2 1/2 cup
Water - 3 1/2-4 cups
Rice - 2 tbsp

This dish is cooked following instructions of the previous recipe; however, picked over and washed rice is added to the water first. Corn flour is added only when rice is cooked.

Gomi with Cheese

Slice imereti cheese or suluguni cheese into long, thin strips. Cook gomi as described previously, put a thin layer of gomi on a serving plate, top it with layer of cheese slices, and cover cheese with remaining gomi.

Elardzhi

Ingredients:
Corn flour - 1 cup
Water - 2-3 cups
Cheese - 300-400 g

Bring water to boil in a pot, add sifted corn flour, thoroughly mix to break lumps. Stir contents of the pot from time to time during cooking to break any lumps. When porridge thickens add finely chopped cheese (imereti) and cook, stirring all the time, until all the cheese is incorporated.

Chemkva

Ingredients:
Milk - 3-4 cups
Cheese - 500 g
Corn flour - 2-2 1/2 cups

Cut low-salt cheese (imereti) into small pieces, add it to the pot with boiling mil, and cook, stirring, 5-8 minutes. Gradually add sifted corn flour and continue cooking constantly mixing and breaking lumps against walls of the pot. When the porridge thickens, lower the heat but continue cooking 3-5 minutes longer. Transfer cooked chemkva to serving plates and serve hot.

Mchadi

Ingredients:

Corn flour - 3 cups
Water - 1 1/2 cups

Sift corn flour into a bowl, add cold water and mix a dough (the dough should be wet). Dip your hands in water, shape the dough into a ball, put into a preheated skillet, flatten the ball, cover the skillet and bake on the stove. When one side mchadi is cooked - flip it over and continue cooking without covering the skillet.

Mchadi can be baked on a baking sheet in a preheated oven or a hearth.

Mchadi Baked in Stone Ketsi

In a bowl mix sifted corn flour with warm water to get a wet, sticky dough.

Heat up stone ketsi (ed. note - stone or ceramic skillet) in a fire, put dough into it, flatten the dough, cover ketsi with a hot tin sheet, put glowing coals on top of this sheet and bake until done, approximately 40-60 minutes.

Mchadi Baked in Clay Ketsi

Make dough with corn flour as described above. Heat up two clay ketsi, put prepared dough into one ketsi and flatten it with a hand moistened in water. Top the dough with the second ketsi. Add glowing coals to the ketsi on the top and bake until mchadi is cooked.

Another way to bake mchadi in clay ketsi is to put the ketsi with dough close to the fire and bake until mchadi is done.

Mchadi with Beans

Ingredients:
Corn flour - 500 g

Beans - 200 g
Onion - 1
Cilantro and parsley - 2-3 sprigs each
Salt - to taste

Make a dough from corn flour just like described above. Cook and drain beans. Mix beans with diced onion, chopped parsley and cilantro leaves, season with salt and mix well.

Stuff the dough with bean mixture and bake in a preheated skillet or ketsi.

Mchadi with Cheese

This dish is cooked just like "Mchadi with Beans"; however, instead of beans, the dough is stuffed with cut into small pieces imereti cheese.

Mchadi with Butter

While mixing a dough for mchadi, add clarified butter (2 tbsp of butter per 500 g of corn flour) and season it with salt. Bake following instructions described above.

DISHES WITH RICE

Rice Pilaf (A)

Ingredients:
Rice - 500 g
Eggs or potatoes - 2-3
Butter or clarified butter - 200 g
Salt - to taste

Put picked over and thoroughly washed in warm water rice into a pot with boiling salted water and cook until half-done, then drain it in a colander and rinse a few times with cold water.

Meanwhile put some of the butter into a clean pot and put the pot on a stove. When the butter is melted add eggs beaten with some salt to the pot, or, if using potatoes, put thinly sliced potatoes in one layer on a bottom of the pot.

Approximately 3-5 minutes later put parboiled rice in a mound in the pot, add remaining butter, tightly cover the pot and set it over low heat. Wrap moistened towel around the cover to prevent steam from escaping the pot. Cook about 60-70 minutes.

Serve cooked pilaf on a serving plate. Put fried eggs or potatoes on top of the rice.

Pilaf can be covered with a sweet sauce or preserves, in which case fried eggs or potatoes should be set around the rice on the plate. Sauce can also be served on a side.

Rice Pilaf (B)

Pick rice over and wash it. Pour 2 cups of water int a pot, add a little salt, and bring water to boil. When water comes to boil add 30-50 g of butter, clarified butter, or vegetable oil, then add one cup of rice and cook at a simmer until rice absorbs all the water. Do not mix the rice while it is cooking.

When all the water is absorbed add more butter or oil (40-50 g), lower the heat, cover the pot, and cook 30-40 minutes longer.

Pilaf with Lamb Ragout

Ingredients:
Rice - 500 g
Butter - 200 g
Eggs or potatoes - 2-3
Salt - to taste
Lamb - 500 g
Onions - 2-3
Butter or vegetable oil - 70-100 g

Salt - to taste

Cook rice pilaf (A) and at the same time cook lamb ragout as follows: Cut lamb into medium-sized pieces, put it into a preheated skillet and brown on all sides. Season lamb with salt, add diced onions and butter or vegetable oil, and continue cooking until lamb is cooked through.

Put half of the cooked pilaf on a serving plate, top it with lamb ragout, and then cover lamb with remaining pilaf. Top with fried eggs or potatoes.

Pilaf with Lamb or Poultry

Ingredients:
Rice - 500 g
Lamb or poultry - 500 g
Potatoes - 2
Butter - 100 g
Salt - to taste

Cook rice pilaf (A) until rice is half-done. Fry lamb or poultry (chicken, spring chicken, or pheasant) whole, then cut into serving pieces.

Peel and wash potatoes. Slice them across into thin circles.

Melt butter in a wide pot and set potato slices in one layer on the bottom of the pan. About 2-3 minutes from the start of cooking put half of the prepared rice on top of potatoes. Set cooked meat over rice, and top it with remaining rice and add more butter. Cover the pot and put a moistened kitchen towel around the cover to prevent steam from escaping. Lower the heat and cook 30-40 minutes.

Pilaf with Fried Spring Chicken

Ingredients:
Rice - 500 g
Water - 2 cups
Butter - 100 g
Salt - to taste
Spring chicken - 1
Butter - 50-70 g
Seedless raisins - 100 g
Salt and ground black pepper - to taste

Cut spring chicken into pieces and brown it in a sauté pan, then season chicken with salt and ground black peppers, add butter (30 g) and cook it until done.

Melt 70 g of butter in a small skillet, and add picked over and washed seedless raisins. When raisins swell transfer them together with butter into the pan with chicken and mix everything well.

Meanwhile cook rice pilaf (B), transfer some the pilaf to a serving plate, top it with cooked chicken with raisins, and cover with remaining pilaf.

Rice Pilaf with Chicken (A)

Ingredients:
Rice - 2 cups
Chicken - 1
Chicken broth - 4 cups
Salt - to taste

Boil fatty chicken in a pot until done. Strain 4 cups of chicken broth together with fat into a clean pot, return to boil, and once it starts boiling, add picked over and washed rice, cover the pot, and cook until all the water is absorbed.

Remove cover from the pot, gather rice into a mound in

the middle of the pot, cover the pot and keep it over very low heat to let the rice swell. Remove cover from the pot from time to time and shake off any liquid that accumulates on it.

Cut boiled chicken into serving pieces and set it on one side of a serving plate, set rice on the opposite side of the plate.

Rice Pilaf with Chicken (B)

Ingredients:
Rice - 500 g
Chicken - 1
Eggs or potatoes - 2-3
Salt - to taste

Cook fatty chicken in water and cook rice until half-done following instructions of rice pilaf (A).

Skim fat from chicken broth and transfer it to a clean pot. Put this pot on a stove, and when the fat is hot - set a layer of thinly sliced potatoes or pour in beaten eggs. About 2-3 minutes later add prepared rice to the pot, add more fat or a little of chicken broth, cover the pot and cook over low heat 30-40 minutes.

Cut cooked chicken into servings and set them on one side of a serving plate. Mound rice on another side of the plate and set fried potatoes or eggs around it.

Pilaf with Sweet Sauce

Ingredients:
Rice - 500 g
Butter - 200 g
Eggs or potatoes - 2-3
Salt - to taste
Almonds - 200 g

Seedless raisins - 200 g
Pitted prunes - 200 g
Clarified butter - 3/4 cup
Granulated sugar - 1-1 1/2 cups
Honey - 3/4 cup

Cook rice pilaf (A) following recipe. To make sauce - blanch and skin almonds, then put into a clean pot together with 1/2 cup of boiling water and simmer for 15 minutes. Add picked over and washed raisins, pitted prunes, sugar, honey, clarified butter, mix everything well and cook 15 minutes longer.

Transfer cooked pilaf to a serving plate, pour sauce over it, and set fried eggs or potatoes around the rice. If desired -- serve sauce on a side.

Rice Pilaf with Raisins

Ingredients:
Rice - 1 cup
Butter - 100 g
Water - 2 cups
Seedless raisins - 200 g
Granulated sugar - 1 cup
Salt - to taste

Cook rice pilaf (B). When rice is completely cooked - take the cover off the pot and pour granulated sugar and picked over and washed raisins into the middle of the pot. Cover sugar and raisins with rice scooped from the sides, cover the pot, and continue cooking 20-30 minutes longer over very low heat.

Rice Porridge with Milk

Ingredients:
Rice - 1 cup
Milk - 3 cups
Sugar, cinnamon, salt - to taste

Put picked over and washed rice into boiling water (3/4-1 cup) and cook for 10 minutes, then add milk to the pot with rice and continue cooking over low heat, stirring from time to time. About 20-25 minutes later add sugar, and, if desired, salt, mix well, let it simmer 1 minute longer, remove from heat, pour porridge into serving bowls and sprinkle with ground cinnamon.

DISHES WITH CORN AND WHEAT

Boiled Corn Kernels with Walnuts and Raisins

Ingredients:
Shelled walnuts - 100 g
Seedless raisins - 50 g
Honey - 2 tbsp
Powdered sugar - 1 tbsp

Boil young corn on a cob in lightly salted water, then pick kernels off the cobs.

Pass shelled walnuts and raisins through a meat grinder, then add powdered sugar, honey, and corn kernels and mix everything well.

Grilled Corn on a Cob

Put cobs of the corn on a grill, or thread it on a skewer, and grill over hot, glowing coals, turning it frequently.

Kernels should cook through and slightly swell. Grilled corn should be served instantly, wrapped in husk leaves.

Boiled Corn on a Cob

Put whole cobs of corn into a pot (if the cob is too big — break it in half), add boiling water to cover, cover the pot and bring it to boil.

When corn is cooked take it out of the water, set on a serving plate and serve hot. Serve salt and butter on a side.

Corn can also be cooked in salted water, in which case do not serve salt. Only young corn should be cooked this way.

Corn Kernels with Walnuts

Ingredients:
Corn kernels - 300 g
Shelled walnuts - 1/4 cup
Garlic - 1 clove
Cilantro - 2 sprigs
Chili peppers, wine vinegar, salt - to taste

Put picked over and washed corn kernels into an enameled or ceramic pot, cover with warm water, cover the pot, and set it aside for a few hours to soak. Transfer corn kernels into a clean pot, cover with the same water they were soaking in, bring to boil, and cook until corn is cooked. Drain in a colander.

Pound shelled walnuts together with garlic and salt in a mortar. Squeeze walnut oil from the mixture and set aside in a separate container.

Thoroughly pound cilantro with chili peppers, and mix with walnuts and wine vinegar. Add cooked corn to this mixture and mix everything well. Drizzle finished dish with walnut oil.

Kutiya (Wheat Porridge)

Ingredients:
Wheat kernels - 500 g
Granulated sugar - 1 1/2 cups
Honey - 1/2 cup

Wash picked over wheat kernels with cold water, put it into a pot with boiling water, and cook until it is soft and cooked through, and all the water has evaporated. Remove the pot from the heat, add sugar, honey, and mix everything well.

Kutiya with Walnuts and Raisins (Wheat Porridge)

Ingredients:
Wheat kernels - 2 cups
Granulated sugar - 1 cup
Shelled walnuts - 1 cup
Honey - 1/2 cup
Raisins - 200 g

Put picked over and washed wheat kernels into a pot with boiling water, return to boil, and cook until kernels are soft and all the water has evaporated. Remove the pot from the stove, add granulated sugar, honey, crushed walnuts, and raisins, and mix everything well. Kutiya can be made without the honey (quantity of sugar would have to be increased) and without raisins.

Kutiya with Walnuts and Onions (Wheat Porridge)

Ingredients:
Wheat kernels - 3 cups

Onions - 3
Crushed shelled walnuts - 1 cup
Granulated sugar - 1/2 cup
Salt - to taste

Cook picked over and washed wheat kernels as described above; just before the end of the cooking add finely diced onions, and season with salt. When wheat is cooked through - remove the pot from heat and mix in crushed walnut and sugar.

Toasted What Porridge with Butter

Lightly toast picked over wheat kernels in a skillet, then coarsely mill toasted wheat and sift it through a sieve.
Put milled wheat into a pot and cook until half-done, then add bran, mix well, and continue cooking until done. Season porridge with salt and remove from heat.
Transfer cooked porridge to serving plates and top with butter or clarified butter.

Tolokno (Crushed Wheat Porridge)

Ingredients:
Wheat kernels - 2 cups
Granulated sugar - 1/2 cup
Honey - 1 tbsp

Toast picked over wheat kernels in a skillet, then mill them.
Add sugar to 1/2 cup of boiling water and simmer until all the sugar is dissolved, then remove from heat and let it cool. Pour syrup over ground wheat, then add honey, and mix everything well.
Tolokno can be cooked without honey. Finished tolokno can be sprinkled with picked over seedless raisins and

blanched almonds. Tolokno can also be cooked with corn kernels.

PASTRY AND SWEETS

Hachapuri (Stuffed Bread) (A)

Ingredients:
Milk - 500 ml
or Matsoni - 2 cups
Eggs - 2
Salt - 1/4 tsp
Wheat flour - as much as necessary
Cheese Imeretinsky - 500 g
Eggs - 2

Cut Imeretinski cheese into thin, flat slices, put into a ceramic or enameled pot, cover with cold water, and leave to soak for 2-5 hours (depending on the saltiness of cheese). Drain the cheese in a colander, and, when all the water is drained, squeeze with your hand, transfer into a clean bowl, thoroughly mash it, add 2 eggs, and, if cheese is not too fatty, a tablespoon of butter, thoroughly mix everything and divide into four parts. If cheese is too young - not salted or low-salt - it does not have to be soaked. Just mash it, pass it through a sieve, or pass it through a meat grinder, and mix it with eggs.

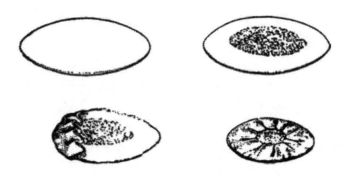

Make not very stiff dough with milk, salt, and wheat flour, or with matron, eggs, and what flour. Divide prepared dough into four parts, roll each part thinly, put prepared cheese in an even layer in the middle of each piece of dough, bring the sides of the dough up and either completely pinch the dough over the cheese, or shape it in the form of a Danish.

Hachapuri should have the size of the skillet in which it will be cooked.

Use cast iron skillet to cook hachapuri. Heat the skillet up, put hachapuri in, seam-side down, cover the skillet and bake covered in a preheated oven. When one side is cooked, flip hachapuri over and bake on the other side, leaving the skillet uncovered. Brush baked hachapuri with melted butter and serve hot. Cooled hachapuri should be warmed up before serving.

Hachapuri (Stuffed Bread) (B)

Ingredients:
Milk - 1 cup
Egg - 1
Butter - 50 g
Sugar - 1 tsp
Salt - 1/2 tsp
Wheat flour - 3 cups
Cheese - 500 g
Egg - 1
Butter - 50 g

Prepare cheese stuffing following instructions of the previous recipe.

Sift the flour, make a well in the middle of the flour, add 50 g of butter, egg, salt, sugar, pour in milk, mix a dough, divide it in half, and roll each half into a thin circle. Put prepared cheese stuffing in an even layer in the middle of each circle of dough and pinch the sides of the dough together so that the cheese stuffing is completely enclosed.

Heat a skillet with 25 g of butter, put prepared hachapuri into the skillet - seam side down, and cover the skillet. Bake in a preheated oven. When one side is baked, flip hachapuri over and continue baking uncovered.

Hachapuri (Stuffed Bread) (C)

Ingredients:
Milk - 2 cups
Salt - 1/4 tsp
Wheat flour - as much as necessary
Cheese - 500 g
Egg yolks - 2
Cheese - 50 g

Prepare the dough following instructions of the Hachapuri (A) recipe, roll it into a ball, then roll it out in a very thin circle, brush it with clarified butter and fold it twice. Sprinkle the work surface with some flour and roll the dough out again into a thin circle. Pick mashed low-salt cheese in the middle of the dough and pinch the sides together over cheese.

Hachapuri should be the size of the skillet in which it is cooked.

Warm up a cast-iron skillet, put hachapuri in, seam-side up, and bake in a preheated oven until done.

Mix egg yolks with mashed cheese, brush baked hachapuri with egg-mixture, return it to the oven, and bake until nicely browned.

Hachapuri (Stuffed Bread) (D)

Ingredients:

Matsoni (yogurt) - 2 cups
Egg - 1
Baking soda - 1/2 tsp
Butter - 200-250 g
Wheat flour - as much as necessary
Cheese - 500-600 g
Egg - 1
Butter for brushing - 2 tsp

Mash low-salt cheese and mix it with an egg. Add baking powder to matsoni, beat it in, add egg, then add wheat flour and make not a very stiff dough. Divide the dough into four parts, roll each one into a thin circle, brush with butter, then fold sides in, in a shape of an envelope, then roll each of these "envelopes" out into thin circles again.

Brush one of the circles with butter, cover with another circle, brush it with butter, put an even layer of prepared cheese on top and pinch sides of the dough together to completely enclose the stuffing. Put hachapuri seam-side down into a preheated cast-iron skillet, and bake in a preheated oven. Brush baked hachapuri with melted butter. Repeat the process with the third and fourth circles of dough.

Rich Dough Hachapuri (Stuffed Bread)

Ingredients:
Eggs - 2
Milk - 1 1/2 cups
Baking soda - 1/2 tsp
Vinegar - 1 tbsp
Clarified butter - 2 tbsp
Wheat flour - as much as necessary
Cheese - 500 g
Eggs - 2
Clarified butter - 1 tbsp

Mix raw eggs with 2 tablespoons of clarified butter and beat well, then add baking soda (mixed with a small quantity of vinegar) and milk, mix well, then add wheat flour (enough to make not a very stiff dough) and make a dough. Divide the dough into two equal parts, roll out each until 1/2 cm thick. Put one sheet of dough into a baking sheet sprinkled with flour. Make cheese stuffing by mashing the cheese and mixing it with eggs and clarified butter. Set cheese stuffing on top of the first sheet in an even layer, cover it with the second sheet of dough and pinch sides of both sheets of dough together. Bake in a preheated oven.

Hachapuri with Yeast Dough

Ingredients:
Water or milk - 1 cup
Lard or butter - 2 tbsp
Egg - 1
Salt - 1/2 tsp
Cheese - 600-700 g
Egg - 1
For brushing:
Egg - 1/2
Milk - 2 tsp
Clarified butter - 2 tsp

Prepare yeast dough with sponge or straight method and divide it into two equal parts. Roll each half into a thin circle. Put cheese in the middle of each circle and pinch sides together leaving the middle open - like a Danish. Transfer hachapuri to a baking sheet sprinkled with flour, brush with egg beaten with milk, and bake in a preheated oven.

Put 1 tsp of butter in the middle of each hachapuri and serve hot.

Hachapuri with Beans

Make a simple dough for hachapuri from wheat flour and water, roll it out thinly, put an even layer of prepared beans on top of the dough, then cook following instructions of hachapuri (A) or hachapuri (B).
To make bean stuffing — cook beans until soft, drain in a colander, and pass them through a sieve. Transfer bean puree to a clean pot, add melted lard (2 tbsp of lard for 500 g of dry beans), season beans with salt and sauté until heated through, then cool.

Hachapuri with Potatoes

Make a simple dough for hachapuri from wheat flour and water, roll it out thinly, put an even layer of potato stuffing on top of the dough, then cook following instructions of hachapuri (A) or hachapuri (B).
To prepare potato stuffing boil peeled potatoes until cooked through. Season potatoes with salt, thoroughly mash them. Let the stuffing cool before using.

Hachapuri with Cheese and Potato Stuffing

Thoroughly crumble cheese and mix it with mashed potatoes (one part of cheese to three parts of potatoes by weight).
Make a simple dough for hachapuri from wheat flour and water, roll it out thinly, put an even layer of prepared

stuffing on top of the dough, then cook following instructions of hachapuri (A) or hachapuri (B).

Hachapuri with Beet Greens

Finely chop fresh beet greens, season with salt, and set them aside for 30-40 minutes. Thoroughly squeeze beet greens with your hand, add crumbled cheese (Imeretisnky, unsalted). Stuff simple dough with this mixture and bake just like hachapuri.

Brindzhula

Make a thin batter just like for pancakes with salted water and wheat flour. Pour it into a preheated baking pan or ketsi to form 2-3 cm thick layer, then sprinkle crumbled unsalted imeretinsky cheese about 3-4 cm thick, and bake in a preheated oven until done.

If using ketsi to bake this dish - cover it with a sheet of tin and top the tin with glowing coals.

Gvedzeli

Make a simple dough, just like for hachapuri. Crumble imereti fresh unsalted cheese (400-500 g), add chopped hard-boiled egg and mix everything well.
Roll the dough into a thin sheet, spread prepared cheese stuffing on half of the sheet. Top stuffing with hard-boiled eggs cut into quarters lengthwise (3-4 eggs). Top the stuffing with the other half of the dough and pinch sides together. Bake in a preheated oven.

Hachapuri

Hachapuri can be baked with any dough: puff pastry, rich dough, yeast dough, bread dough, or unleavened dough, and can have any shape - round, square, open, closed. The best cheese to use in stuffing is fresh unsalted imereti cheese; however, hachapuri can also be made with and type of fresh cheese (feta or any other).

Nazuki

Ingredients:
Wheat flour - 4 cups
Eggs - 2
Milk - 3 cups
Fresh yeast - 1/3 cups
Sugar - 1 cup
Clarified butter - 1 1/3 cups
Salt - 1 tsp
Ground cinnamon and cloves - 1/2 tsp each

Put 3 cups of sifted wheat flour into a bowl. Gradually add boiling milk (1 1/2 cups) constantly mixing with a whisk to break any clumps. Cover the bowl with the dough with a clean towel and set it aside for one hour. Gradually add remaining 1 1/2 cups milk to the dough, 1/3 cup not very thin yeast, sugar, eggs, salt, cinnamon, cloves, and remaining 1 cup of flour to the dough, mixing well to incorporate. Leave the dough to rise in a warm place. When the dough has risen, punch it down while adding warm butter and more flour - enough to get a soft dough. Knead until the dough pulls away from the sides of the bowl, then leave it again in warm place for 1 1/3 - 2 hours.

Transfer the dough to a work surface dusted with flour, cut it into pieces, shape each piece into a ball, and then roll each ball into an oblong shape, transfer to a baking sheet dusted with flour, make a grooves or indentations with a dull side of a knife, brush with an egg-yolk beaten with a small quantity of water or milk, and bake in a preheated oven.

If desired - use lard instead of clarified butter in this recipe.

Pie

Ingredients:
Eggs - 2
Granulated sugar - 1 1/2 cups
Sour cream - 1 cup
Clarified butter - 3/4 cup
Baking soda - 1/2 tsp
Lemon zest - 1/2 tsp
Salt - 1/4 tsp
Wheat flour - As much as necessary
Crumb mixture:
Wheat flour - 1/2 cup
Clarified butter - 2-3 tbsp

Beat whole eggs with sugar until white, then gradually add sour cream, clarified butter, lemon zest, and enough flour to mix a soft dough. Mix baking soda into the dough.

In a separate bowl thoroughly mix 1/2 cup of flour with 2-3 tbsp of clarified butter.

Transfer prepared dough into a buttered baking pan, smooth the top, then crumble separately mixed flour with butter over the dough, and bake in a preheated oven.

Pie with Raisins and Walnuts

Ingredients:
Wheat flour - 1 kg
Shelled walnuts - 300 g

Seedless raisins - 2 cups
Clarified butter - 1 1/3 cup
Granulated sugar - 2 cups
Simple syrup - 1/2 cup
Salt - to taste

Mix a dough with wheat flour, water, and salt. Melt 2 tbsp of clarified butter in a skillet, then add picked over and washed seedless raisins. Sauté until raisins swell. Remove the skillet from heat, add crushed walnuts, granulated sugar, and mix everything well.

Divide the dough into 4 parts and roll each one out into a thin sheet.

Set one of the sheets of dough on a baking sheet sprinkled with flour, brush it with melted clarified butter, and top with an even layer of about 1/3 of walnut and raisin mixture. Set another sheet of dough on top of walnut stuffing and repeat the process of brushing the dough with clarified butter and topping it with walnut and raisin mixture. When the pie is covered with the final sheet of dough - pinch the sides of the dough together and brush the top with egg-yolk beaten with a small quantity of water or milk. Make a shallow cuts in a shape of diamond in the dough. Bake in a preheated oven until done.

When the pie is done deepen the cuts made previously and pour prepared simple syrup over pie.

Walnut Pie

Ingredients:
Eggs - 4, separated
Granulated sugar - 3 cups
Lemon zest - 1 tsp
Shelled walnuts - 1 1/2 cups

Milk - 1 cup
Clarified butter - 1 cup
Pitted prunes - 100 g
Raisins - 100 g
Salt - 1/2 tsp
Fruit jam - 2 tbsp
Wine vinegar - 1 tbsp
Baking soda - 1 tsp
Wheat flour - 800 g
Egg yolk - 1
Milk - 2 tsp
Walnuts, granulated sugar - for decoration

Beat egg yolks with sugar until white. Mix a dough by gradually add grated lemon zest, melted butter, salt, warm milk, wine vinegar, baking soda mixed with wine vinegar, crushed walnuts, and 500 g of flour to the beaten egg yolks.

Continue mixing the dough while adding raisins, finely chopped prunes, fruit jam, whipped egg-whites, and, finally, remaining 300 g of flour.

Transfer the dough to a buttered baking pan, smooth the top of the dough with your hand greased with clarified butter, brush the top with egg yolk beaten with milk or water, decorate with walnut halves and sprinkle with granulated sugar, and bake in a preheated oven.

Lightly cool baked pie, then remove from the pan.

Puff Pastry Cake with Walnuts

Ingredients:
Eggs - 2
Wine vinegar - 1 tbsp
Salt - 1/2 tsp
Water - 500 ml
Wheat flour - as much as necessary
Lard - 250 g

Shelled walnuts - 2 cups
Raisins - 1 1/2 cups
Sugar - 3 cups
Egg yolk - 1
Milk or water - 2 tsp

Thoroughly mix eggs, wine vinegar, and salt with water, then, gradually adding flour, mix not a very stiff dough. Divide the dough into four parts, roll each piece of dough out thinly into a rectangle, brush it with melted lard, fold in a shape of an envelope, brush with lard once more, and put into a cold place to rest. Repeat this process four times. Finally, roll each piece of dough thinly, brush with lard, fold in a shape of an envelope and roll it out thinly to a size of the baking sheet it will be baked in. Transfer rolled out sheet to the baking sheet, prick in a few places with a tip of a knife and bake in a preheated oven. Brush the final sheet of puff pastry with milk or egg yolk mixed with water before baking.

To make stuffing pass shelled walnuts, raisins, and granulated sugar through a meat grinder twice. If desired - add ground cinnamon (1 tsp).

Assemble the cake by alternating baked pastry and walnut stuffing layers. Final layer should be the pastry brushed with milk or egg wash before baking. Carefully cut the cake into diamonds.

Honey Cake

Ingredients:
Eggs - 3
Honey - 1 cup
Granulated sugar - 1 cup
Ground cinnamon - 1 tsp

Ground cloves - 1/2 tsp
Baking soda - 1 tsp
Salt - 1/4 tsp
Wheat flour - 3 cups
Egg yolk - 1
Milk or water - 2 tsp
Almonds or walnuts - to taste

Mix flour with granulated sugar, baking soda, ground cinnamon and cloves. Pour prepared flour into a mound on a clean board, make a well in the middle of the mound, put eggs, honey, and salt and mix a dough.

Transfer prepared dough into a buttered baking pan, smooth the top, brush it with egg yolk beaten with milk or water, decorate with almonds or walnuts, and bake in a preheated oven.

Tea Cake

Ingredients:
Eggs - 2, separated
Granulated sugar - 1 1/2 cups
Clarified butter - 2 tbsp
Fruit jam - 2 tbsp
Wheat flour - 2 cups
Tea - 1 cup
Baking soda - 1 tsp
Wine vinegar - 1/4 cup
Salt - 1/4 tsp
Fruit jam - 3/4 cup
Toasted walnuts - 3/4-1 cup
Butter - 2 tsp
Crushed breadcrumbs - 1/2 tbsp

Brew a strong tea (steep two teaspoons of tea leaves for 1 1/4 cups of boiling water, then strain).

Melt granulated sugar (1/2 cup) until caramelized. Gradually add strained tea (do this carefully to avoid being burned by steam) and mix. When all the sugar has melted - remove caramel from heat and let it cool.

Meanwhile beat egg yolks with sugar (1 cup) until white, add a mixture of melted butter and fruit jam, then add cooled tea caramel, mix everything well. Add wine vinegar mixed with baking soda, quickly stir it in, then gradually add salt and flour while mixing all the time. Finally fold in whipped egg whites. Transfer the dough into a buttered and sprinkled with crushed breadcrumbs or flour baking pan. Bake in a preheated oven.

Cool baked cake, brush the top with fruit jam and sprinkle with toasted walnuts.

Kada (A)

Ingredients:
Wheat flour - 1 1/2 cups
Butter - 100 g
Water - 1/2 cup
Salt - 1/4 tsp
Stuffing:
Wheat flour - 3 tbsp
Butter - 300 g
Sugar - 3/4-1 cup

Sift flour into a mound on a work surface, make a well in the middle of the mound, pour 1/2 cup of water and add 1/4 tsp of salt and quickly mix a dough. Roll the dough out to a sheet about 1 cm thick, brush it with butter (100 g), fold it twice, and leave in a cold place for 10 minutes. Roll the dough out again, and fold it twice and return to the cold place for another 10 minutes. Repeat the process 2-3 times (the dough is not brushed with butter these times).

Meanwhile prepare stuffing - toast 3 full tablespoons of flour in a skillet until it is lightly covered, add 100 g of butter and sauté everything together. Remove the skillet from heat and add sugar to it. Mix everything well.

Divide prepared dough into 2 parts. Roll each half into a thin circle or rectangular sheet, spread half of the stuffing over each sheet, roll each sheet into a roll, then twist it and slightly flatten with your hand. Transfer to a baking sheet lightly dusted with flour, and bake in a preheated oven.

Kada (B)

Ingredients:
Wheat flour - 3 cups
Butter - 200 g
Salt - 1/2 tsp
Baking soda - 1/3 tsp
Matsoni (yogurt) - 1 cup
Egg - ½
Stuffing:
Clarified butter - 1/2 cup
Granulated sugar - 1 cup
Wheat flour - 1 1/2 cups
Salt - 1/2 tsp
Egg - ½
Milk or water - 2-3 tsp

Sift flour into a mound on a work surface, make a well in the middle of the mound, put butter and salt into the well and chop it with a knife into very small pieces. Gather flour mixed with butter into a mound, make a well in the middle and put matsoni mixed with baking soda and half of an egg into this well. Mix a dough, divide it into three parts and put it into a cold place.

Meanwhile prepare stuffing - beat clarified butter with a wooden spoon, add granulated sugar and beat it together with butter. Add flour and salt to creamed butter and mix everything together. Divide this mixture into three parts, then divide each part into three parts to get nine parts. Roll one pieces of chilled dough into a very thin circle, then crumble a piece of prepared stuffing over the dough. Fold the dough in half and pinch sides together, then roll it out thinly and crumble another piece of stuffing over it. Fold the dough in half again and pinch sides together. Roll it out thinly and crumble the third piece of stuffing over it. Fold the dough and pinch the sides; however, do not roll it out

305

this time, just flatten it with your hand. Cut the prepared dough into eight wedges, transfer to a baking sheet, brush with egg mixed with water or milk, and bake in a preheated oven.

Gozinaki

Ingredients:
Shelled walnuts - 800-1000 g
Honey - 1 kg

Lightly toast shelled walnuts in a skillet, then thinly slice them.

Pour honey into a pot for cooking preserves, put the pot on the stove, and simmer honey constantly stirring. When honey is reduced so that a drop of it on a plate will not spread, add prepared walnuts to the honey, and continue cooking until the honey caramelizes. Transfer the mixture to a clean, moistened with water, board and spread it using a spoon or a rolling pin also moistened with cold water until honey mixture forms 1/2 - 1 cm thick layer.

Lightly cool prepared gozinaki and cut it into a diamonds.

To make a crunchy gozinaki - add 1/2 cup of sugar to the honey and walnuts while the mixture is still cooking. Gozinaki can be made with hazelnuts or almonds; however, when using almonds - blanch the nuts and peel them.

PRESERVES

Cooking Preserves

Use only white and clean sugar while cooking preserves. Put sugar into a tub or a pot used cooking preserves and add cold or hot water. Put the tub on the stove and bring to boil mixing all the time - until all the sugar dissolves. Syrup is ready after 1-2 minutes of simmering. Remove syrup from heat, add berries or fruits to it, then return it back to the stove and bring to boil. Lightly shake the tub to get berries or fruits to submerge in the syrup (berries or fruits have to be covered by syrup).

Preserves should be cooked over medium heat. Skim the foam rising to the top with a spoon or a skimmer. When the foam stops forming and the boiling slows down the preserves are almost ready. From this point on it requires constant attention; otherwise it might burn and acquire an unpleasant flavor. On the other hand, if preserves are removed from heat too early - it will be too liquid and will start fermenting after a while.

To preserve color and prevent crystallization in preserves from low-acid fruit or berries, like apricots or white cherries, it is recommended to add 1/4-1/2 tsp of lemon acid to the preserves for each 1 kg of sugar almost the end of the cooking.

To determine if preserves are cooked drip one drop of preserves onto a tea plate - the drop has to keep its shape and does not spread on the surface of the plate. Fruits or berries should not float to the top of the syrup but should be evenly distributed throughout the syrup. Good quality preserves should be clear and have a color of the berries or fruits used in its preparation.

Sour Cherry Preserves

Ingredients:
Sour cherries - 1 kg
Sugar - 1 kg
Water - 3/4-1 cup

Pick sour cherries over, wash in cold water. Add sugar to the pot(tub) for cooking preserves, add water, mix and bring to boil. Add cherries to the prepared syrup and cook until done (approximately 2 hours), shaking the pan from time to time and skimming foam.

Pitted Sour Cherry Preserves (A)

Ingredients:
Pitted sour cherries - 1 kg
Sugar - 1 kg
Cooking liquid - 3/4 cup

Pick sour cherries over, wash in cold water, then remove pits. Put cherry pits into a pot, cover with water, and bring to boil. Remove the pot from the heat and strain cooking liquid. Put sugar into a pot (tub) for cooking preserves, add strained cooking liquid and bring it to boil. Add prepared berries to the simmering syrup and cook until done (approximately 2 hours). Lightly shake the pot with cherries and skim the foam as it gathers on top of the syrup.

Pitted Sour Cherry Preserves (B)

Ingredients:
Pitted sour cherries - 1 kg
Sugar - 1 kg
Water - 1/2-3/4 cup

Remove pits from the picked over and washed in cold water sour cherries. Put sugar into a pot (tub) for cooking preserves, add water, mix and bring it to boil. Add prepared cherries to the syrup and cook until done (2 hours), shaking the pot from time to time and skimming foam.

Rainier Cherry Preserves

Ingredients:
Rainier cherries - 1 kg, pitted
Sugar - 1 kg
Water - 1/2 cup
Vanilla extract - to taste

Pick over rainier cherries, wash them in cold water and take out the pits. Add sugar and water into a pot (tub) for cooking preserves, add water and cook simple syrup. Add cherries into the syrup, carefully shake the pot to force berries to submerge, and cook until done (2-2 1/2 hours). Add vanilla extract to taste.

Rainier Cherry Preserves Cooked Without Water

Ingredients:
Rainier cherries - 1 kg, pitted
Sugar - 1 kg
Vanilla extract - to taste

Pick over and wash rainier cherries in water. Pit cherries and wash in cold water again - submerging and draining them three times. Set washed cherries in layers in a pot (tub) for cooking preserves, sprinkling each row of cherries with sugar. Put the pot on the stove and cook until done (2-2 1/2 hours). Add vanilla extract to taste. If desired - add slices of lemons to the cherries before the start of cooking.

Raspberry Preserves

Ingredients:

Raspberries - 3 kg
Sugar - 1 kg
Grain alcohol - 1/4 cup

Pick over raspberries, set berries in rows in large bowl, sprinkle each row with sugar (500 g), drizzle with alcohol, and put into a cool place for 5-6 hours. Transfer raspberries into a pot (tub) for cooking preserves, add remaining 500 g of sugar and cook until done (40-60 minutes), shaking the pot from time to time.

Strawberry Preserves

Ingredients:
Strawberries - 1 kg
Sugar - 1 kg
Water - 1/2 cup

Carefully pick over strawberries taking care not to damage the berries and remove stems. Cook a syrup from sugar and water in a pot (tub) for cooking preserves, remove the pot from heat. Add berries to the syrup, carefully shake the pot to get strawberries to submerge in the syrup, return the syrup to simmer and cook until done (60-80 minutes).

Strawberry Preserves Cooked Without Water

Ingredients:
Strawberries - 1 kg
Sugar - 1 kg

Put picked over strawberries in layers in a bowl, sprinkling each layer with sugar (500 g) and leave in a cool place for 5-6 hours. Transfer berries with all the released juices into pot (tub) for cooking preserves, add remaining 500 g of sugar, bring to simmer and cook until done (40-60 minutes), shaking the pot from time to time.

Wild Strawberry Preserves

Ingredients:
Wild strawberries - 1 kg
Sugar - 1 kg
Water - 1/2 cup
Cognac or brandy - 1 tbsp

Put picked over wild strawberries into a bowl, top it with sugar (500 g), drizzle with cognac or brandy and set aside in a cool place for a couple of hours. Strain juice released from berries, add 1/4 cup of water, remaining 500 g of sugar, and make a syrup. Put berries into the syrup. Rinse the bowl used top macerate berries and pour this water into the pot as well. Carefully shake the pot to force berries to submerge in the syrup, return syrup to simmer and cook until done (60-80 minutes).

Red Currants Preserves

Ingredients:
Red currants - 1 kg
Sugar - 1 kg
Water - 3/4-1 cup

Pick over red currants and remove stems, wash berries in cold water and drain them in a colander. Put sugar into a pot (tub) for cooking preserves, add water and make a syrup. Add red currants to the syrup, carefully shake the pot to force berries to submerge in the syrup, and cook until done

(50-60 minutes).

Blueberry Preserves

Ingredients:
Blueberries - 1 kg
Sugar - 750 g
Ground cinnamon - 3 g
Ground cloves - 1 g

   Carefully pick over blueberries, put into a colander and wash under a running water, then let all the water drain. Transfer berries into a pot (tub) for cooking preserves, add sugar, bring it to simmer, and cook until done (50-60 minutes) shaking the pot from time to time. Add ground cinnamon in cloves to the pot during cooking.

Blackberry Preserves

Ingredients:
Blackberries - 1 kg
Sugar - 1 kg

   Pick over blackberries and remove stems. Set berries in layers a pot (tub) for cooking preserves, sprinkling each layer with sugar, and set aside in a cool place for 4-5 hours. Put the pot on a stove and bring it to simmer. Cook until done (1-1 1/4 hours) shaking the pot from time to time.

Dogberry Preserves

Ingredients:
Dogberries - 1 kg
Sugar - 1 kg

Water - 1-1 1/2 cups

Pick over dogberries and wash them in cold water. Add sugar into a pot (tub) for cooking preserves, pour in water, mix it and bring to boil. Add prepared dogberries into the syrup and cook until done (2 hours). Carefully shake the pot during cooking and skim the foam rising to the top.

White Grape Preserves

Ingredients:
White grapes - 1 kg
Sugar - 1 kg
Water - 1/2-3/4 cup

Wash large clusters of ripe white grapes, remove seeds from the grapes, mix with sugar (500 g) and leave for 3-4 hours in a cool place. Make a syrup with remaining sugar and water and let it cool. Add prepared grapes to the syrup, carefully shake the pot to submerge berries in the syrup, return to simmer, and cook 1 1/2-2 hours.

Barberry Preserves

Ingredients:
Barberries - 1 kg
Sugar - 1.5 kg
Water - 2-2 1/2 cups

Wash picked over barberries in cold water. Make a syrup, let it cool, then pour it over prepared barberries and set aside for 1 day. Following day drain the syrup, bring it to simmer, cool it, pour it over berries and leave to infuse for one more day. Next day drain the syrup again, bring it to simmer, let it cool, pour it over berries, return to simmer and cook preserves until done.

Tomato Preserves

Ingredients:
Unripe small tomatoes - 1 kg
Sugar - 1200 g
Water - 1 1/2 cups

Pick over small unripe plum tomatoes, wash them in cold water and put into a pot (tub) for cooking preserves. Make a syrup with sugar and water, let it cool slightly, then pour it over prepared tomatoes and set it aside for one day. Following day drain the syrup into a clean pot, bring it to simmer, pour it over tomatoes again and set tomatoes aside for one more day. Repeat the process the next day; however, this time continue cooking preserves over low heat until done.

Melon Preserves

Ingredients:
Peeled melon - 1 kg
Sugar - 1 kg
Water - 1 cup
Cognac or brandy - 1 tbsp

Cut the rind off a hard, unripe melon, remove seeds from inside, the cut the flesh of the melon into long rectangle pieces using a carving knife. Put prepared melon into the pot (tub) for cooking preserves, sprinkle with 500 g of sugar, drizzle with cognac or brandy, and leave for 2-3 hours in a cool place. Meanwhile make syrup with remaining sugar, pour hot syrup over prepared melon and set it aside to infuse for one day. Following day drain the syrup from the melon, bring it to simmer, pour it back over melon, and cook preserves until done.

Quince Preserves

Ingredients:
Quinces - 1 kg, peeled
Sugar - 1 kg
Cooking liquid - 1-1 1/2 cups

Wash quinces, peel them, cut in half, remove cores, then cut each half into wedges.

Put peels from quinces into a pot, cover with water, bring to boil, and let them simmer for 1-2 minutes, then remove the pot from heat and strain the liquid. Put prepared quinces into a clean pot, add strained cooking liquid so it just barely covers the fruit and cook (10-15 minutes, depending on ripeness of fruit) until quinces become soft. Take quinces out of the pot with a skimmer and set them in one layer on a plate. Strain cooking liquid. Put sugar into a pot (tub) for cooking liquid, add strained cooking liquid and make a syrup. Put quinces into the simmering syrup and cook until done (2-2 1/2 hours).

Preserves with Whole Peaches

Ingredients:
Peaches - 1 kg
Sugar - 1 kg

Peel peaches washed in cold water and prick in a few places with a thin wooden pin. Put prepared peaches into a pot (tub) for cooking preserves, add sugar and leave in a cool place. About 4-5 hours later put the pot on the stove, bring to simmer and cook until done (2-2 1/2 hours).

Peach Preserves

Ingredients:
Peaches - 1 kg
Sugar - 1 kg

Peel washed peaches, cut them into wedges, and set cut peaches in layers in a pot (tub) for cooking preserves, sprinkle each layer with sugar, and leave in a cool place. About 4-5 hours later put the pot on a stove, bring to a simmer, and cook until done (2-2 1/2 hours).

Blackthorn Preserves

Ingredients:
Blackthorn - 1 kg
Sugar - 1 kg
Water - 1-1 1/2 cup

Wash picked over blackthorn with cold water, prick in a few places with a thin wooden pin. Cook syrup with sugar and water and let it cool. Put prepared blackthorn into the syrup and set it aside for one day. Take berries out of the syrup and bring syrup to boil. Return blackthorn to the syrup and cook until done (1 1/2-2 hours), skimming foam as it rises to the top.

Cherry Plum Preserves

Ingredients:
Cherry plums - 1 kg

Sugar - 1 kg
Water - 3/4-1 cup

Wash picked over cherry plums with cold water, prick in
a few places with a thin wooden pin. Cook syrup, pour it
over prepared cherry plums, and set it aside for one day.
Take plums out of the syrup and bring the syrup to boil.
Return plums to the syrup and cook until done (1 1/2-2
hours).

Tkemali Preserves

Ingredients:
Tkemali plums - 1 kg
Sugar - 1 1/2 kg
Water - 1 cup

Pick over and wash tkemali. Make a syrup and let it cool
a little. Put prepared tkemali plums into the syrup, return to
simmer and cook until done (2 hours).

Crabapples Preserves

Ingredients:
Crabapples - 1 kg
Sugar - 1 kg
Water - 1 1/2-2 cups

Pick over crabapples leaving the stems on, and wash
them in cold water. Prick crabapples in a few places with a
thin wooden pin, put into a bowl and pour boiling water
over them and leave for 15 minutes. Make a syrup. When
crabapples are cool - transfer them to a simmering syrup and
cook until done (2-3 hours).

Rose Petals Preserve

Ingredients:
Rose petals - 1 kg
Sugar - 4 kg 500 g
Water - 7 cups

Remove petals from red or pink roses, remove white base of each petal, mix with 600 g of sugar, rub petals between palms and thoroughly squeeze them. Put squeezed petals into a jar and pour 200 g of sugar over it, then add squeezed juice, cover the jar, and set it aside for one day. Take rose petals out of the jar, rub them between palms and squeeze them again. Set squeezed juice aside in a covered container. Remaining petals should weight 1 kg.

Put sugar (3 kg 700 g) into a pot (tub) for cooking preserves, add water and bring it to boil. Add squeezed rose petals to the syrup and cook over low heat until done. Add squeezed juice shortly before the end of cooking.

Green Walnuts Preserves

Reading through this recipe made us thankful that these days we can just buy green walnut preserves online or at your local food importer.

Ingredients:
Unripe walnuts – 100
Hydrated lime - 500 g
Alum - 1 tbsp
Sugar - 2 kg + 1 cup
Cinnamon - 2 tsp
Cloves – 10
Cardamom – 5
Vanilla extract - to taste

318

Peel medium-sized unripe walnuts removing the green outer skin, cover with cold water so that walnuts are completely submerged, and leave for three days, changing water three-four times a day. Drain the walnuts on the forth day and prick each one with a fork in a few places. Sprinkle walnuts with hydrated lime, cover with cold water, and leave it for three more days. Drain walnuts and thoroughly wash them under a running water. Cover washed walnuts with cold water and set aside for four days, changing water three times a day. On a fifth day drain the walnuts and parboil them for 15 minutes, then drain.

Bring water to boil in a clean pot, add alum, then add walnuts and boil for 15 minutes, then drain them in a colander. Once walnuts are drained put the into a boiling water for 5 minutes, then drain again. In another pot bring water to boil, put 1 cup of sugar into this water, then add walnuts and cook for 30 minutes. Drain in a colander.

Put 7 cups of water into a pot (tub) for cooking preserves, add sugar and bring everything to boil. Add walnuts and spices wrapped into a small piece of cheesecloth to the boiling syrup and cook until done. Walnuts should be glistening black when cooked completely. Add vanilla extract to the cooked preserves.

Apricot Preserves (A)

Ingredients:
Apricots - 1 kg
Sugar - 1 kg
Water - 1-1 1/2 cups

Wash picked over, firm, not overripe apricots with cold water and prick in a few places with a thin wooden pin. Make a syrup, pour it over prepared apricots and set aside for one day. On the following day drain the syrup and bring it to boil, add apricots to the boiling syrup and cook until done.

Apricot Preserves (B)

Ingredients:
Apricots - 1 kg
Sugar - 1 kg
Water - 3/4-1 cup

Wash picked over, firm, not overripe apricots with cold water, and prick in a few places with a thin wooden pin. Make a syrup with 500 g of sugar and 1 cup of water, pour it over prepared apricots, return to simmer and cook 3-5 minutes, then remove from heat and set aside for 5-6 hours. Drain the syrup and bring it to boil, then pour it back over apricots, add remaining 500 g of sugar and cook over low heat until done.

Forelle Pears Preserves (A)

Ingredients:
Forelle pears - 1 kg
Sugar - 1 kg
Water - 1 cup

Carefully remove the core from firm, not overripe Forelle pears, peel them but leave the stem attached, and put into a cold water. Make a syrup, then put prepared pears into the syrup, and cook until done.

Forelle Pears Preserves (B)

Ingredients:

Forelle pears - 1 kg
Sugar - 1 kg
Water - 1 1/2 cups

Wash firm, not overripe Forelle pears with cold water, and prick in a few places with thin wooden pin. Make a syrup in a pot, add prepared pears to the syrup and let them simmer for 5-10 minutes, then remove from heat and set aside for 5-6 hours. Remove pears from the syrup, return syrup to boil, return pears to the syrup and cook until done.

Pear Preserves

Ingredients:
Pears - 1 kg
Sugar - 1 kg
Pear cooking liquid - 1 1/2 cups
Cloves - 4-5

Peel and core firm, ripe pears and cut them into wedges lengthwise. Put prepared pears into a pot, cover with cold water, bring to boil and simmer 15-20 minutes. Put sugar into a pot (tub) for cooking preserves, add pear cooking liquid, mix everything and bring to boil. Add pears and cloves into the simmering syrup and cook until done.

Eggplant Preserves

Ingredients:
Eggplants - 24-27
Sugar - 2 kg and 1/2 cup
Hydrated lime - 30 g
Alum - 1/2 tbsp
Vanilla extract - to taste

Wash young eggplants, peel them leaving the stem untouched. Cut each eggplant into quarters lengthwise, put cut eggplants into water to prevent browning. When all eggplants are prepared transfer them into another container, sprinkle with hydrated lime, cover with water, and set aside for 1 1/2 hours. Thoroughly wash eggplants under a running water, put into boiling water and parboil for 3 minutes, then drain in a colander. Bring fresh water to boil in a pot, add alum to the pot, then add eggplants to the pot and parboil for 3 minutes. Drain eggplants in a colander and squeeze with your hand. Fill pot with fresh water, bring it to boil, add 1/2 cup of sugar to it, and, when the sugar is dissolved, add eggplants to it, parboil for 5 minutes, then drain in a colander and squeeze with your hand. Prepare syrup with remaining sugar, add eggplants to it, and cook until done. Add vanilla extract to the cooked preserves.

Watermelon Rind Preserves (A)

Ingredients:
Watermelon rind - 1 kg
Sugar - 1 kg and 1/2 cup
Hydrated lime - 200 g
Alum - 1/2 tbsp
Water - 3 cups

Choose a watermelon with a thick rind, remove all the flesh and peel the outer green skin off. Cut prepared rind into smaller (5-6 cm long) pieces, prick each piece in a few places with a fork, put into a pot, sprinkle with hydrated lime, cover with water and set aside for one hour. Take watermelon rinds out of the lime solution and thoroughly wash them under a running water. Put rinds into a pot, cover with boiling water and parboil for 10 minutes, then drain in a colander. Wash the pot, then fill it with boiling water, add alum and return the pot to boil. Add rinds to the pot when the water comes to boil and parboil them for 10 minutes, then drain in a colander. Wash the pot again, add boiling water and 1/2 cup of sugar to it, return to boil and put rind the pot. Parboil rinds for 10 minutes then drain in a colander. Wash the pot yet again, add 3 cups of boiling water and remaining sugar. Add watermelon rinds to the boiling syrup and cook until done. Add vanilla extract to the pot just before removing it from heat.

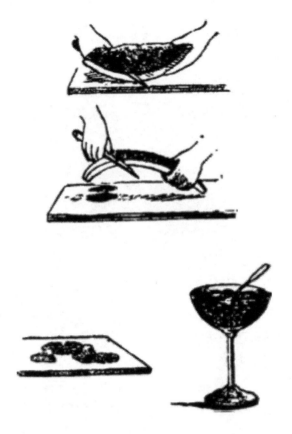

Watermelon Rind Preserves (B)

Ingredients:
Watermelon rind - 1 kg
Sugar - 1,200 g
Baking soda - 1 1/2 tsp
Water to dissolve baking soda - 6 cups
Water for syrup - 3 cups
Vanilla - to taste

Remove flesh from a watermelon with a thick rind, then peel green skin off of it. Cut prepared rind into medium, 5-8 cm long, pieces, and prick each piece in a few places with a fork.

Dissolve 1 1/2 tsp of baking soda in one cup of hot water, then mix it with 5 cups of cold water. Pure prepared watermelon rinds into this solution, cover, and set aside for 4 hours. Pour 600 g of sugar into a pot (tub) for cooking preserves, add 3 cups of water, bring to boil and simmer 10-15 minutes.

Meanwhile take watermelon rinds out of baking soda solution and wash under a running water, then them put into the boiling syrup, return to boil, and simmer for 15 minutes, then remove from heat and set aside for 12 hours.

Add remaining sugar to the pot with watermelon rinds, bring everything to boil and cook until done - approximately 3 hours. About 2 minutes before the end of cooking add vanilla extract to preserves.

Eggplant preserves can be cooked following the same instructions.

Fig Preserves (A)

Ingredients:
Figs - 1 kg
Sugar - 1 kg
Water - 1 1/2-2 cups

Pick over ripe figs and prick each one in a few places with a thin wooden pin. Put sugar into a pot (tub) for cooking preserves, add water, and make a syrup. Add prepared figs into the syrup and cook until done (2 1/2-3 hours).

Fig Preserves (B)

Ingredients:
Figs - 1 kg
Sugar - 1 kg
Water - 2 cups

Put ripe figs into a pot (tub) for cooking preserves. Cook a syrup and pour it over figs. Leave to infuse for 1 day. Drain syrup into another pot, bring it to boil and simmer for 15-20 minutes, then pour it over figs and set aside for one more day. Following day put the pot with figs on the stove, bring it to boil, and cook until done, skimming foam from time to time.

PICKLES AND MARINADES

Whole Fermented Cabbage

Ingredients:
White cabbage - 1 kg
Celery stalks - 150 g
Dried herbs - 100 g
Garlic - 50 g
Salt - 2 tbsp
Chili peppers - to taste

Select medium-sized, whole, firm heads of white cabbage. Remove any wilted outer leaves. Scrape the bottom of the core of the cabbage and make two perpendicular cuts in it, or cut each head in half or in quarters and remove the core. Put prepared cabbage into a pot with boiling water for 3-5 minutes, then take it out and let it cool.

Bring 2 cups of water to boil in a clean pot, add 1 tbsp of salt, add celery and garlic to the pot, simmer for 2-3 minutes, then remove from the pot and let them cool. Cool broth as well.

Wash and dry a glass jar, put half of the prepared cabbage into the jar, add cooled celery and garlic, chili peppers (and bay leaves if desired), top with remaining cabbage. Add 2 cups of cooled broth and 2 cups of cold water, then top with dried herbs (savory, basil, tarragon, mint, and dill), sprinkle with 1 tbsp of salt. Put a round wooden cover over cabbage and top with a heavy weight (large, thoroughly washed stone), cover with a clean kitchen towel or cheese cloth, seal the jar, and leave it in a dry cool place with a constant temperature. When cabbage settles down add more cabbage to keep the jar full. In about 7-10 days taste for salt and add more if needed.

Make sure that during fermentation cabbage is always covered with brine; otherwise, the mold will spoil it. Add more salted cold water whenever the level of brine goes down. If mold appears on top of the brine carefully skim it off, thoroughly wash the stone and scald it with boiling water.

It is recommended to make fermented cabbage in November.

Shredded Fermented Cabbage

Ingredients:
Cabbage - 1 kg
Salt - 1-1 1/2 tbsp
Carrots - 300-400 g
Chili peppers and bay leaves - to taste

Remove wilted outer leaves from small, firm heads of green or white cabbage, cut each head in half or into quarters and remove cores, then finely shred cabbage. Mix shredded cabbage with salt in a bowl, cover the bowl, and set it aside for 10-15 minutes. Rub cabbage between palms to make it soft. Set thin layers of cabbage alternating with layers of thinly sliced carrots and chili peppers with bay leaves in a clean crock.

Tamp each layer of cabbage with a wooden tamper hard enough to release juice. Dense packing of cabbage insures that there is no air between layers and prevents spoiling.

Lay the cabbage up to the top of the crock, making sure that released juice does not overflow the its edge. Cover cabbage with a thoroughly washed and scalded with boiling water wooden cover, and top it with a heavy weight (washed stone). In 3-4 days bubbles will appear on top of the juice indicating the start of fermentation process. During this time pierce cabbage in a few places all the way to the bottom of the crock to let the gasses formed due to fermentation to escape. Make sure that cabbage is completely submerged in juice. If there was not enough juice released during packing - add brine to cover (3/4-1 tsp of salt to 1 cup of water). Remove any white film forming on top of the juice and wash wooden cover and weight with boiling water.

Marinated Cabbage

Ingredients:
Cabbage - 1 kg
Wine vinegar - 1 1/4 cups
Water - 2 1/2 cups
Allspice – 10
Bay leaf – 1
Salt - 1 tbsp

Finely shred cored cabbage, mix it with salt (1/2 tbsp), lightly rub between palms, squeeze, transfer into a jar, add cooled marinade, close the car with waxed paper, and keep in a dry, cool place.

To make marinade pour wine vinegar and water into a clean pot, add salt (1/2 tbsp), sugar, allspice, bay leaf, bring it to boil, then let it cool.

Cabbage Fermented with Beets

Ingredients:
Cabbage - 1 kg
Beets - 300-400 g
Celery stalks - 150-200 g
Dried herbs - 100-150 g
Garlic - 50 g
Salt - 2-2 1/2 tbsp
Chili peppers - to taste

Prepare cabbage following instructions of the "Whole Fermented Cabbage" recipe, the only difference being that every layer of cabbage should be alternated with a layer of peeled and halved or quartered beets.

Brined Beets

Ingredients:
Beets - 1 kg
Celery stalks - 150 g
Parsnips - 150 g
Dill - 100 g
Garlic - 20 g
Salt - 1 tbsp
Chili peppers and bay leaves - to taste

Thoroughly wash beets with a brush, but do not peel. Put prepared beets into a pot with boiling water, return water to boil, and parboil for 8-10 minutes, then remove the pot from heat. Leave the beets in the cooking liquid until cool enough to handle, then peel them.

Add salt into a pot with boiling water (2 cups), then add celery, parsnip, and garlic, simmer for 2 minutes, then remove from heat and cool (vegetables separately and broth separately).

Put cooled beets into a clean jar alternating with layers of celery, parsnips, garlic, dill, and chili peppers (and bay leaves if desired). Add cooled brine to the jar (2 cups), then top with cold water (1-2 cups). Beets should be covered with brine.

Marinated Beets

Ingredients:
Beets - 1 kg
Wine vinegar - 2-2 3/4 cups
Water - 2-2 1/2 cups
Salt - 1-1 1/2 tsp
Allspice or whole black peppers – 10
Cloves - 5-6
Bay leaves - 1-2
Sugar - to taste

Wash beets with a brush, but do not peel or cut the root off, put them it into a pot, cover with water and cook until done. Remove the pot from heat and let beets cool in the cooking liquid. Peel beets and cut into smaller pieces, put cut beets into a jar, add pickling liquid to cover. Seal the jar with a parchment paper and store in a cool, dry place.

To prepare marinade mix wine vinegar with water in a pot, add sugar, salt, allspice or whole black peppers, cloves, bay leaves, bring everything to boil, then cool before using.

Brined Carrots

Ingredients:
Carrots - 1 kg
Onion – 1
Sugar - 1 tbsp
Salt - 1 tbsp

Peel and wash carrots, finely shred them and mix with sugar and salt.

Peel onion and thinly slice it across into rounds. Tightly pack prepared carrots and onion into a jar, cover the jar with muslin cloth and tie it with a kitchen twine. Store in a cool, dry place.

Brined Bladdernut Buds

Preparation is somewhat similar to capers.

Ingredients:
Bluddernut buds - 1 kg
Salt - 1 tbsp

Pick over flower buds of a bladdernut tree, wash them in cold water, then thoroughly squeeze them. Put prepared bladdernut buds in layers into a cask sprinkling each layer with salt and packing it down with a wooden spoon.

When the cask is filled with packed bladdernut buds cover them with sterilized wooden cover and top it with a heavy weight (washed stone).

Brined Green Tomatoes (A)

Ingredients:
Green tomatoes - 1 kg
Salt - 1 tbsp

Garlic - 50 g
Herbs (celery leaves, parsley, dill, savory, basil) - 200 g
Dried dill - 50 g
Chili peppers - to taste

Select small, firm green tomatoes of different shapes (round or plum variety), wash them in cold water and drain in a colander. Make a lengthwise slash in each tomato.

Finely chop herbs (celery leaves, parsley, savory, basil, dill), garlic, chili peppers, add salt and mix everything together. Stuff prepared herb mixture into the slashed of the green tomatoes. Put stuffed tomatoes in tightly packed rows in a jar, cover with a wooden circle and top with a weight (thoroughly washed stone). Seal the jar and store in a cool, dry place.

Brined Green Tomatoes (B)

Ingredients:
Green tomatoes - 1 kg
Salt - 1 tbsp
Celery leaves - 200 g
Parsley - 150 g
Dill - 100 g
Garlic - 50 g
Water - 3 cups
Bay leaf – 1
Chili peppers - to taste

Wash firm green tomatoes with cold water and drain in a colander.

Put celery leaves and parsley into 3 cups of boiling water for 3-5 minutes, then remove and cool. Add salt to the infusion and cool it as well.

Set tomatoes into tight layers in a jar, alternating with layers of celery leaves, parsley, dill, crushed garlic, chopped chili peppers, and bay leaf. Pour cooled brine into the tightly filled jar (to cover tomatoes), cover with a wooden cover and top with a weight, seal the jar and store in a cool, dry place.

Brined Green Tomatoes (C)

Ingredients:
Green tomatoes - 1 kg
Salt - 1 tbsp
Celery leaves - 300 g
Dried dill - 100 g
Garlic - 50 g
Water - 3-4 cups
Chili peppers - to taste

Wash firm, not very large green tomatoes with cold water, dip them into boiling water for 2-3 minutes, then put into cold water for 15-20 minutes. Drain in a colander.

Put celery leaves into boiling water for 1-2 minutes, then take it out and let it cool. Add salt to the celery infusion and let it cool.

Set tomatoes in tight rows in a jar, alternating each row with cooled celery, sliced garlic and chili peppers. When jar is filled with tomatoes add brine to cover the tomatoes, then top with remaining celery and dried dill. Cover with a wooden cover and top with a thoroughly washed stone. Seal the jar and store in a cool, dry place.

Green Tomatoes with Walnuts

Ingredients:
Green tomatoes - 1 kg
Shelled walnuts - 1 cup
Coriander seeds - 1 tsp
Garlic - 1-2 cloves
Wine vinegar, chili peppers, salt - to taste

Wash firm green tomatoes in cold water, put into a bowl and cover with boiling water for 15-20 minutes, then drain in a colander. Cut each tomato in half or in quarters - depending on their size.

Thoroughly pound shelled walnuts, garlic, and salt in a mortar, and squeeze oil from the walnut mixture into a separate container. Add crushed chili peppers, crushed coriander seeds, and wine vinegar to the walnut mixture and mix well. Mix prepared tomatoes with the walnut mixture, tightly pack into jars, pour walnut oil over, thoroughly wipe the edges of jar necks and hermetically seal them. Store in a cool, dry place.

Brined Eggplants

Ingredients:
Eggplants - 1 kg
Celery leaves - 1 cup
Parsley, savory, and dill - 1/2 cup
Garlic - 50 g
Salt - 1 1/2 tbsp
Chili peppers - to taste

Thoroughly wash unpeeled, small, elongated eggplants in cold water and make a 3-4 cm lengthwise slash in each one. Put eggplants into a pot with boiling water and parboil for 7-10 minutes, then transfer into a bowl with cold water for 20-30 minutes. Drain in a colander.

Put celery leaves into 4 cups of boiling water, infuse for 3-5 minutes, then take them out and cool. Add salt to the celery-infused water, remove it from heat and cool.

Finely chop herbs (celery leaves, parsley, savory, dill), garlic, chili peppers, mix everything with salt and stuff prepared eggplants with this mixture. Tightly pack eggplants into jars, pour cooled brine to cover eggplants, cover with a clean wooden cover, and top with a heavy weight (a washed stone). Cover jars with clean cloth and store in a cool, dry place.

Fried Eggplants in Wine Vinegar

Ingredients:
Eggplants - 1 kg
Wine vinegar - 1/2-3/4 cup
Salt - to taste

Cut washed, peeled eggplants lengthwise into 1-2 cm slices, sprinkle with salt and keep under weight for 25-30 minutes, then squeeze with hand.

Warm up vegetable oil in a skillet and fry prepared eggplants over medium heat. Tightly pack fried eggplants in jars and cover with wine vinegar. Thoroughly wipe edges if jar necks and hermetically seal them with parchment paper. Store in a cool, dry place.

Fried Eggplants

Ingredients:
Eggplants - 1 kg
Onions - 200 g
Vegetable oil - 3/4 cup
Salt - to taste

Fry eggplants in vegetable oil as described in previous recipe.

Brown finely diced onions in vegetable oil, mix with fried eggplants, then add a little more vegetable oil and fry onions together with eggplants. Tightly pack cooked eggplants in jars, top with a 3-4 cm layer of tempered vegetable oil. Thoroughly wipe edges of jar necks, then hermetically seal with parchment paper. Store in a cool, dry place.

Eggplants with Walnuts and Sautéed Onions

Ingredients:
Eggplants - 1 kg
Shelled walnuts - 1-1 1/2 cups
Onions - 100-150 g
Wine vinegar - 1/2 cup
Water - 1/2 cup
Garlic - 1-2 cloves
Coriander seeds - 1 tsp
Imereti saffron - 1 tsp
Ground cloves and cinnamon - 1 tsp
Tempered vegetable oil - as needed
Chili pepper and salt - to taste

Thoroughly wash unpeeled eggplants with cold water, make a lengthwise slash in each one, put into a pot, add enough boiling water to cover eggplants half-way, bring the pot to boil, and cook approximately 20 minutes (making sure not to overcook).

Transfer cooked eggplants to a clean board, cover with another board and top with a weight. Keep eggplants under weight for 12-15 hours to drain all the water and bitterness. Finely dice onions and sauté them in vegetable oil, then add 1/2 cup of water, mix well, let it boil for 2-3 minutes, then remove from heat.

Mix walnuts pounded together with garlic, chili peppers, coriander seeds, Imereti saffron, and salt with cooled sautéed onion, wine vinegar, and ground cloves and cinnamon.

Stuff prepared eggplants with walnut mixture through the slashes, tightly pack them into jars together with remaining stuffing. Top the jars with a 2-cm layer of tempered vegetable oil (heated, then cooled). Thoroughly wipe jar necks with a cloth or paper towels, and seal with parchment paper. Store in a cool, dry place.

Whole Eggplants with Walnuts (A)

Ingredients:
Eggplants - 1 kg
Onions - 100 g
Shelled walnuts - 1 1/2 cups
Garlic - 2-3 cloves
Coriander seeds - 1 tsp
Imereti saffron - 1 tsp
Dried suneli - 1 tsp
Chili peppers, wine vinegar, celery, salt - to taste

Thoroughly wash small unpeeled eggplants with cold water, cut eggplants lengthwise almost all the way through, put into a pot, add hot water to cover half-way, and cook for approximately 20 minutes.

About 5 minutes before the end of the cooking add celery leaves and stalks to the pot. Remove the pot from heat and let everything cool.

Transfer cooked eggplants to a cutting board, cover with another board, and top with a heavy weight. Keep under weight for 18-20 hours.

Pass shelled walnuts, garlic, coriander seeds, and chili peppers through a meat grinder 3 times. Add crushed Imereti saffron and dried suneli to the walnut mixture, mix everything well, then squeeze oil into another container and set it aside. Finely dice onions and add it to the walnut mixture together with wine vinegar diluted with water (to taste), mix everything.

Stuff prepared eggplants with walnut mixture, wrap blanched celery stalks around stuffed eggplants, tightly pack eggplants into jars, and top with walnut oil. Thoroughly wipe necks of jars with a cloth or a paper towel and seal with parchment paper. Store in a cool, dry place.

Whole Eggplants with Walnuts (B)

Ingredients:
Eggplants - 1 kg
Onions - 200 g
Shelled walnuts - 1 cup
Vegetable oil - 100 g
Garlic - 1-2 cloves
Coriander seeds - 2 tsp
Wine vinegar, chili peppers, salt - to taste

Sprinkle diced onions with salt and let it stand for 1-2 hours, then squeeze.

Mix walnuts, pounded together with garlic, coriander seeds, chili peppers, and salt, with prepared onions and wine vinegar (if desired - dilute vinegar with water).
Wash small eggplants and slash them in half without cutting all the way through, sprinkle with salt, put into a bowl and keep it covered for 2-3 hours, then thoroughly squeeze them.

Heat vegetable oil in a heavy skillet. Fry eggplants unfolded cut side down until nicely browned, then cool. When eggplants are cool enough to handle - stuff them with walnut mixture. Tie stuffed eggplants with a kitchen twine and return into the skillet. Fry on all sides until soft, then let eggplants cool and remove the twine.

Tightly pack cooked eggplants into jars, top with a 3-cm layer of tempered oil. Thoroughly wipe edges of jar necks with a cloth or a paper towel and seal them with parchment paper. Store in a cool, dry place.

Sliced Eggplants with Walnuts (A)

Ingredients:
Eggplants - 1 kg
Shelled walnuts - 1/4 cup
Wine vinegar - 1/2 cup
Vegetable oil - 3/4 cup
Coriander seeds - 1/2 tsp
Dried suneli - 1 tsp
Imereti saffron - 1 tsp
Celery leaves - 3/4 cup, finely chopped
Parsley and cilantro - 1/2 cup each
Garlic - 2-3 cloves
Chili peppers and salt - to taste

Cut washed and peeled small eggplants into 6-8 slices, put into a bowl, season with salt, cover the bowl, and set aside for 3-4 hours. Squeeze eggplants with hand, and fry in a skillet in hot vegetable oil over medium heat. Let eggplants cool.

Mix walnuts pounded together with coriander seeds, garlic, chili peppers, Imereti saffron, and dried suneli, with finely chopped herbs (celery leaves, parsley, cilantro), diced onions, and wine vinegar diluted with water. Mix walnut mixture with cooked eggplants, tightly pack it in jars, top with a 2-cm layer of tempered (heated and cooled) vegetable oil. Thoroughly wipe necks of jars with a cloth or a paper towel, seal them with parchment paper, and store in a cool, dry place.

Sliced Eggplants with Walnuts (B)

Ingredients:
Eggplants - 1 kg
Shelled walnuts - 1 kg
Cilantro - 3 sprigs

Garlic - 2 cloves
Coriander seeds - 1 tsp
Wine vinegar, chili peppers, salt - to taste

Put washed and peeled small eggplants into a pot with boiling water, parboil them for 3-5 minutes, then drain in a colander.

Squeeze cooled eggplants, then cut them across into circles and squeeze again taking care to preserve the shape of the slices.

Pound shelled walnuts together with cilantro, garlic (1 clove), and salt, squeeze oil from the mixture and set it aside. Separately pound coriander seeds, salt, garlic, and chili peppers, then mix it with crushed walnuts and wine vinegar, add prepared mixture to cooked eggplants and tightly pack everything into jars. Top jars with walnut oil and tightly seal them. Store in a cool, dry place.

Sliced Eggplants with Walnuts (C)

Ingredients:
Eggplants - 1 kg
Shelled walnuts - 3/4-1 cup
Coriander seeds - 1 tsp
Garlic - 2 cloves
Wine vinegar - 3/4 cup
Water - 1/4 cup
Onions - 200 g
Chili peppers, salt - to taste

Cut washed and peeled small eggplants across, sprinkle with salt, and set it aside for 1-2 hours. Squeeze eggplants and fry them on all side in hot vegetable oil in a hot skillet. Let eggplants cool.

Finely dice peeled onions, sprinkle with salt and set aside for 1-2 hours, then squeeze.

Pound walnuts together with cilantro, chili peppers, garlic, and salt in a mortar. Add prepared onions and wine vinegar to the crushed walnuts and mix well.

Set cooked eggplants in layers in a jar alternating with layers of walnut mixture. When jars are almost full top eggplants with tempered (heated and cooled) vegetable oil. Wipe necks of jars with a cloth or a paper towel and hermetically seal them. Store in a cool, dry place.

Eggplants with Sweet Bell Peppers

Ingredients:
Eggplants - 1 kg
Sweet bell peppers - 300 g
Shelled walnuts - 1 cup
Celery leaves, cilantro, dill - 1 cup, finely chopped
Parsley, basil, savory - 1/2 cup, finely chopped
Onions - 300-400 g
Garlic - 50 g
Wine vinegar, salt - to taste

Cut washed, unpeeled eggplants lengthwise, put into a boiling water and cook for 15-20 minutes. Drain cooked eggplants, put the on a cutting board, cover with another board and weight with some heavy load. Keep then under weight for 8-10 hours, then cut into medium-sized pieces. Put sweet bell peppers into boiling water for 5 minutes, then cool them, squeeze excess water, and cut into large pieces.

Mix walnuts crushed with garlic and salt with finely chopped herbs (celery leaves, cilantro, parsley, basil, savory, dill), diced onions, and wine vinegar. Add prepared eggplants and sweet bell peppers to the walnut and herb mixture.

Tightly pack eggplants into jars and top them with tempered (heated and cooled) vegetable oil. Seal jars and store them in a cool, dry place.

Sliced Marinated Eggplants

Ingredients:
Eggplants - 1 kg
Onions - 150-200 g
Wine vinegar - 3/4 cup
Water - 1/2 cup
Allspice - 1 tbsp
Bay leaf – 1
Vegetable oil - 1/2-3/4 cups
Salt - 1 tbsp

Cut washed and peeled small eggplants across into circles, sprinkle with salt, cover, and set aside for 3-4 hours. Squeeze eggplants and fry over medium heat in a skillet in hot vegetable oil.

Thinly slice peeled onions. In a clean pot bring to boil wine vinegar mixed with water, add allspice, bay leaf, and salt, let it simmer for a short while, then cool.

Set a layer of sliced onions on a bottom of a jar, top with two layers of eggplant slices, then another layer of onions, and so on . Repeat the process of alternating layer of onions with 2 layers of eggplants until the jar is almost full, then add cooled marinade and top everything with a 2-cm thick layer of tempered (heated and cooled) vegetable oil. Thoroughly wipe the neck of the jar with a cloth or a paper towel and seal with parchment paper. Store in a cool, dry place.

Whole Marinated Eggplants

Ingredients:
Eggplants - 1 kg
Celery leaves - 3/4 cup, finely chopped

Herbs (savory, basil, cilantro) - 1/2 cup, finely chopped
Dill - 1/2 cup, finely chopped
Celery stalks - as needed
Garlic - as needed
Wine vinegar - 1 1/2 cups
Water - 2 cups
Salt - 1 tbsp

Dip washed and peeled small eggplants into boiling water for 1-2 minutes, then drain in a colander, let them cool, and make a 3-4 cm long lengthwise slash in each.

Put celery stalks into boiling water for 1 minutes, then cool. Add 1/2 tbsp of salt to the celery infusion, add wine vinegar, return to boil, then remove from heat and let it cool.

Scald garlic with boiling water. Mix finely chopped herbs (celery leaves, savory, basil, cilantro, and dill) with 1/2 tbsp of salt. Stuff prepared eggplants with the herb mixture, add one clove of garlic into each one, and wrap them with blanched celery stalks.

Tightly pack prepared eggplants into jars and top with cooled marinade. Thoroughly wipe the necks of the jars and seal them. Store in a cool, dry place.

Red Chili Peppers

Pass red chili peppers through a meat grinder, then add salt and wine vinegar (use just a small quantity of wine vinegar - it should not affect the flavor of vinegar to the preparation), pack this mixture into small jars and seal them. Use pickled peppers as a seasoning for boiled or fried meat, poultry, or fish.

Tkemali Sauce

Ingredients:
Tkemali plums - 1 kg

Water - 1/4 cup
Coriander seeds - 1 tsp
Garlic - 4-5 cloves
Chili peppers, pennyroyal, salt - to taste

Wash picked over tkemali plums with cold water, cut each in half, put into a pot with a little bit of water, bring to boil, and simmer until the skins separate from the fruit. Pass contents of the pot through a sieve, discard skins and pits. Put tkemali puree into a pot and simmer, stirring all the time, until desired thickness is achieved.

About 5 minutes before the end of cooking add crushed chili peppers, garlic, coriander seeds, pennyroyal, and salt. Pour cooked sauce into bottles through a funnel, top with a tablespoon of vegetable oil and seal with sterilized corks. Store in a cool, dry place.

Spicy Tomato Sauce

Ingredients:
Tomatoes - 1 kg
Coriander seeds - 1 tsp
Dried suneli - 1 tsp
Garlic - 2-3 cloves
Chili peppers, salt - to taste

Cut firm, ripe, washed tomatoes into quarters, put into an enameled pot, and set it aside for 24 hours. Drain released watery juice from the pot, put the pot on a stove and bring to simmer. Simmer until tomato skins separate . Pass tomatoes through a sieve and discard seeds a skins. Transfer tomato puree into a clean pot and cook it down until desired thickness. Stir the puree frequently to prevent scorching.

About 5 minutes before the end of cooking add crushed coriander seeds, garlic, chili peppers, dried suneli, and salt.

Pour cooked sauce into bottles and seal following instructions of the previous recipe.

Table of Approximate Weights of Some of Ingredients (in Grams)

Ingredient Name	1 cup (250 cm3)	Tablespoon	Teaspoon	1 Piece
Flour, grains, sugar, etc.				
Wheat flour	160	25	10	–
Potato flour	200	30	10	–
Crushed breadcrumbs	126	15	5	–
Semolina	200	25	8	–
Buckwheat	210	25	7	–
Pearl barley	230	25	8	–
Oatmeal	90	12	6	–
Barley groats	180	20	7	–
Rice	230	25	9	–
Sago	180	20	7	–
Millet	220	30	10	–
Beans	220	30	10	–
Unshelled peas	200	–	–	–
Shelled peas	230	25	10	–
Lentils	210	–	–	–
Tolokno (Crushed wheat)	140	22	8	–
Crushed walnuts	120	20	6-7	–
Granulated sugar	200	30	12	–
Powdered sugar	190	25	7-8	–

Salt	325	30	10	–
Poppy seeds	155	15	5	–
Black pepper	–	–	5	–
Allspice	–	–	4.5	–
Ground red pepper	–	–	1	–
Mustard	–	–	4	–
Cloves	–	–	4	–
Ground cloves	–	–	3	–
Cocoa powder	–	20	10	–

Milk and milk products

Clarified butter	245	20	5	–
Butter	210	40	15	–
Rendered pork fat	–	12	–	–
Melted lard	200	40	–	–
Lard	230	60	–	–
Milk	250	20	5	–
Dry milk	120	20	6	–
Condensed milk		30	12	–
Sour cream	250	25	10	–

Vegetables and other products

Carrot, medium	–	–	–	75
Potato, medium	–	–	–	100
Onion, medium	–	–	–	75

Cucumber, medium	–	–	–	100
Parsnip	–	–	–	50
Tomato paste	–	30	10	–
Tomato puree	220	25	8	–
Jam	–	25	–	–
Gelatin (leaf)	–	–	–	2.5
Gelatin (powdered)	–	15	5	–
Vinegar	250	15	5	–
Raisins	165	25	–	–
Dried blueberries	130	15	–	–
Egg, large	–	–	–	55-65
Egg, medium	–	–	–	50-55
Egg, small	–	–	–	45-50
Egg yolk	–	–	–	20
Egg white	–	–	–	30

SAMPLE MENUS

Sample Lunch Menu with Two Dishes and an Appetizer for Winter Season

Georgia has a great tradition of serving thoroughly cleaned and washed herbs with meals (lunch and dinner) during any season of the year. Depending on a season following herbs can be served - parsley, dill, cress, tarragon, basil, savory, scallions, and so on.

Sunday
Option I
Various herbs
Suluguni Cheese on a Skewer
Spinach with Walnuts
or Sturgeon with Walnut Sauce
Mchadi
Soup-Chihirtma with Chicken (A)
Roasted Suckling Pig
or Tenderloin Shashlik

Option II
Various herbs
Hachapuri
White Cabbage with Walnuts (B)
or Boiled Fish with Vinegar Sauce
Soup-Artala (A)
Satsivi with Turkey (half of a bird), Gomi
Fried Turkey (half of a bird)

Option III
Various herbs
Cheese, Mchadi
Spinach Braised in Vegetable Oil
Soup-Kharcho (Vegetarian), Gomi or Mchadi

Pilaf with Sweet Sauce

Monday
Option I
Various herbs
Cheese, Mchadi
Beans with Walnuts
Pork Soup
Rice Pilaf (A)

Option II
Various herbs
Trout with Sauce
Soup with Walnuts (Vegetarian), Gomi
Beans with Clarified Butter and Eggs

Option III
Various herbs
Suluguni, Mchadi
Soup with Red Beans
Spinach with Butter and Eggs (A)

Tuesday
Option I
Various herbs
Potato Croquettes
Soup-Chihirtma with Chicken Giblets
Chicken with Walnuts and Pomegranate, Mchadi

Option II
Various herbs
Gomi with Cheese
Boiled Tripe with Spice Sauce
Soup-Kharcho with Sturgeon
or Stellate Sturgeon with Walnuts, Gomi
Beef Tenderloin Pot Roast

or Beef with Prunes

Option III
Various herbs
Spinach Braised in Vegetable Oil
Cheese Soup (Gadazelili), Gomi
Boiled Eggs with Walnut Sauce, Gomi or Mchadi

Wednesday
Option I
Various herbs
Suluguni
Liver Braised with Pomegranate
Soup-Kharcho with Beef (A), Gomi
Tolma with Beef
or Kupaty

Option II
Various herbs
Cheese
Beets with Dogberries
Soup-Bozartma with Goose (half of a bird)
Roasted Goose with Dried Dogberries (half of a bird)

Option III
Various herbs
White Cabbage with Walnuts (A), Mchadi
Soup with Beans on Vegetable Oil
Rice Pilaf with Raisins

Thursday
Option I
Various herbs
Beef Tongue with Spicy Garnish, Mchadi
Chicken Soup (half of a bird)

Boiled Chicken with Walnut Sauce (half of a bird), Mchadi or Gomi

Option II
Various herbs
Braised Beef Offal
Sour Cabbage with Walnuts
Soup-Kharcho with Eggs, Gomi
Roasted Beef Tenderloin with Wine

Option III
Various herbs
Cheese, Mchadi
Beans with Walnuts and Pomegranate
Milk Soup with Eggs and Herbs
Braised Pumpkin with Rice and Raisins

Friday
Option I
Various herbs
Cheese, Mchadi
Boiled Chicken (half of a bird)
Fish in Pomegranate Sauce
Soup-Chihirtma with Chicken (half of a bird)
Suckling Pig on a Spit
or Salmon, Sturgeon, or Stellate Sturgeon on a Skewer

Option II
Various herbs
Leeks with Walnuts (A,B)
Soup-Kharcho with Beef (B), Gomi
Pilaf with Chicken (A,B)

Option III
Various herbs
Sturgeon Head in Broth

Potato Croquettes (B), Mchadi
Bean Soup with Butter and Eggs
Spinach with Butter and Eggs

Saturday
Option I
Various herbs
Beets with Walnuts
Pork Offal with Suneli, Mchadi
Soup-Kharcho with Pork, Gomi
Sturgeon or Stellate Sturgeon on a Skewer
or Chicken Braised with Walnuts (A,B)

Option II
Various herbs
Cheese, Mchadi
Bean Croquettes
Soup with Goose and Dried Dogberries (half of a bird)
Satsivi with Goose (half of a bird), Gomi or Mchadi

Option III
Various herbs
Boiled Potatoes with Walnuts, Mchadi
Soup-Chihirtma (Vegetarian)
Satsivi with Eggs
or Satisivi with Beans, Gomi or Mchadi

Sample Lunch Menu with Two Dishes and an Appetizer for Spring Season

Sunday
Option I
Various herbs
Boiled Fish with Vinegar Sauce
Soup-Bozbashi (B)
Chahohbili with Young Chicken

or Tolma with Grape Leaves (A,B)

Option II
Various herbs
Suluguni Cheese
Sassaparil (Ekala) with Walnuts, Mchadi
Lamb Soup with Meatballs (B)
Shashlik-Basturma with Lamb

Option III
Various herbs
Cauliflower Leaves with Walnuts, Mchadi
Soup-Chihirtma (Vegetarian)
Cauliflower with Butter and Eggs

Monday
Option I
Various herbs
Boiled Young Lamb
Soup-Bozartma with Lamb
Roasted Leg of Lamb with Garlic

Option II
Various herbs
Cheese, Mchadi
Braised Heart and Liver of Lamb with Tarragon
Soup-Chihirtma with Chicken or Lamb
Satsivi with Poultry (A, B)
or Cooked Poultry with Satsebeli-Bazha Sauce, Gomi or
Mchadi

Option III
Various herbs
Cauliflower with Walnuts, Mchadi
Soup-Shechmandi with Sour Fruit Leather
Rice Pilaf (B)

Tuesday
Option I
Various herbs
Suluguni, Mchadi
Hard-Boiled Eggs with Walnut Sauce
Soup-Bozbashi (B)
Rice Pilaf with Lamb Ragout

Option II
Various herbs
Boiled Beans with Herbs
Lamb Soup with Rice
Lamb Offal on a Skewer

Option III
Various herbs
Cheese, Mchadi
Radish Greens with Walnuts
Soup-Chihirtma (Vegetarian)
Kaurma with Potatoes

Wednesday
Option I
Various herbs
Poached Catfish with Cilantro and Vinegar
Soup-Kharcho with Lamb or Beef (B)
Lamb with Cherry Plums (A,B)

Option II
Various herbs
Cheese, Mchadi
Beans with Walnuts and Wine Vinegar (A)
Soup-Bozartma with Chicken
Baked Sturgeon, Stellate Sturgeon, or Salmon

Option III
Various herbs
Sasaparilla (Ekala) with Tkemali, Mchadi
Soup-Shechmandi with Buttermilk
Spring Chicken or Young Chicken on a Skewer

Thursday

Option I
Various herbs
Cheese, Mchadi
Soup-Artala (B)
Young Chicken with Walnut Sauce

Option II
Various herbs
Fresh Fish with Garlic and Wine Vinegar
Soup-Kharcho with Chicken and Walnuts (B), Gomi
Asparagus with Butter and Eggs
Option III
Various herbs
Asparagus with Walnuts, Mchadi
Soup with Asparagus (Vegetarian)
Pilaf with Young Lamb or Poultry

Friday

Option I
Various herbs
Fish with Garlic Sauce
Soup-Kharcho with Chicken, Turkey, or Goose (A) (half of a
bird)
Satsivi with Chicken, Turkey, or Goose (half of a bird), Gomi
or Mchadi

Option II
Various herbs
Beans Sauteed in Vegetable Oil
Soup-Bozbashi with Meatballs (A)
Tenderloin Shashlik-Basturma

Option III
Various herbs
Nettles with Butter and Eggs
Soup with Walnuts
Rice Porridge with Milk

Saturday

Option I
Various herbs
Beans with Walnuts and Wine Vinegar (B)
Soup-Bozartma with Chicken or Turkey
Poultry Braised with Walnut Sauce
Option II
Various herbs
Dried Salted Fish with Tkemali, Mchadi
Soup with Lamb Shilaplavi (A)
or Chahohbili with Lamb

Option III
Various herbs
Cheese, Mchadi
Nettle with Walnuts
Soup-Shechmandi with Garlic
Pilaf with Fried Spring Chicken

Sample Lunch Menu with Two Dishes and an Appetizer for Summer Season

Sunday

Option I
Various herbs
Hachapuri
Green Beans with Walnuts, Mchadi
Soup-Bozbashi with Meatballs (B)
Chicken Tabaka
or Fried Spring Chicken Stuffed with Giblets

Option II
Various herbs
Cheese, Mchadi
Green Beans Salad
Tomatoes and Eggs Salad with Walnut Dressing
Soup-Chihirtma with Young Chicken
Lamb Shahslik with Eggplants

Option III
Various herbs
Eggplant Caviar (A)
Soup-Shechmandi with Yogurt and Rice (B)
Green Beans with Butter and Eggs (A)

Monday
Option I
Various herbs
Young Beet Greens with Walnuts
Summer Soup
Chahohbili with Young Chicken

Option II
Various herbs
Soup-Chrianteli with Sour Cherries or Blackberries
Green Beans with Butter and Eggs (B)

Option III
Various herbs

Cheese, Mchadi
Green Beans with Tkemali
Soup with Tomatoa (B)
Vegetarian Chahohbili

Tuesday
Option I
Various herbs
Green Beans with Walnuts (B)
Soup-Buglama with Lamb and Eggplants
Chahohbili with Lamb (B)

Option II
Various herbs
Cheese, Mchadi
Soup with Unripe Grapes
Lamb with Green Beans (A)

Option III
Various herbs
Adzhapsandali (B)
Soup-Shechmandi with Yogurt (Matsoni) (A)
Green Beans with Caramelized Onions and Eggs

Wednesday
Option I
Various herbs
Adzhapsandali (B)
Soup-Bozartma with Spring Chicken
Satsivi with Green Beans
or Sautéed Green Beans

Option II
Various herbs
Green Beans with Walnuts and Vinegar
Soup with Dogwood Berries and Walnuts

Braised Lamb with Eggplants and Tomatoes

Option III
Various herbs
Roasted Eggplants with Walnuts
Soup-Shechmandi with Yogurt and Rice (B)
Eggplants with Eggs

Thursday
Option I
Various herbs
Eggplant Caviar (B)
Lamb Soup with Vegetables
Tolma with Lamb (A)

Option II
Various herbs
Eggplants with Sweet Bell Peppers
Soup With Tomatoes (B)
Chahohbili with Spring Chicken and Tomatoes

Option III
Various herbs
Green Beans with Tomatoes and Walnuts
Soup-Shechmandi with Herbs
Lamb with Green Beans (B)

Friday
Option I
Various herbs
Adzhapsandali (D)
Lamb Soup with Meatballs
Tolma with Lamb

Option II
Various herbs

Cheese, Mchadi
Sweet Bell Peppers with Walnuts
Soup-Shechmandi with Yogurt (B)
Young Chicken with Tomatoes and Eggs

Option III
Various herbs
Cheese, Mchadi
Asparagus Salad
Cheese Soup (Gadazelili)
Chahohbili with Giblets and Tomatoes

Saturday
Option I
Various herbs
Tomatoes with Walnut Sauce, Mchadi
Soup-Bozbashi with Eggplant and Green Beans
Lamb Meatballs Fried in a Skillet

Option II
Various herbs
Tomatoes Braised with Walnuts, Mchadi
Soup-Chihirtma with Tomatoes
Beef Fried with Green Beans

Option III
Various herbs
Asparagus with Walnuts
Asparagus Soup
Fried Spring Chicken with Garlic Sauce

Sample Lunch Menu with Two Dishes and an Appetizer for Fall Season

Sunday
Option I

Various herbs
Eggplants with Walnuts (A,B), Mchadi
Soup-Bozbashi (A)
Roast Lamb
or Lamb on a Spit

Option II
Various herbs
Green Beans with Matsoni
Soup with Beef and Tomatoes
Quickly Cooked Kupaty
or Chahohbili with Spring Chicken (A,B)

Option III
Various herbs
Eggplant Caviar with Pomegranates
Bean Soup with Butter and Eggs
Eggplants with Meat
or Basturma with Fish

Monday
Option I
Various herbs
Fried Eggplants with Garlic and Herbs
Soup-Kharcho with Beef and Walnuts
Chahohbili with Beef

Option II
Various herbs
Sturgeon or Stellate Sturgeon with Broth (A,B,C)
or Poached Fish with Tomatoes
Soup-Chihirtma with Chicken (B) (half of a bird)
Chicken with Green Beans (half of a bird)

Option III
Various herbs

Eggplants Fried in Lamb Tail Fat
Soup-Shechmandi with Dogwood Berr.
Fried Lamb with Pomegranate (A)

Tuesday
Option I
Various herbs
Green Tomatoes with Carrots and Garlic
Soup-Bozartma with Young Chicken (half
Chicken with Tomato-Walnut Sauce (half o chadi

Option II
Various herbs
Braised Eggplants
Lamb Soup with Peas
Tolma with Lamb (B)

Option III
Various herbs
Suluguni Cheese on a Skewer, Mchadi
Soup-Kharcho with Bread
Eggplants Stuffed with Lamb Tail Fat

Wednesday
Option I
Various herbs
Eggplants Fried in Vegetable Oil and Stuffed with Nuts
Soup-Tatariahni with Beef (A)
Beef Tenderloin with Eggplants

Option II
Various herbs
Eggplants Fried in Vegetable Oil with Garlic-Vinegar Suce
Soup-Kharcho with Chicken and Walnuts (A) (half of a ird)
Fried Chicken with Pomegranates (half of a bird)

ith Walnuts (A), Mchadi

natoes (A)

its with Rice and Tomatoes

der with Barberries

T

C

ps

Fants with Tomato Sauce

Sma with Lamb

Cd Apples Tolma Stuffed with Lamb

oh with Pomegranate Sauce

O

Verbs

Len Walnuts (B), Mchadi

Sohlama

Chli with Beef Tenderloin

OrII

Vaherbs

ChMchadi

MuFlounder, or Trout with White Wine

or sh in Sauce

Peap with Rice

Bral Lamb with Pomegranate Sauce

Fric

Optn I

Varius herbs

Gree Tomatoes with Walnuts (A)

Soup Kharcho with Beef or Lamb (A)

Rice ilaf with Raisins

or Fish with Eggplants

Option II
Various herbs
Cheese, Mchadi
Green Tomatoes with Vegetable Oil
Soup-Tatariahni with Beef (B)
Shashlik Fried in a Skillet
or Fried Eggplants with Rice and Tomatoes

Option III
Various herbs
Eggplants Grilled on a Skewer with Garlic
Soup-Shechmandi with Yogurt and Rice (B)
Chanahi (A,B,C)

Saturday
Option I
Various herbs
Roasted Eggplants with Walnuts and Pomegranates
Soup-Bozbashi with Meatballs (B)
Lamb with Green Beans and Matsoni
or Shashlik-Chahohbili

Option II
Various herbs
Tomatoes with Walnut Sauce
Soup-Kharcho with Chicken, Turkey, or Goose (B) (half of a bird)
Satsivi with Poultry (A,B,C,D) (half of a bird)
or Rice Pilaf with Chicken (A,B)

Option III
Various herbs
Catfish in Sauce
or Fish in Tomato Sauce
Cheese Soup (Gadazelili)

T. P. SULAKVELIDZE

Satsivi with Eggplants, Gomi
or Kidneys on a Skewer with Pomegranate Sauce

Made in the USA
Middletown, DE
06 June 2016